MOAB IS MY
WASHPOT

MOAB IS MY WASHPOT

Stephen Fry

HUTCHINSON
LONDON

1 3 5 7 9 10 8 6 4 2

This edition first published in 1997 by Hutchinson

Random House (UK) Limited
20 Vauxhall Bridge Road, London SW1V 2SA

Random House Australia (Pty) Limited
20 Alfred Street, Milsons Point, Sydney,
New South Wales 2061, Australia

Random House New Zealand Limited
18 Poland Road, Glenfield, Auckland 10, New Zealand

Random House South Africa (Pty) Limited
Endulini, 5A Jubilee Road, Parktown 2193, South Africa

A CIP record for this book is available from the British Library

Papers used by Random House UK Limited are natural,
recyclable products made from wood grown in sustainable forests.
The manufacturing processes conform to the environmental
regulations of the country of origin.

ISBN 0 09 1801613

Typeset by MATS, Southend-on-Sea, Essex
Printed and bound in Great Britain by
Mackays of Chatham PLC, Chatham, Kent

For You

The Book of D., Verse 10, Chapter 11

To live is to war with trolls in heart and soul. To write is to sit in judgement on oneself.

Henrik Ibsen

The interests of a writer and the interests of his readers are never the same and if, on occasion, they happen to coincide, this is a lucky accident.

W. H. Auden

The author and publishers thank the following for permission to reproduce extracts and song lyrics:

Enemies of Promise by Cyril Connolly – © by permission of the Estate of Cyril Connolly c/o Rogers Coleridge & White Ltd, 20 Powis Mews, London W11 1JN.

Looking Back by Norman Douglas – The Society of Authors as the Literary Representative of the Estate of Norman Douglas.

Hitler: A Study in Tyranny by Alan Bullock – reprinted by permission of Hamlyn (a division of Reed Books Limited).

Portnoy's Complaint by Philip Roth – © 1969 Philip Roth, reprinted by permission of Random House Inc., 201 East 50th Street, New York, NY 10022, and Jonathan Cape, Random House UK, 20 Vauxhall Bridge Road, London SW1V 2SA.

'Notes on the English Character' from *Abinger Harvest*, and *Obituary of Roger Fry*, both by E. M. Forster – by permission of King's College Cambridge, and The Society of Authors as the literary representative of the E. M. Forster Estate.

Review of E. M. Forster's *Abinger Harvest*, by Desmond MacCarthy, from *The Sunday Times* 22 March 1936 © Times Newspapers Limited 1936.

'I'm a Believer'. Words and music by Neil Diamond © 1966 Stonebridge Music/Sony/ATV Music Publishing, and © 1966, Screen Gems-EMI Music Inc, USA. All Rights Reserved. International Copyright Secured. Reproduced by permission of Screen Gems-EMI Music Ltd, London WC2H 0EA.

'Sport'. Words and music by Vivian Stanshall © 1969, reproduced by permission of EMI Music Publishing Ltd, London WC2H 0EA.

Every effort has been made to seek copyright permission, and the publishers apologise for any inadvertent breach.

Joining In

'Look, Marguerite ... England!'
Closing lines of *The Scarlet Pimpernel*, 1934

FOR SOME REASON I recall it as just me and Bunce. No
one else in the compartment at all. Just me, eight years and
a month old, and this inexpressibly small dab of misery
who told me in one hot, husky breath that his name was
Samuelanthonyfarlowebunce.

I remember why we were alone now. My mother had
dropped us off early at Paddington Station. My second term.
The train to Stroud had a whole carriage reserved for us.
Usually by the time my mother, brother and I had arrived on
the platform there would have been a great bobbing of boaters
dipping careless farewells into a sea of entirely unacceptable
maternal hats.

Amongst the first to arrive this time, my brother had found
a compartment where an older boy already sat amongst his
opened tuck-box, ready to show off his pencil cases and conker
skewers while I had moved respectfully forward to leave them
to it. I was still only a term old after all. Besides, I wasn't
entirely sure what a conker skewer might be.

The next compartment contained what appeared to be a tiny
trembling woodland creature.

My brother and I had leaned from our respective windows

to send the mother cheerfully on her way. We tended to be cruelly kind at these moments, taking as careless and casual a leave of her as possible and making a great show of how little it mattered that we were leaving home for such great stretches of time. Some part of us must have known inside that it was harder for her than it was for us. She would be returning to a baby and a husband who worked so hard that she hardly saw him and to all the nightmares of uncertainty, doubt and guilt which plague a parent, while we would be amongst our own. I think it was a tacitly agreed strategy to arrive early so that all this could be got over with without too many others milling around. The loudness and hattedness of Other Parents were not conducive to the particular Fry tokens of love: tiny exertions of pressure on the hands and tight little nods of the head that stood for affection and deep, unspoken under-standing. A slightly forced smile and bitten underlip aside, Mummy always left the platform outwardly resolute, which was all that mattered.

All that taken care of, I slid down in my seat and examined the damp shivering thing opposite. He had chosen a window seat with its back to the engine as if perhaps he wanted to be facing homewards and not towards the ghastly unknown destination.

'You must be a new boy,' I said.

A brave nod and a great spreading of scarlet in downy, hamstery cheeks.

'My name's Fry,' I added. 'That's my bro talking next door.'

A sudden starburst of panic in the fluffy little chick's brown eyes, as if terrified that I was going to invite my bro in. He probably had no idea what a bro was.

The previous term I hadn't known either.

'Roger, Roger!' I had cried, running up to my brother in morning break. 'Have you had a letter from –'

'You call me bro here. Bro. Understood?'

I explained everything to the broken little creature in front of me. 'A bro is a brother, that's all. He's Fry, R. M. And I'm Fry, S. J. See?'

The hamster-chick-squirrel-downy-woodland thing nodded

to show that it saw. It swallowed a couple of times as if trying to find the right amount of air to allow it to speak without sobbing.

'I was a new boy last term,' I said, a huge and perfectly inexplicable surge of satisfaction filling me all the way from gartered woollen socks to blue-banded boater. 'It really isn't so bad, you know. Though I expect you feel a bit scared and a bit homesick.'

It didn't quite dare look at me but nodded again and gazed miserably down at shiny black Cambridge shoes which seemed to me to be as small as a baby's booties.

'Everybody cries. You mustn't feel bad about it.'

It was it this point that it announced itself to be Samuelanthonyfarlowebunce, and to its friends Sam, but never Sammy.

'I shall have to call you Bunce,' I told him. 'And you will call me Fry. You'll call me Fry S. J. if my bro is about, so there won't be any mix up. Not Fry Minor or Fry the Younger, I don't like that. Here, I've got a spare hankie. Why don't you blow your nose? There'll be others along in a minute.'

'Others?' He looked up from emptying himself into my hankie like a baby deer hearing a twig snap by a water pool and cast his eyes about him in panic.

'Just other train boys. There are usually about twenty of us. You see that piece of paper stuck to the window? "Reserved for Stouts Hill School" it says. We've got this whole carriage to ourselves. Four compartments.'

'What happens when we get . . . when we get there?'

'What do you mean?'

'When we get to the station.'

'Oh, there'll be a bus to meet us. Don't worry, I'll make sure you aren't lost. How old are you?'

'I'm seven and a half.'

He looked much younger. Nappy age, he looked.

'Don't worry,' I said again. 'I'll look after you. Everything will be fine.'

I'll look after you.

The pleasure of saying those words, the warm wet sea of

pleasure. Quite extraordinary. A little pet all to myself.

'We'll be friends,' I said. 'It won't be nearly as bad as you expect. You'll see.'

Kindly paternal thoughts hummed in my mind as I tried to imagine every worry that might be churning him up. All I had to do was remember my own dreads of the term before.

'Everyone's very nice really. Matron unpacks for you, but you've got to take your games clothes down to the bag room yourself, so you'll have to know your school number so as you can find the right peg. My number's one-o-four which is the highest number in the school's history, but twelve boys left last term and there are only eight or nine new boys, so there probably won't ever be a one-o-five. I'm an Otter, someone'll probably tell you what House you're in. You should watch out for Hampton, he gives Chinese burns and dead legs. If Mr Kemp is on duty he gives bacon slicers. It's soccer this term, my bro says. I hate soccer but its conkers as well which is supposed to be really good fun. My bro says everyone goes crazy at conker time. Conkers bonkers, my bro says.'

Bunce closed up the snotty mess in the middle of my hankie and tried to smile.

'In two weeks' time,' I said, remembering something my mother had told me, 'you'll be bouncing about like a terrier and you won't even be able to remember being a bit nervous on the train.'

I looked out of the window and saw some boaters and female hats approaching.

'Though in your case,' I added, 'you'll be *buncing* about . . .'

A real smile and the sound of a small giggle.

'Here we go,' I said. 'I can hear some boys coming. Tell you what, here's my *Ranger*. Why don't you be reading it when they come in, so you'll look nice and busy.'

He took it gratefully.

'You're so kind,' he said. 'I've never met anyone as kind as you.'

'Nonsense,' I replied, glowing like a hot coal.

I heard the grand sounds of approaching seniors.

'Okay then, Mum,' someone said.

'Don't say "okay", darling. And you will write this time, won't you?'

'Okay, Mum.'

My bro and I never called our parents Mum and Dad. It was always Mummy and Daddy until years later when Mother and Father were officially sanctioned. Towards adulthood we allowed ourselves to use, with self-conscious mock-Pooterism, Ma and Pa.

Last term, I had put my hand up in an art lesson and said, 'Mummy, can I have another piece of charcoal?' The form had howled with laughter.

There again, during the first weeks of summer holidays I often called my mother 'Sir' or 'Matron'.

Bunce buried himself in the Trigan Empire, but I knew that he was listening to the sounds too and I could tell that the confidence and loudness of the other boys' voices terrified him. He clutched the sides of the comic so hard that little rips appeared on the outer pages.

On the way to Paddington after lunch I had felt more dread, infinitely more terror and despair at the prospect of school than I had the term before. During the long summer holiday Roger had told me to expect this. Homesickness was much worse the second and third terms than it was the first. Bunce had come as a godsend therefore, something to take my mind off my own fears.

The door to our carriage slid open with a loud bang.

'Oh God, it's Fry's Turkish Delight. And what the hell are you doing by the window?'

'Hello, Mason,' I said.

'Come on, shove over.'

Bunce started to rise like a courteous old commuter offering his seat to a heavily-packaged woman. 'Would you like ... ?' he began huskily.

'No, I want Fry's seat, if he hasn't stunk it out yet.'

Well there it was. I felt my face flush scarlet as I got up mumbling something inaudible, and removed myself to the corner seat farthest from the window.

For five minutes I had enjoyed the sensation of someone

looking up to and admiring me. Bunce had respected me. Believed in me. Trusted me. Now the little puppy would see that the rest of the school treated me as if I was no one. Just another tiresome squit. I sat in my new seat, trying to look unconcerned and stared down at my bare knees and the grazes and indentations of gravel still there from a bicycle fall. Only yesterday afternoon I had been riding along the lanes listening to skylarks high in the huge Norfolk skies and watching partridges tread stubble in the fields. Three weeks ago I had had my eighth birthday party and been taken to see *The Great Race* at the Gaumont in Norwich.

Mason settled himself into his conquered seat and looked across at Bunce with great curiosity and an air of faint repugnance, as if Bunce might be of a breed he had never run into before and hoped never to encounter again.

'You,' said Mason, kicking across at him. 'Have you got a name then?'

The reply came as something of a shock.

'I have got a name,' said Bunce, rising, 'but it's none of your bloody business.'

Mason looked stupefied. There was nothing in the least bad about him. In taking my seat and remarking on my smell he had meant no particular insult, he was merely exercising the natural privilege of seniority. Seniority is pay-back time. He had been treated like a worm when he was small, now it was his turn to treat those under him like worms. He was ten, for heaven's sake. He was allowed to wear *long trousers*. At prep school, ten is to eight what forty is to twenty in adult life.

'I'm going over there,' said Bunce, pointing to the seat next to mine. 'It smells better over there.' He threw himself down beside me with a determined bounce on the springs and then ruined everything by bursting into tears.

Mason was denied the chance of any response to this astonishing eruption by the entrance into the compartment of Kaloutsis and his parents. It was not at all done for Family to board the train, but Kaloutsis was Greek and his parents serenely above the finer points of English protocol.

'Ah, and here's a little one,' cried Mrs Kaloutsis, swooping down on Bunce. 'And no one looking after you?'

'Thank you,' Bunce snivelled, 'but Fry S. J. is looking after me very well indeed. *Very* well. Very well *indeed*. I had a smut in my eye and he lent me his handkerchief.'

Train boys were generally the sons of military or colonial parents, and had flown in to London Airport to be picked up by uncles, aunts or godparents who would take them on to Paddington. Most other boys at Stouts Hill were driven to school by their parents.

The reserved compartments filled up over the next quarter-hour with deeply tanned boys returning from hot weeks in places like Northern Rhodesia, Nigeria, India, Aden, the West Indies and Ceylon. One boy, Robert Dale, whom I liked, sat opposite me and Bunce and told us about India. Dale's father edited an English language newspaper in Bombay and Dale always shouted 'Aiee!' when he was in pain. It had amazed me greatly when I first heard him stubbing his toe against the foot of the bed in the dormitory, since I had never imagined that expressions of pain could vary. I had thought 'Ouch!' and 'Ow!' were the same all over the world. I had suffered a hot and bothered exchange in my first French lesson, for example, when I was told that the French for 'Oh!' was '*Ah!*'

'Then how do they say "Oh", sir?'

'They say "*Ah*."'

'Well then, how do they say "Ah"?'

'Don't be stupid, Fry.'

I had sulked for the rest of the lesson.

Dale took off his shoes and socks and leaned back. He had the most splendidly fine feet, with a perfect, even spread of toes. At the beginning of every autumn term boys like him who spent their school holidays in Africa, Asia or the West Indies would show off by running across gravel barefoot without any pain. By the end of the term, with winter set in, their feet would have lost their natural tough layers of callused skin and they would be just the same as the rest of us.

A guard looked in and performed a brief headcount. He gazed into the middle distance and told us that the last boy who

had rested his foot on a seat had been arrested by the police at
Didcot and put in prison, where he still languished on a diet of
bread and water.

'Sounds better than school food,' said Dale.

The guard grunted at our giggles and left. Boaters were
thrown on to luggage-racks, feet put up on seats and talk
turned to soccer, what had been done in the hols, who was
going to be made prefect and the whole Edwardian schoolboy
novel nonsense. Mason seemed to have forgotten all about
Bunce's strange outburst and was delighting the boy opposite
with underarm farts.

After one of those squealing, juddering, stomach-dropping
false starts with which trains so tactlessly articulate human
emotion, we pulled ourselves out of the great shed of
Paddington and steamed west.

The Gloucestershire town of Stroud, sanctified by the memory
and to the memory of Laurie Lee, produces – or used to produce
– almost all the baize that Britain and her dominions ever
thought to use. Baize for the doors into servants' quarters, baize
for billiards, snooker and pool, baize for card tables, baize for
casinos, auction-rooms and baize to drape over the cages of
songbirds to fool them into thinking it night. Some miles to the
south of Stroud stands the Bury, a great green hill over whose
shoulders one might believe the weavers of the Slad Valley once
threw a huge bolt of their baize as a giant billboard to show off
their product to the world. The small village of Uley snuggles
itself into the thicker nap at the base of this fuzzy-felt hill and
sleeps there contentedly, unaware of triple-thick shakes, pay-
per-view Fight Nights, Lottery Winsday and driver's side air
bags. The village of Uley still believes in Gestetnered parish
magazines, dividend tea, sherbet dips, Heinz salad cream and
half-timbered Morris vans. The village of Uley grows lobelias
and alyssum on the front fringes of lawn that bank up to warm
ham-stone cottages out of which rumble the deep tones of Long
Wave wireless. The village pub of Uley radiates a warm vapour
in which are mingled the vanilla richness of pipe tobacco and the
malty hum of Usher's Ales. The village church of Uley has its

fragrance too, a compound of Esso Blue, Mansion furniture wax and hymn books in a state of permanently suspended decay.

High on a mound half a mile away stands Stouts Hill School, a dashing castle of knapped flint, all turrets and arrow-slits and skirted by a dragon-fly flicking, carp-snapping, mallow-flaming lake. The lane from Stouts Hill to the village winds steeply down to the Dursley road. There is horse shit there, dropped in caramac-coloured lumps by warm-sided bay mares ridden by gymkhana-jolly girls who blush fiercely when they meet your eye.

There is horse shit there all right.

In the village of Uley nought-percent-financed Daewoos lurk behind remotely controlled carport doors, satellite dishes glitter from the roofs, copal-varnished slices of barked Do-It-All elmwood proclaim Mulberry Lodge, South Fork and El Adobe. A blackboard outside the village pub vibrates in three-coloured chalk with the promise of Happy Hour, pool, premium guest beers and big screen satellite TV. The smell of stale lager and Doritos leaks up the main street to the church, where laserprinted A4 pages flap announcements from the chancel wall promising car boot sales and outreach fellowship retreats in Wales. Lard-arsed fatties in Russell Athletic sweatshirts swap Sensual Love Guide CD-ROMs with their neighbours as their Nike-ticked kids line up burger cartons on the barbecue patio and zap them with turbo-boosted water guns. The girls smear blusher on their cheeks and poke their tongues out fiercely when they meet your eye. Stouts Hill the school has closed now, to be replaced by Stouts Hill the time-share holiday home.

Well, maybe it's not so bad. Somewhere between warm gloop and cold water is the tepid truth about the village of Uley, which gets on with life as charmingly as it can. There was a time when the very Mansion furniture wax, dividend tea and gymkhana girls of sentimental memory were themselves modern and noisomely resented intrusions; books will one day be written that recall CD-ROMs and Russell Athletic sweatshirts in a nostalgic melancholy haze as fervent and foolish as any.

We will cut, just for a moment, to London. These days I have a flat in St James's, that elegant parcel of metropolitan clubland bordered by Piccadilly, Pall Mall, St James's Street and Lower Regent Street. It suits, I suppose, my self-image – or rather that image of me others have that I often weak-mindedly allow to become my self-image – to live in St James's. St James's has long been the natural habitat of the upper class English bachelor. Here he may browse for shirts and ties in Jermyn Street, for hats and shoes in Lock's and Lobb's, for foodstuffs in Fortnum's, for literature in Hatchards and the London Library, and for company in Brooks's, White's, Boodle's, Buck's or (if tragically pushed) in the improbably named East India, Devonshire, Sports and Public School's Club where the best school curry in all London can be found, served with sultanas and slices of banana, washed down with lukewarm London tap water poured into stout little Duralex glasses. I have lived in St James's for the last five years, not a proper English upper class bachelor at all, but tired of Islington, the proper home for people like me, and never at ease west of Hyde Park Corner or south of the Strand.

From my window I can see the clock face of Christopher Wren's handsome church of St James. Behind it – the other side of Piccadilly – Sackville Street leads up to Savile Row and the great Nash curve of Regent Street. In the year 1961 my parents visited Sackville Street, examining each doorway in turn until they came upon a brass plaque on which was written:

GABBITAS & THRING
SCHOLASTIC AGENCY

In the year 1977 I too visited Sackville Street, looking for the brass plaque that still said:

GABBITAS & THRING
SCHOLASTIC AGENCY

I don't suppose that any writer will ever be able to come up with a partnership that quite matches the ludicrous perfection of the names Gabbitas and Thring.

What is a Scholastic Agency?

Oh, tish now, and come, come, come . . . you know perfectly well.

A scholastic agency is a kind of public and prep school dating agency. It acts as a private sector pimp, procuring staff for short-handed schools, placement for jobless teachers and schools for parents at a loss to know where their little ones might thrive. That second service was of interest to me in 1977, and the third to my mother and father in 1961.

They wanted to find a prep school for my brother Roger and for me. I was four years old then and Roger well on his way to six. Today of course, what with the establishment of social equality, the smashing of the class system and the achievements of a Nation More At Ease With Itself, by the time your offspring have reached four and five it is *far* too late to be looking for schools: demand for private education is so high that children must be put down for admission not at birth but *in utero*, ideally before their first cells have divided.

There may be some reading this who are hazy (and proudly so) about the precise meanings of 'prep school' and 'public school'.

A prep school is an establishment designed, as the name implies, untypically for a British institution, to prepare a child. In this instance the preparation is for public school. Public school, as the name decidedly does *not* imply, very typically for a British institution, is wholly private. Public schools undertake to guide, mould and instruct pupils aged between thirteen and eighteen. Prep schools accept their intake from somewhere in the region of eight, nine or ten years old, and prepare them for the Common Entrance Examination, a test recognised by all the public schools. Different public schools are satisfied by different CE results. Thus Winchester, which has an interest in only the cleverest boys, would expect CE marks way above seventy per cent, while Malvern and Worksop and Monckton Combe by way of example, might be content with percentages in the nether fifties or upper forties. There is, it follows, no absolute pass mark in the Common Entrance. Public Schools can decide whom they take according to their need to have a fully pupilled and profitable school roll, according to their own sense of academic reputation, according to a candidate's athletic, musical or artistic qualities, or according to his status as offspring of an old boy or a Great, Rich and Desirable Parent.

At the time of my infancy, the early 1960s, nearly all prep and public schools were single-sex boarding schools. Today, girls are involved to a much greater degree, sometimes only in the Sixth Form, sometimes all the way through. Parents are more reluctant to pack their children off early and may choose to have them attend as day pupils or weekly boarders. Headmasters are younger than they were and more likely to be married. Parents expect more say in the running of a school, to attend more PTA meetings and to complain more vocally about living conditions, discipline and the curriculum. Heating, diet, facilities, syllabus and discipline seem far less Spartan now than they were twenty years ago. But these changes aside, the system, so far as I have been able to ascertain, is much as it was.

It is common enough, all things being equal, for a father to send his sons to the prep school he attended as a boy himself. My father, however, had been a chorister at St Paul's Cathedral and attended its choir school. My brother and I were unlikely to follow in his footsteps. The sound of Roger and Stephen Fry singing, even before Dame Nature had her impertinent pubic way with us, could cause people to stab themselves in the throat with sharpened pencils, jump from high windows, claw out their own inner ears, electrocute their genitals, put on a Jim Reeves record, throw themselves cackling hysterically into the path of moving buses . . . anything, anything to take away the pain. The cathedral choir school of St Paul's with its fussy, outworn emphasis on tunefulness and harmony was never going to be an option. Hence Gabbitas and Thring.

Young Mr Thring – or it may have been old Mr Gabbitas – recommended Stouts Hill Preparatory School, Uley, Near Dursley, Glos. Something in my mother's manner had told them that a friendly, warm place was required and few schools came friendlier than Stouts Hill: friendliness was its most notable feature. The school glowed with a kindly familial warmth that enfolded even the most sensitive, apron-clutching child. Founded and headmastered by one Robert Angus, it was effectively run by his four daughters, Carol, Sue, Paddy and Jane. These four Angus girls, young Mr Gabbitas said – and old Mr Thring signified his agreement by giving the desk a mighty thump – were considerate, charming, enthusiastic, sweet-natured and fun. The pupils all rode (for Miss Jane loved ponies and horses to distraction); there was fishing, boating and ice-skating on the lake; traipsing, nutting and blackberrying in the abundant outlying copses and woods; sailing and bird-spotting at Slimbridge and as much running, jumping, cricketing, ruggering, soccering, Latining, Greeking and Common Entrance preparing as the most doting parent could hope for. The diet was well balanced and nutritious, the school uniform amusing and stylish and the fees as frighteningly expensive as any parent could scream at. Every single Gabbitas and each several Thring was united in his commendation of Stouts Hill, Uley, Glos. and they were not afraid who knew it. My parents and Roger too, after a visit of inspection later in the year, approved warmly.

When my brother began his first term there the Fry family lived in Chesham, Buckinghamshire. When my turn came to follow him in the summer term of the year 1965, we had moved to Norfolk, the other side of England, two hundred British miles distant from Gloucestershire.

When people today hear that I was sent away to board at a school two hundred miles from home at the age of seven they often raise a disapproving eyebrow, snort a contemptuous snort or fling up a despairing hand at the coldness, cruelty and neglect of parents who could do such a thing to a child of such tender years: the words 'bosom' and 'snatching' and phrases like 'how could any . . . ?' and 'at such an age' and 'no wonder the British are so . . .' are often used.

There is great stupidity in this reaction, or at least minimal imagination, which is more or less the same thing, but morally worse. What is forgotten by those who dislike the idea of children being sent away at an early (or any) age is the matter of expectation and custom. The rightness or wrongness of private boarding education is a separate issue and I change my opinion about it as regularly as I change my socks, the desktop pattern on my computer screen and my views on God.

When I was seven years old every child that I knew of my own age went away to boarding school. Again the rightness or wrongness of being friendly only with children from similar backgrounds is a separate issue. The point is that my father had been to boarding school, my mother had been to boarding school, all the friends I had in the world went away to boarding school. It was what one did. It was Life as I knew it. A child of seven does not question such a circumstance: it is the way of the world. If I had *not* been sent away I should have wondered what was wrong with me. I should have felt neglected and left out. At a local day school I most emphatically should *not* have felt more loved or more cared for, far from it. Going round to play with friends in the school holidays and listening to their stories of boarding school would have left me feeling miserably excluded and inexplicably singled out for strange and unusual punishment. I know this for a fact, for I *did* spend a term at a primary school and, sweet and friendly as the place was, I couldn't wait to leave and join my brother.

Had we lived in Central London I dare say it might have been different. As it was we were hidden in the mysterious interior of rural East Anglia, where the nearest shop was a twenty-minute bicycle ride away and the nearest friends many miles farther. There was no door-bell ringing and can-Stephen-come-out-to-play-ing in Booton, Norfolk: no cool friends called Zak and Barnaby and Luke, no parks, no Saturday morning cinema clubs, no milk-shake parlours, no buses, no visiting ice-cream vans, no roller-skating rinks. When city-bred friends saw the house I lived in, they cooed with envy and delight at the idea of so much space with so much nature all around. I used to coo with envy when I stayed in a terraced house in suburban London and saw fitted carpets, central heating and drawing-rooms that were called sitting-rooms and had televisions in them.

It is also true that the ineptly hidden distress of my mother at the end of the school holidays gave me more direct, clear testament of absolute love than most children are ever lucky enough to receive at such an early age. That I was fucked up as a child and then as a youth, I cannot deny. That my fucked-up-edness sprang from a sense of betrayal, desertion or withheld love I will not allow.

Roger, my adorable brother, was and is far from fucked up after all, and he was the first to be sent away and might reasonably be expected to have felt the greater sense of abandonment, there being no elder in whose footsteps he might follow. Jo, my adorable sister, wasn't sent away at all, as girls weren't by then. She was fairly fucked up as a teenager but arguably *because* of the very fact that she didn't go to boarding school. Private education may be a divisive abomination, it may leave its product weird and ridiculous in all kinds of insanitary and peculiar ways, it may have held back the social development of this country, it may be responsible for all kinds of disasters and unpleasantnesses, but in my case it never left me feeling starved of parental love and attention. I think it safe to say that I would have been a fucked up youth had I been given a secondary modern, comprehensive or grammar school education. Whether at boarding school, day school or at home with governesses and private tutors, I would always have been as screwed up as an unwanted letter from the *Reader's Digest*. Wherever I had been, whatever I had done, I should have experienced an adolescence of sturm, drang, disaster and embarrassment.

This is all speculation. The facts are that my brother went to Stouts Hill, my sister was born and then the family moved to Norfolk.

Leaving Buckinghamshire meant leaving Chesham Prep, a day school where I had been having my pre-prep education. The town of Chesham perches itself between London Underground's Metropolitan Line and the Chiltern Hills embarrassedly unsure as to its status: country town or Metroland *banlieu*? Chesham Prep had four Houses – a House being a nominal administrative subdivision or *gau*, that is, not a physical building. I was in Christopher Columbus, and sported its blue badge with great pride. It took me many years to understand or truly believe that Columbus was actually Italian. Even to this day I can't fully accept it. Why would a school in the heart of England choose a foreign hero? Perhaps they were unaware of his nationality themselves. It was common knowledge that the British discovered everything – trains, democracy, television, printing, jets, hovercrafts, the telephone, penicillin, the flush lavatory and Australia, so it was reasonable to assume Christopher Columbus must have been a Briton. Francis Drake boys – or was the other House Nelson . . . or Walter Raleigh perhaps? I can't quite remember – wore badges of flaming vermilion. Chesham Prep was a co-educational school and my girlfriend, the object of my warm six-year-old affection, was Amanda Brooke, from whose soft charcoal lambswool V-neck glowed Florence Nightingale's proud primrose yellow. Her sister Victoria's jersey flashed with the lime green of Gladys Aylward, Innkeeper of the Sixth Happiness. Victoria was Roger's girlfriend, which kept things neat and in the family, so to speak.

It shames me to remember that eleven years and a couple of expulsions later, at seventeen and on the run from home, I was to return to Chesham, stay as a guest of the Brooke girls and steal a Diner's Club card from their father before running off on a wild nationwide spending spree that ended in prison and disgrace.

It was in the playground of Chesham Prep that I tripped and fell on my face one morning and broke my nose. At the time my nose was a cute little button – if any part of me has ever been cute – and the accident, although bloody and loud, was unremarkable in the life of a small child. Over the years however, my nose grew and grew and it became apparent by the time I was fourteen that, like its owner, it was not growing straight. From time to time through my teens and beyond I would say, 'I must get this damned nose straightened one day . . .' to which a gushing chorus would always reply, 'Oh no, Stephen, you mustn't . . . it's so *distinguished.*' There is of course nothing distinguished about a bent nose. A duelling scar may rightly be called distinguished, as might a slightly cleft chin or a glamorously imperceptible limp, but a bent nose is idiotic and unpleasant. I suppose people were trying to be kind and protect me from the humiliation of discovering that, even after an operation to straighten my ridiculous nose, I would still look a mess. The trauma of finding out that a straight-nosed Stephen looked every bit as unappetising as a bent-nosed Stephen might have tipped me completely over the edge.

We keep our insignificant blemishes so that we can blame them for our larger defects. The problem of my bent nose comes to mind when I have regular arguments with a friend on political subjects. He is firmly of the opinion that the existence of the monarchy, the aristocracy and the House of Lords is absurd, unjust and outdated. It would be hard to disagree with that. He believes, however, that in the name of liberty and social justice they should be abolished. This is where we part company. I think of the monarchy and aristocracy as Britain's bent nose. Foreigners find our ancient nonsenses distinguished, while we think them ridiculous and are determined to do something about them one day. I fear that when we do get rid of them, as I suppose we shall, we are going to let ourselves in for the psychic shock of discovering that the process has not made us one jot freer or one ounce more socially equitable a country than France, say, or the United States of America. We will remain just as we are, about *as* free as those countries. We are probably not quite as free at the moment (whatever free might mean) or as socially just (ditto) as the Benelux countries or Scandinavia, and as it happens, Scandinavia and the Benelux countries have monarchs. There will be great psychological damage done to us if we take the step of constitutional cosmetic alteration. The world would stare at us and whisper and giggle about us excitedly, as people always do when friends have had some sort of plastic surgery. We would unwind our bandages, present our new, straight-nosed constitution to the international community and await the fawning compliments and gasps of admiration. How hurt we will be when we see that the international community is actually yawning and, far from being dazzled by the blaze of justice and freedom and beauty that radiates from our features, they are rather indignant that instead of dining in splendour and pageantry with a crowned monarch, their heads of state will in future be lunching at President Hattersley's Residence or sipping tea with Lady Thatcher in some converted People's Palace. Britain would suddenly have no absurd minor blemish to blame for its failures, which are of course no more than the defects of being human. If we concentrated on our real defects; if we blamed our weakness of political will for impeding the achievement of greater social justice rather than pretending that it is all the fault of harmless warts and daft mannerisms, then we might indeed be better off. The trouble with doing a thing for cosmetic reasons is that one always ends up with a cosmetic result, and cosmetic results, as we know from inspecting rich American women, are ludicrous, embarrassing and horrific. But of course, I am a sentimentalist, and sentimentalists will hunt for any excuse to maintain the more harmless fripperies of the *status quo*.

Hey, we are straying far from our sheep, as they say in France. I was at Chesham Prep, six years old with a budding bent nose and I was going to tell you all about the boy from the Cape.

At Chesham Prep, my form mistress Mrs Edwards gave us all italic pencils which we were allowed to sharpen with knives. She wrote with flat-sided chalk on the blackboard and italic lettering was ever her theme, her message, her purpose and her passion. We were not allowed to write so much as our own names with italic pencils until we had covered page after page of our rough books, first with wavy lines going up and down, up and down, up and down, next with all the letters of the alphabet unjoined, and finally with all the letters of the alphabet joined up in approved style. To this day, every six months or so, at a stationer's, I will buy an Osmiroid calligraphic writing set and practise my italic shapes, thick thin, thick thin, thick thin. I will rule constraining lines and write the alphabet within them, and then I will write the same favourite words from those days: I have always especially loved the way italic tools will render the dots on the letters 'i' and 'j', thus –

i j

– so I take great pleasure in the look of words like –

jiving ~ skiing ~ Hawaii ~ jiujitsu

– and most especially –

Fiji ~ Fijian

After a few days of this kind of arseing about, I will leave the lids off the pens, the nibs will go dry and the special ink will harden into a gummy resin. A week or so later I throw the whole kit away and wonder what the hell I have been playing at.

In the middle of my last term in Mrs Edwards' class a very pretty boy with fair hair and a wide smile arrived. He had come from Cape Town and Mrs Edwards adored him. His italic lettering was as gorgeous as he was and I found myself torn between resentment and infatuation. The boys I fell for subsequently were usually very neat and very well behaved. Far too well behaved for my liking.

Every action and gesture of the boy from Cape Town (who might have been called Jonathan, although perhaps that's a trick of affinity – something to do with the publishers Jonathan Cape) reminded me of my clumsiness of line. My upstrokes were bulky and badly proportioned, his were graceful and pure; my fingers were always inky while his were always clean, finished off with perfect nails. He had out-turned lips that were most luscious then, but are today probably of that strangely opened out, overmoist quality as common to ex-colonials of the southern hemisphere as sandy eyelashes and wide hips. I expect now he looks like Ernie Els or Kerry Packer. Shame.

Perhaps the boy from Cape Town set the pattern for all the love that lay in store for me. Strange thought. I haven't ever

recalled him to mind before this minute. I hope this book isn't
to become regression therapy. How unpleasant for you. I do
wonder though if he still writes in italics as he did when we
were infants, thirty-four years ago.

   Sex of course, meant nothing to me. Bottoms and willies
featured greatly in life at Chesham from the age of three
onwards and they gave perpetual amusement, suffused with
intense, muffled delight. There was a boy called Timothy who
sat next to me in Mrs Edwards' class. We would pull the back
of our shorts and underpants down as we sat at our desks, so
that we could feel our bare bottoms against the wooden seats.
From the front, to Mrs Edwards' eye, everything would look
normal. This excited me hugely: both the bareness of bottom
and the secrecy were inexplicably delicious. Not to the point of
erection you understand, at least not so far as I remember.
Timothy and I would sometimes go into the woods together to
play what we called Rudies. Rudies involved peeing up against
a tree in as high an arc as we could manage or watching each
other poo. All very mysterious. I can't pretend that I find
anything appealing in that sexual arena today, although I know
that many august personages are highly pleased by the idea.
One is always hearing about those who pay prostitutes to
empty their bowels on to glass-topped coffee-tables under
which the client lies in a frenzy of excitement, pressing his face
up against the excremental outpush. We think this all very
English, but as a matter of fact a trawl through the grosser areas
of Internet Usenet postings will show that Americans, as in all
things *outré*, win the palm with ease. I haven't looked in on the
newsgroup alt.binaries.tasteless for a year or so now but it's
quite clear there's a big world of scatological weirdness out
there. The French come next: I don't suppose anyone who has
done so will forget the experience of reading de Sade's *The One
Hundred and Twenty Days of Sodom* and those elegantly
disengaged descriptions of the bishop's way with coffee. Then
there was that French intellectual and structuralist hero who
liked to lie in a trough in gay bars and be pissed on by
strangers. No, it may come as a disappointment to you, but the
fact is we British are no weirder than anyone else when it

comes to sexual oddity, we just *think* we are, which is the basis of our weirdness. Just as it is the *love* of money that it is the root of all evil, so it is the *belief* in shamefulness that is the root of all misery.

I can't for the life of me remember where the woods were that we visited for our rather tame rudies or who Timothy was. His name wasn't Timothy of course, and if he is reading this book now he has probably forgotten the escapades entirely and is reciting it to his wife by the fireside as an example of how he was always right about that disgusting Stephen Fry chap.

I have no memories of early 'sex-games', as the Kinsey and Hite people like to call them, which involved the opposite sex. A girl did once show me her knickers and I remember finding the elastic and the colour unappealing. I can't recall wanting to know or see more. A friend of mine at university, asked when he knew he was gay, said that he distinctly remembered at the moment of his birth looking back up there and saying, 'Well! That's the last time I'm ever going up one of *those* . . .' I have since shamelessly used this as my own explanation of When I Knew.

I liked girls greatly, except when they bullied me or pursed their lips prissily and said, 'Um! Telling on *you* . . .'

The inelegance of my italics, the shimmering beauty of Jonathan Cape and those occasional rudies with Timothy aside, my six-year-old life is hidden for the moment in an impenetrable mist. I know that I could read well at three and write accurately at four, and that I never ever learned my times table.

In Chesham we dwelt in a very Betjemanesque kind of road called Stanley Avenue. Sherwood House where we lived has since been pulled down and replaced by a housing estate that calls itself a Close. I suppose that means Sherwood House must have been large, but I only remember a few details: a stained glass entrance porch; a booth where a black telephone with a sliding drawer under it lived – the dial had the letters in red so that one could easily call PUTney 4234 and CENtral 5656. I loved to bang the hard bakelite cradle up and down and listen to the hollow, echoing clicks it sent down the line. Sounds are not as evocative as smells, but to anyone over the age of thirty-five the old dialling and hanging-up tones are as instant a transport to the past as the clunking of half-crowns and the *thlop* of the indicator flipping up on an old Austin motorcar.

I was intensely fascinated by the telephone. Not in the way of a teenage girl chattering for hours lying on her stomach with her thighs pressed together and ankles crossed in the air, but intrigued by how it changed people. In those days, when you were cut off you would rattle the cradle and shout, 'Operator! Operator!' Older people still do it. They don't know that it's as fruitless as pulling at a servant's bell or asking for the Left Luggage office.

They don't know that in the world today . . .

THERE'S NO ONE THERE

They don't know that the Bible is a Customer Service Announcement and that purgatory is when St Peter puts you on hold and sends you into a self-contained menu-driven loop of tone button operated eternity to the sound of Vivaldi's 'Spring'.

The very word 'Hello' only earned its sense of a greeting after the American phone companies hunted about for a new word with which telephonic conversations could politely, unsuggestively and neutrally be initiated, much as the BBC in the 1930s threw open the debate as to what someone who watched television might be called. The wireless had listeners, should television have watchers? Viewer, of course, was the word decided upon. In the case of telephony, the aim was to stop people saying 'Who is that?' or 'How do you do?' or even 'Howdy'. 'Good morning' and 'Good day' had a somewhat valedictory flavour, as well as being of doubtful use in a country divided up into so many time zones. Prior to the 1890s 'hello!' had simply been an exclamation of surprise and interest, with obvious venery overtones. By the turn of the century everyone was writing songs and newspaper articles about 'Hello Girls' and beginning to use the word in real life as salutation's vanilla-flavoured, everyday, entry-level model.

My favourite telephone fact, for this was the time, as I approached seven, that I began to collect facts instead of butterflies, stamps or football cards, was that Alexander Graham Bell was said to have made the following entirely endearing remark soon after he had invented the telephone: 'I do not think I am exaggerating the possibilities of this invention,' he said, 'when I tell you that it is my firm belief that one day there will be a telephone in every major town in America.'

In those days, my father actually went out to work, so I suppose I associate the telephone with my mother and Chesham, its laurels and shrubs and nearby ticking Atco mowers and with a suburban idyll so soon to be replaced in Norfolk by spooky attics, rural isolation and permanent paternal presence. Sherwood House in my mind is where *Just William*'s William lived, it is where Raffles and Bunny went when they wanted to relieve a *parvenue* of her pearls, it is where Aunt Julia had her Wimbledon fastness in Wodehouse's Ukridge stories. In Sherlock Holmes it is the house of the Norwood Builder and the mysterious Pondicherry Lodge. In fact, it is easier for me to remember Sherwood House by opening a page of any one of those books and allowing the flood of image to take over than it is for me to sit down and make a concentrated attempt at genuine recall.

My mother occasionally taught English to foreign students and history at nearby colleges and schools, but I think of her at a typewriter in the dining room, with myself curled under her feet staring into a gas fire and listening to *Mrs Dale's Diary*, *Twenty Questions* and *The Archers*. Or hearing her voice rise in pitch and volume and decrease in speed and sense when the telephone had rung and she had hurried through to the booth in the hall to answer it. I swear it is less than five years since I last heard her say down the line in her kindest clear-and-slow-for-foreigners voice:

'If you are in a call-box, press button B . . .'

Buttons A and B must have vanished from payphones twenty years ago.

That is my image of infancy. Just me, glowing in the

combined warmth of the gas fire, my big-bellied mother and her Ferguson wireless. If it felt in a sociable mood, our Siamese cat would join us, but in my memory we are alone. Sometimes we will get up, my mother stretching, hands on hips and, after she has found a headscarf and a raincoat, we will leave the house. We visit the hairdresser's, the Home and Colonial Stores, the Post Office, and finally Quell's where I noisily hoover up a raspberry milkshake while my mother closes her eyes in bliss as she spoons in a melon or tomato sorbet. On the way back we feed stale crusts to the ducks in the park. All the way there and back, she will talk to me. Tell me things. What words mean. Why cars have number-plates. How she met Daddy. Why she must go into hospital soon to have a baby. She makes up stories about a koala called Bananas. In one adventure Bananas comes to England to visit relations at Whipsnade for Christmas and suffers terribly because of the cold, the foolish animal having packed only his shorts, swimming trunks and sandals in the expectation that Buckinghamshire would be boiling hot in December. I giggle, as we children do, at the stupidity of those who don't know things that we have only just been taught ourselves.

Life has been downhill ever since. Or do I mean uphill?

As we reach Stanley Avenue, we race for the house and, pregnant as she is, Mother always *nearly* wins. She was athletic at school and kept goal for the England schoolgirls' hockey team.

There were *au pair* girls at Chesham, German or Scandiwegian usually, there was Mrs Worrell who scrubbed, there was Roger and in the evenings, there was the terrifying prospect of Father. But in my memory there is Mother at the typewriter (once she loudly said 'fuck' forgetting I was under her chair) and there is me, gazing into the blue and orange flames.

One morning I was off school, whether shamming or genuinely sick I can't remember. Mother came into my bedroom, hands wearily pressed against hips, and told me that the time had come for her to go into hospital. Roger had once attempted to tell me how pregnancy came about. One or both

of us became a little confused and the picture in my head was
that of my father as a kind of gardener, dropping a small seed
into my mother's tummy-button and watering it with his pee.
A peculiar image I suppose, but to a race of Martians no
stranger than the unwieldy truth.

The upshot of all this was a baby girl, Joanna. Her middle
name Roselle came from my mother's own Viennese mother. It
became my particular joy to help feed and dress this new sister
and my most burning ambition to be the first person she smiled
at.

I was now officially a middle child.

The next week we left Chesham and headed for Norfolk.

2

It is January 1965. Roger, who is eight, has returned to Stouts
Hill for his second term. I am considered a spot too young. I
am due to follow him in the summer so in the meantime I
attend for one time-marking term a Church of England
primary school in the village of Cawston, a mile from our new
house in Booton.

Cawston Primary School was run by John Kett, descended
from Kett of Kett's Rebellion, the Kett who ended his days
hanging from chains on the ramparts of Norwich Castle. The
twentieth-century descendant is a kindly figure who writes
books on Norfolk dialect and is much loved and looked up to
by everyone for miles around. Whether he shares his noisome
ancestor's belief in eastern independence I could not say, but I
am certain that were today's fashion for devolution to be
continued into the ancient kingdoms of England, he would be
a very natural candidate for King of Anglia – perhaps with
Delia Smith as his consort.

'I need a volunteer,' Miss Meddlar said one day.

My hand shot up. 'Oh, Miss, me Miss! Please Miss!'

'Very well, Stephen Fry.' Miss Meddlar always called me by

both names. It is one of my chief memories of primary school, that of being Stephen Fry all the time. I suppose Miss Meddlar felt first names were too informal and surnames too cold and too affected for a decent, Christian village school. 'Take this to Mr Kett's class please, Stephen Fry.'

'This' was a sheet of paper bearing test results. Spelling and Adding Up. I had annoyed myself by getting one answer wrong in the spelling round. I had spelled the word 'many' with two 'n's. Everyone else had made the same mistake but compounded the error by using an 'e', so Miss Meddlar had given me half a point for knowing about the 'a'. I took the sheet of paper from her knowing that my name headed the list with nineteen and a half out of twenty.

Out in the corridor I walked towards Mr Kett's classroom door. I stood there ready to knock when I heard laughter coming from inside.

No one in life, not the wartiest old dame in Arles, not the wrinkledest, stoopingest Cossack, not the pony-tailedest, venerablest old Mandarin in China, not Methuselah himself, will ever be older than a group of seniors at school. They are like Victorian photographs of sporting teams. No matter how much more advanced in years you are now than the age of those in the photograph, they will always look a world older, always seem more capable of growing a bigger moustache and holding more alcohol. The sophistication with which they sit and the air of maturity they give off is unmatchable by you. Ever.

The laughter from inside Mr Kett's room came from nine- and ten-year-olds, but they were nine- and ten-year-olds whose age I will never reach, whose maturity and seniority I can never hope to emulate. There was something in the way their laughter seemed to share a mystery with Mr Kett, a mystery of olderness, that turned my knees to water. I pulled back my hand from the door just in time to stop it from knocking, and fled to the changing room.

I sat panting on a bench by the lockers staring miserably at Miss Meddlar's sheet of paper. I couldn't go through with it. I just couldn't walk into that senior classroom.

I knew what would happen if I did, and I rehearsed the scene in my head, rehearsed it in such detail that I believed that I actually *had* done it, just as a scared diver on the high board finds his stomach whooming with the shock of a jump he has made only in his mind.

I shivered at the thought of how the scene would go.

I would knock.

'Come in,' Mr Kett would say.

I would open the door and stand at the threshold, knees wobbling, eyes downcast.

'Ah. Stephen Fry. And what can I do for you, young man?'

'Please, Mr Kett. Miss Meddlar told me to give you this.'

The seniors would start to laugh. A sort of contemptuous, almost annoyed laughter. What is this squidge, this fly, this *nothing* doing in our mature room, where we were maturely sharing a mature joke with Mr Kett? Look at him . . . his shorts are all ruckled up and . . . my God . . . are those StartRite sandals, he's wearing? *Jesus* . . .

My name being first on the list would only make it worse.

'Well, Master Fry. Nineteen and a half out of twenty! A bit of a brain box, by the look of things!'

Almost audible sneers at this and a more muttered, angry kind of laughter. *Spelling*! *Adding up* for Christ's sake . . .

No, it was intolerable. Unthinkable. I couldn't go in there.

I wanted to run away. Not home. Just away. To run and run and run and run. Yet I was too frightened to do that either. Oh dear. Oh double dear. Such terrible, terrible misery. And all because I had done well. All because I had stretched up my hand so high and squealed 'Oh, Miss, me Miss! Please Miss' so loudly and so insistently.

It was all wrong, the world was all wrong. I was Stephen Fry in a changing room in a small school in Norfolk and I wanted to be someone else. Someone else in another country in another age in another world.

I looked down at Miss Meddlar's piece of paper. My name at the top was running saltily into the name of Darren Wright below. Darren Wright had fourteen marks out of twenty. Fourteen was a much more sensible mark. Not at all embarrassing. Why couldn't *I* have scored fourteen?

I screwed the paper into a ball and stuffed it into a wellington boot. It was Mary Hench's wellington boot. It said so in clear black writing on Elastoplast stuck to the inside. Mary Hench and I were friends, so maybe she wouldn't tell if she found it.

I stood up and wiped my nose. Oh *dear*.

Over the next ten years I was to find myself alone in changing rooms many, many times more, the longest ten years of my life. This occasion was innocent and infantile, those future visits guiltier and more wicked by far. To this day institutional changing rooms make my heart beat with a very heavy hammerblow of guilt. The feeling of wanting not to be Stephen Fry, wanting to be someone else in another country in another age, that was to return to me many times too.

I left this ur-changing room, this primal prototype of all the changing rooms that were to be, and had no sooner sunk tremblingly back into my seat in Miss Meddlar's classroom than the bell went for morning break.

As was my habit I joined Mary Hench and the other girls at the edge of the playground, hard by the painted hopscotch lines. She was a large girl, Mary Hench, with gentle brown eyes and a pleasant lisp. We liked to bounce tennis balls against the wall and talk about how stupid boys were while we watched them playing football and fighting in the middle of the playground. Soft, she called them. Boys were soft. Sometimes I was soft, but usually I was daft, which was a little better. With Mary Hench was Mabel Tucker, the girl I sat next to in Miss Meddlar's. Mabel Tucker wore National Health spectacles and I of course called her Table Mucker which she hated. She would shout out loudly in class when I farted, which I did not believe to be playing the game.

'Please, Miss. Stephen Fry's just farted.'

Not on. Outside of enough. You were supposed to giggle secretly and delightedly or pull your sweater up over your nose. To draw adult attention to the event was quite monstrously wrong. Besides, I wasn't sure that adults *knew* about farting.

Just as break was coming to an end, I saw, out of the corner of my eye, Miss Meddlar surveying the playground. I tried to hide behind Mary Hench, who was bigger than me, but she told me not to be so soft and pushed me ahead.

'Stephen Fry,' said Miss Meddlar.

'Yes, Miss?'

'Mr Kett says that you never did give him that sheet of paper.'

Boys and girls were pushing past me on their way back to their classes.

'No, Miss. That's right, Miss. He wasn't in his classroom. He must have gone out. So I left it on his desk.' Said airily. Jauntily. Insouciantly.

'Oh. Oh I see,' Miss Meddlar looked a little confused, but in no sense incredulous.

With a calm 'if there's nothing further?' cock of the eyebrow, I moved on.

At lunch Mr Kett came to my table and sat down opposite me. I felt a thousand eyes burning into me.

'Now then, young man. What's this about me not being in the classroom this morning? I never left my classroom.'

'Well, I knocked, sir, but you didn't answer.'

'You knocked?'

'Yes, sir. As you didn't answer I went away.'

'Miss Meddlar says you said you left the mark sheet on my desk.'

'Oh no, sir. As you didn't answer my knock I went away.'

'I see.'

A pause, while, all hot and prickly, I looked down at my lunch.

'Well, if you give me the mark sheet now then . . .'

'Sir?'

'I'll take it now.'

'Oh. I lost it, sir.'

'You *lost* it?'

'Sir. In break.'

A puzzled look spread over Mr Kett's face.

Get to know that puzzled look, Stephen Fry. You will see it many times.

For Narcissus to find himself desirable, the water he looks into must be clear and calm and sweet. If a person looks into a turbulent pool his reflection will be dark and disturbed. That was Mr Kett's face, rippled with dark perturbation. He was being lied at, but lied at so *well* and for so impenetrable a reason.

I can see his perplexity so clearly. It looms before me now and the turbulence in his eyes makes me look very ugly indeed.

Here was a bright boy, very bright. He came from a big house up the road: his parents, although newcomers to Norfolk, seemed nice people – even qualifying for what used to be called *awfully* nice. Their boy was only here at this little school for a term before he went away to prep school. Kett was a man of his village and therefore a man of the world. He had seen bright children before, he had seen children of the upper middle classes before. This boy seemed presentable enough, charming enough, decent enough and here he was telling the lie direct without so much as a blush or stammer.

Maybe I'm over-refining.

There is very little chance that John Kett remembers that day. In fact, I know he doesn't.

Of course I'm over-refining. I'm reading into the incident what I want to read into it.

Like all teachers, John Kett overlooked and pardoned those thousands of revelatory moments in which the children under his care exposed the animal inside them. Every day he must bid good morning to men and women, parents now themselves, whom once he witnessed thrashing about in mad tantrum, whom once he saw wetting themselves, whom once he saw bullying or being bullied, whom once he saw bursting into terrified screams at the sight of a tiny spider or the sound of distant thunder, whom once he saw torturing ladybirds. True, a cold lie is worse than animal savagery or hot fright, but that lie is and always was, my problem, not John Kett's.

This Affair of the Test Results in Mary Hench's Wellington Boot is a big episode for me simply because I remember it so clearly: it is significant, in other words, because I have decided that it is significant and that in itself is of significance to me. I suppose it seems to mark in my mind the beginning of what was to become a pattern of lonely lies and public exposures. The virtue of this particular lie was that it was pointless, a pure lie, its vice that it was so consciously, so excellently done. When Kett sat down to question me at the lunch table I had been nervous – mouth dry, heart thumping, hands clammy – but the moment I began to speak I found I became more than simply nerveless, I became utterly confident and supremely myself. It was as if I had discovered my very purpose in life. To put one over, to dupe: to deceive not only without shame, but with pride, with real pride. *Private* pride, that was always the problem. Not a pride I could share in the playground, but a secret pride to hug to myself like miser's gold or pervert's porn. The hours leading up to exposure would have me sweating with fear, but the moment itself would define me: I became charged, excited and happy, while at the same time maintaining absolute outward calm and confidence, able to calculate in microseconds. Telling lies would bring about in me that state the sportsman knows when he is suddenly in form, when the timing becomes natural and rhythmic, the sound of the bat/racket/club/cue sweet and singing: he is simultaneously relaxed and in deepest concentration.

I could almost claim that the moment the police snapped the cuffs about my wrists eleven years later was one of the happiest of my life.

Of course, someone might try to make the connection between all this and acting. When acting is going well, the same feeling of mastery of time, of rhythm, control and timing comes over one. Acting, after all, is lying, lying for the pure exquisite joy of it, you might think. Only acting isn't that, not to me at any rate. Acting is telling truth for the pure, agonising hell of it.

People always think that actors make good liars: it seems a logical thought, just as one might imagine that an artist would make a good forger of other people's signatures. I don't think there's any especial truth in either assumption.

Things I often heard from parents and schoolteachers.

'It's not that you *did* it, but that you *lied* about it.'

'*Why* did you lie?'

'It's as if you actually *wanted* to get caught.'

'Don't lie to me, again, Fry. You're a terrible liar.'

No I'm not, I used to think to myself. I'm a brilliant liar. So brilliant that I do it when there isn't even the faintest chance of being believed. That's lying for the sake of it, not lying purely to achieve some fatuous end. That's *real* lying.

All of this *is* going to return us to Samuel Anthony Farlowe Bunce before long.

First I will tell you what in reality John Kett chooses to remember about me. One by-product of slebdom is that those who taught you are often asked to comment about your young self. Sometimes they do it in newspapers, sometimes they do it in public.

A few years ago I was asked by John Kett's successor to open the Cawston School Fete, or Grand Summer Fair, to give it its due title.

Anyone who grew up in the country twenty or thirty years ago knows a lot about fetes. Fetes worse than death, as my father called them with self-ironising ho-ho jocularity.

At East Anglian country gatherings there was dwile flonking – now sadly being replaced by the more self-conscious urban appeal of welly throwing. There was bowling for a pig – in those days country people knew how to look after a pig, I expect today's average Norfolk citizen if confronted by such an animal would scream, run away and sue. There was throwing a wet sponge at the rector (or vicar – generally speaking Norfolk villages thought it smarter to have a rector than a vicar – I believe the difference is, or was, that the bishop chooses a vicar and the local landowner chooses a rector). There were bottle stalls, bran tubs filled with real bran, Guess the Weight of the Ram for a Penny competitions, coconut shies and tractor or traction engine rides for sixpence.

If my brother, sister and I were very lucky, a local fete might offer Harry Woodcock, a local watchmender and seller of ornaments, whose shop sign proclaimed him to be:

Harry Woodcock
"The Man You Know"

Woodcock went from fete to fete carrying with him a bicycle wheel attached to a board. The wheel had radiating from its centre like the minute hand of a clock an arrow which was spun for prizes. Nicky Campbell does much the same thing on British television, and Merv Griffin's American original *The Wheel of Fortune* has been showing on ABC for decades. Harry Woodcock blew such professionals out of the water and left them for dead. He wore extravagantly trimmed pork-pie hats and pattered all the while like a cockney market trader. East End spiel in a Norfolk accent is a very delicious thing to hear.

My sister approached me during one such Saturday afternoon fete just as I was estimating how many mint imperials there might be in a huge jar that an archdeacon bore beamingly about a thronged deanery garden.

'You'll never guess who's here . . .'

'Not . . . ?'

'Yup. The Man You Know.'

And off we scampered.

'Hello there, young man!' boomed The Man You Know, tipping his hat as he did to everyone and everything. 'And young Miss Fry too.'

'Hello, Mr Man You Know,' we chorused, striving with a great effort of will not to dissolve into a jelly of rude giggles. We paid a shilling and received a tickety-boo each. These were blocks of polished wood with a number from nought to twenty painted on each side. All tickety-boos were to be to tossed back into a basket, to another tip of the hat, after each spin of the wheel. The Man You Know had attempted some grace with the brush when painting the numbers, giving each digit a little flourish. I could picture him the day he made them – they were decades old by this time – his tongue would have been poking out, as it did when he examined broken watches, while he sissed and haahed out his breath and ruined each wooden block with too much of an effort to be decorative and neat. My sister, who had and has great talent with brush and pen, could have stroked out twenty numbers in twenty seconds and each one would have been graceful and fine and easy. There was a mournful clumsiness about The Man You Know, his dignity and his tickety-boos.

As indeed there was about his patter.

'Roll, bowl or pitch. You never do know, unless you ever do know. Lady Luck is in a monstrous strange mood this afternoon, my booties. She's a piece, that Lady Luck and no mistake. A lucky twenty tickety-boos and a lucky twenty numbers, each one solid gold, or my name's not Raquel Welsh. You can't accoomerlate, less you specerlate, now if that aren't the truth I'm not the Man You Know. And I am, oh yes, but I am. I yam, I yam, I yam, as the breadfruit said to Captain Bligh. Here's a fine gentlemen: two more punters needed fore I can spin, better give me a bob, sir – you might win a present to keep that wife a yours from straying. Thanking you kindlier than you deserve. Here comes a lovely lady. My mistake, it's the curate, no, that *is* a lovely lady. Up you step, my bootiful darling, I shan't let you go – that's either a shilling for a tickety-boo or you give me the biggest smacker of a kiss that you ever did give in all your born days. Blast, another shilling. I'd rather a had the kiss. Lays and gen'men . . . The Man You Know is about to spin. The world . . .' here he would hold his finger exaggeratedly to his lips, 'the world . . . she hold her breath.'

And so the world did hold her breath. The world, she held her breath and the wheel ticked round.

Well, the world has stopped holding her breath. She has exhaled and blown us a gust of bouncy castles and aluminium framed self-assembly stalls that sell strange seamed tickets of purple pulped paper that you rip open and litter the grass with when you find that you have not won a huge blue acrylic bear. The side-shows we queue for now are the Ride in the All New Vauxhall 4x4 Frontera (courtesy Jack Claywood Vauxhall Ltd.), the Virtual Reality Shoot Out and the chance to Guess the RAM of the Compaq PC, kindly provided by PC Explosion of Norwich.

Hang on, I hear the voice of Mary Hench telling me that I've gone soft. Thinking about the countryside can do that to me.

When I was a literature student one was for ever reading that all great literature was and always had been about the tension between civilisation and savagery:

- Apollo and Dionysus
- Urbs et rus
- Court and forest
- City and arcadia
- Pall Mall and maypole
- Town and country
- High street and hedgerow
- Metropolis and Smallville
- Urban sprawl and rural scrub

It is fitting that as I write this I am half-listening to David Bellamy, Jeremy Irons and Johnny Morris as they address a mass rally gathered in Hyde Park. They are warning the nation about the danger being done to the countryside by urban ignorance and misplaced metropolitan sentimentality. The *point d'appui* of the rally was to save fox-hunting, but it seems to have turned into something bigger.

I've just turned on the television . . . it *is* a huge crowd, almost as large as the number of townies who flock to the Yorkshire Dales every Sunday, but these people, I suspect, will at least leave the park tidy and free of litter.

I suppose some rat-faced weasel from New Malden will be interviewed at any minute to give the other side of the hunting debate.

Bingo! I'm right. Though by the sound of him he's from Romford rather than New Malden. And he's just described fox-hunting as 'barbaric', which is peculiar since he's the one with the stutter. Forgive the pedantry of a frustrated classicist.

They should have asked a fox instead.

'Would you rather be hunted by hounds, gassed, trapped, poisoned or shot, old darling?'

'Well, since you mention it, I'd rather be left alone.'

'Ng . . . but given that that isn't an option?'

'No? Thought not. It never is, is it?'

'Well, you know. Lambs. Chicken farms. Hysterical people hearing you rootling through their wheelie bins at night.'

'I like a nice wheelie bin.'

'Yes, that's as may be, but which way would you rather be killed?'

'Think I'll stick to dogs if it's all the same to you. A fox knows where he is with hounds. My direct ancestors have lived in the same place, hunted by hounds every winter, for three hundred years. Hounds are simply hopeless when you come down to it.'

That's enough about town and country. I was supposed to be telling you about John Kett and the Cawston Village Fete. As it happens, there's a story about a mole fast approaching, so animals won't be left out.

Opening the Cawston School Fete counted as both duty and pleasure. I was an Old Boy, I had a connection, something to *do*, other than wander about with my hands behind my back like minor royalty inspecting a dialysis machine. I could revisit the changing room for example, savour once more the poster-paint tang of the art cupboard and see if the hopscotch rink had been repainted since Table Mucker's championship season.

The Cawston Fete was not quite the miracle of yesterdecade, but – an alarming exhibition of tae kwan-do given by local boys aside – there was enough of a smell of oversugared sponge cake and faintly fermenting strawbails to remind me of when the world was young and guilty.

I wandered from stall to stall in a sort of daze, interrupted now and then by the shy murmur of, 'I don't suppose you'll remember me . . .'

Table Mucker had grown an explosive pair of breasts and a large brood of daughters the eldest of whom looked ready to start production on her own. Mary Hench grinned at me from behind a downy moustache and a fierce girlfriend (clearly boys were still soft in her book) while John Kett himself seemed unchanged from the man whose puzzled eyes had lived with me in silent reproach for twenty-five years.

'Well, young man, I expect everything seems to have shrunk since last you were here.'

I agreed and he turned the subject to moles.

Moles?

Other people at the fete had mentioned moles too, with twinkles or with amused, nose-tapping suggestiveness on my arrival and as I made the traditional preliminary inspection of cake-stand and bottle-stall.

My parents' gardeners were a pair of brothers called Alec and Ivan Tubby who battled to keep the tennis court – as well as the improbable pride of our garden, the badminton lawn – free of moles. Was there some connection there?

Mole-catching is a great art and most practitioners (the fluorescent jacketed Rentokil variety always excepted) stand silently for great lengths of time staring at lawns and fresh molehills. After perhaps half an hour of this agonising inactivity they will at last make a move and pad softly towards apparently random places in the grass where they insert a number of traps. Over the next couple of days three or four dead moles will be pulled out. I suppose while they were standing doing nothing the mole-catchers were in fact reading tiny trembles in the earth, or patches of darker or lighter grass that gave them some suggestion as to where the moles were headed. The mole-hills themselves are not much of a clue of course: once they've dug them, the gentlemen in black velvet move themselves off. The trick is to guess in which direction they have gone.

Back in 1965, during the first weeks of my term at Cawston Primary School I had become more and more depressed about my inability to win a star for the Nature Table.

Every week, we pupils in Miss Meddlar's class would have to bring something in for a classroom display of biological *objets trouvés*. The prize exhibit would win a star. One week Mary Hench brought in a sandwich tern's egg, taken from a nest on the coast at Brancaster. After Miss Meddlar had established in her own mind the truthfulness of Mary Hench's assertion that the nest had been abandoned and the egg cold when happened upon (I didn't believe Mary Hench for a second, I remain convinced to this day that the wicked girl had simply clapped her enormous hands and shooed away a sitting mother, so insane and diabolical was her ambition to win more stars than anyone else and the Junior Achievement Cup and five shilling book token that went with them) a star was awarded. I had entertained high hopes that week for my badger's skull, boiled, vigorously scrubbed clean with Colgate toothpaste for a whiteness you can believe in and total fresh breath confidence, and attractively presented in a Queen's Velvet envelope box packed with shredded red cellophane. I was to do the same dental cosmetic job on a less easily identifiable bone (I was sure that it was human) some years later, and win my third Blue Peter Badge – and a third Blue Peter Badge, as the world knows, is instantly converted into a Silver Blue Peter Badge. But all these happy achievements lay a long way ahead. For the moment, I was starless. But my blood was up. I was going to win a star and make Mary Hench howl with envy if I had to commit murder to do it.

Glory never arrives through the front door. She sneaks in uninvited round the back or through an upstairs window while you are sleeping.

Grim weeks of effort and nature-trailing followed. I tried a starfish, a thrush egg, a collection of pressed campions and harebells and a boxful of shards of that willow pattern ironstone china that the Victorians buried in the earth for the sole purpose of disappointing twentieth-century treasure seekers. None of these met with the least success. By the eighth week of term I knew that Nature Table Star List by heart.

> Mary Hench
> Mary Hench
> Jacqueline Wright
> Ian Adams
> Jimmy Speed
> Mary Hench
> Mary Hench

One Sunday evening, as I was wheeling round and round the

stable block at home on my bicycle, racking my brains for an idea of what to offer up the next morning, Ivan Tubby approached me with something small and soft and dark cupped in his hands.

'Found a mole,' he said.

This was not a mole that had been squashed and spiked in a gin-trap, it was a mole that seemed to have died very recently of natural causes. Perhaps its mother and father had been trapped and it had popped up to see what was going on and where dinner was and then discovered with a shock that it couldn't see at all and in any case wasn't supposed to be above the ground with the Up There people and the Seeing Animals. In whatever manner it met its end, this was a young mole in the most excellent condition, its pink snout and spreading shovel paws still warm and quite perfectly shaped.

I begged to be allowed to keep him and Ivan generously consented, although as it happened he had marked him down as a treat for his cat.

The next morning I bicycled down the mile-long lane to Cawston in a fever of excitement, the mole packed in straw in my saddlebag. This was to be my day of triumph.

'Here we have a common European mole,' I would tell the class, Pear's *Family Cyclopaedia* having been thoroughly exhausted on the subject of moles the night before. 'Moles eat their own weight every day and can actually starve to death within twelve hours if they don't have enough food. A mole is capable of burrowing up to eighteen feet in one hour. Thank you.'

I imagined executing a small bow and receiving delighted applause from all but a frustrated, white-lipped Mary Hench, whose feeble puss-moth caterpillar or pathetic arrangement of barn owl pellets would go unnoticed.

I parked the bicycle and rushed to Miss Meddlar's, slowing down as I arrived in the doorway, so as to look cool and casual.

'Well now, you're very early this morning, Stephen Fry.'

'Am I, Miss? Yes, Miss.'

'And what's that you have there? Something for the nature table?'

'Yes, Miss. It's a –' I started, excitedly.

'Don't tell me now, child. Wait until class. Put it on the table and . . . well now *whatever* is going on?'

A violent explosion of giggles and screams could be heard coming from the playground. Miss Meddlar and I went to the window and tried to crane round and look towards the source of the uproar. Just then, Jimmy Speed, a chaotic, ink-stained boy, the kind who grins all the time as though he believes everyone to be quite mad, burst into the room.

'Oh, Miss, Miss. You'll never guess! You'll never ever guess!'

'Guess what, Jimmy Speed?'

'That's Mary Hench, Miss! She's brought a donkey in for the nature table. A real live donkey! Come out and see. That's ever so beautiful, though how he will fit on the table, that I do not know.'

'A donkey!' Miss Meddlar went pink with excitement, straightened her skirt and headed for the door. 'A donkey. Good heavens!'

I looked down at my little mole and burst into tears.

It was at the end of the week, just as everyone in the school was beginning to talk of things other than Mary Hench and her donkey, that Mr Kett came up to me in the playground and drew me aside.

'Hello there, young man,' he said. 'You look a little down in the dumps if I might say so.'

'Do I, sir?'

'You do, sir,' he said. 'I remember a joke I heard as a boy in the pantomime. Cinderella, that was. In Dereham, years before the war. One of the ugly sisters, she said, "Whenever I'm down in the dumps, I buy myself a new hat." And the other ugly sister replied, "So that's where you get them from then." I remember that as if it were yesterday.'

Only, said in his light Norfolk accent it came out as, '. . . I remember that as if it were yisty.'

'So,' he went on, putting a hand on my shoulder. 'What have you been getting down in those dumps?'

'Oh, nothing,' I said, 'only . . .'

'You can tell me, young man. If it's a secret it won't go any further. A boy told me the most amazing secret twenty years ago. Do you know what it was?'

'No,' I asked, perking up. There was nothing I loved better than a secret. 'What was it?'

'I shan't tell you,' said Mr Kett. 'It's a secret. See? That's how good I am at keeping them.'

'Oh. Well, you see, the thing is . . .'

And out spilled some kind of confused description of the disappointment, frustration, rage and despair that burned within me at being trumped by Mary Hench and her double-damned donkey.

'It was a such a *good* mole, you see . . . so *perfect*. Its paws were perfect, its snout was perfect, its fur was perfect. It was the best mole ever. Even though it was dead. *Any* other week it would have won a star. And it's not that stars are so important, it's just that I've never won one for the nature table. Not once. *Ever.*'

'You've had plenty of stars for spelling though, haven't you? So Miss Meddlar tells me.'

'Oh, *spelling* . . .'

'I had a look at your mole. It was a fine mole, there's no question about it. You should be very proud of him.'

That afternoon, as class ended, I went to the nature table, took the creature, now slightly corrupted by time, and wrapped it in a handkerchief.

'Is our mole leaving us?' Miss Meddlar asked, with what seemed to be a gleam of hope in her voice.

'I thought perhaps so,' I sighed. 'I mean, he is getting a bit . . . you know.'

Halfway back home I leaned my bike against a hedge and opened the handkerchief, setting myself scientifically to examine the nature of decay. The body of the mole, once so plush and fine, now matted and patched, appeared to be alive with shiny white ticks. From out of the weeping centre of the carcass, a black insect that had been feasting deep in the wet ooze, seemed suddenly to see me, or at least to see daylight and its chance for freedom. Taking fierce wing with a fluttering clockwork buzz, it launched itself into my eye. I gave a scream and dropped the whole bundle. The flying creature, whatever it was, spun upwards into the air and across the fields.

I felt a wetness around my ankles and looked down. The mole had fallen on to my sandals and exploded there, spreading itself all around my socks and feet. Squealing and shrieking in fright and revulsion, I hopped about flicking with the handkerchief at my shins as though they were on fire.

It was too horrible, nature was too horrible. Nature stank and squelched and vomited with slime, maggots and bursting guts.

I suppose this was the first time I had ever felt an urge not to be. Never an urge to die, far less an urge to put an end to myself – simply an urge not to be. This disgusting, hostile and unlovely world was not made for me, nor I for it. It was alien to me and I to it.

Pieces of the mole lined the foot of the hedge. I rubbed a little at my legs with the once fine, crisp linen handkerchief and then I held it up to the sky. They were the same, the handkerchief and the evening sky. Both spattered with ink and blood. The alien malevolence of a certain kind of late afternoon sunset has frightened me ever since.

'Good heavens, darling,' my mother said. 'Whatever is that smell?'

'Dead mole, what do you think?' I said crossly as I stamped up the back stairs.

'Well, you'd better go straight up and have a bath then.'

'What did you *think* I was doing? Going upstairs to . . . to . . . *play croquet*?'

Not the best put-down ever, but as tart as I could manage.

I didn't think once about the nature table over the weekend. It had rained, which gave me a fine opportunity to stay indoors and ignore nature entirely.

It was only as I bicycled in to school on Monday morning that I realised I had nothing at all for the weekly show and tell.

A stick, I thought. I'll jolly well take in a stick. If they don't want moles, they can make do with a stick. Sticks can be interesting too. Nature isn't all donkeys and otter spraints and tern's eggs and coypu skulls and rotten crawling living things. I'll bring in a dead stick.

So I picked up the first stick I biked past. A very ordinary stick. Dead, but neutral and uncorrupted in its death. And useful too, which is more than you can say for a rotting mole dropping to bits all over your ankles.

I brought the stick into the classroom and dumped it defiantly on the nature table.

'Well now,' said Miss Meddlar, after she had examined the week's crop with the irritating care and slowness of a pensioner paying at a checkout counter. 'Now then, well. Another wonderful effort from you all. I have to say I half expected to see an elephant in the playground, Mary, but that is a lovely jay's feather you've brought in for us, really lovely. But do you know what? The star this week is going to go to . . . Stephen Fry.'

'Hurrh?'

A dozen pairs of disbelieving eyes swivelled between me, Miss Meddlar and the very ordinary dead stick that lay on the nature table like a very ordinary dead stick.

'Come you on forward, Stephen Fry.'

I came me on forward, bewildered.

'This star is not for your stick, although I'm sure it is ever such a fine stick. This star is for you taking away your mole Friday . . .'

'Excuse me, Miss?'

'. . . because I have to say that the dratted thing was stinking out my classroom. He was stinking out the whole corridor, was your mole. I've never been so glad to see anything go in all my born days.'

The class erupted into noisy laughter and, since I was always, and have always been, determined that merriment should never be seen to be at my expense, I joined in and accepted my star with as much pleased dignity as I could muster.

How strange then, how more than passing strange, to discover a quarter of a century later that it was this trivial episode that the school remembered me for, and not for my cold lies and sly evasions.

John Kett was, still is I hope, a lay preacher and a better advertisement for Christianity than St Paul himself. Then again, in my unqualified opinion, Judas Iscariot, Nero and Count Dracula are all better advertisements for Christianity than St Paul ... but that's a whole other candle for a whole other cake. You aren't here to listen to my ignorant ramblings on the subject of theology.

The awful thing is this.

Until this day came twenty-five years on, with John Kett and others and their beaming mentions, I had entirely forgotten the mole and everything to do with it.

At the start of the fete, every time moles had been knowingly alluded to as I Prince Michael of Kented my way from stall to stall, I had pretended that I knew what it was all about, but I was dissembling furiously. I imagined that people might be referring to some television sketch that I had been in and since forgotten all about.

This often happens. I remember a few years ago being angrily yelled at from across the street by a complete stranger. Simply *purple* with fury this man was, shaking his fist and calling me a bastard pigging murderer. I assumed he was someone who didn't like my politics, my television appearances, my sexual preferences, my manner, my voice, my face – *me*. It hardly mattered. He could call me a fat ugly unfunny lefty queer and I would see his point of view. But *murderer*? Maybe it was because I was wearing leather shoes ... it is impossible to tell in these days of serial single issue fanatics. I wheeled round the corner and away. Such people are best avoided. One reads things, you know.

You can imagine my consternation when I realised that this lunatic was dashing round the corner after me in hot pursuit.

'Mr Fry! Mr Fry!'

I turned with what I hoped was a disarming smile, in reality seeking witnesses, policemen or an escape route.

The lunatic was holding up an apologetic hand.

'I suddenly saw that you didn't know what on earth I was talking about,' he said, scarlet with exertion and embarrassment.

'Well, I must confess . . .'

'Speckled Jim!'

'I'm sorry?'

'You know, Speckled Jim!'

Said as if this would clear the matter up entirely.

And then it had indeed dawned.

This man was referring to an episode of a television series in which the character I played, General Melchett, court-martials the hero, Blackadder, for killing, roasting and eating Melchett's favourite carrier pigeon, whose name was Speckled Jim.

At one point during the court-martial, which Melchett rather unsportingly chairs himself, he refers to Captain Blackadder in a loud splutter of mad rage as 'the Flanders pigeon-murderer'. *That* was the phrase this man had been shouting across the street. Not bastard pigging murderer at all . . .

The strange thing about television is that you do it once and then forget about it, while some obsessed fans will watch programmes over and over again and end up knowing the scripts infinitely better than you ever did, even at the time of recording.

Another trap for the unwary comic writer lies in using proper names in sketches. Like many writers I tend to use local placenames as fictional surnames and the surnames of people I know as fictional placenames.

My assumption about the mole references then, had been that I had either appeared in some television programme with a mole, or that I had given the name 'Cawston' or possibly 'Kett' to such an animal. I racked my brains wondering what article I had ever written, or what commercial, sketch, sitcom, radio broadcast, film or play I had ever performed in that had even tangentially involved a mole: mole as small shovel-pawed mammal, mole as buried secret-agent, mole as drilling machinery, mole as unit of molecular weight, mole as melanoma or birthmark, I considered them all. Hugh Laurie and I *had* written a sketch about the kind of people who collect china plates with woodland voles on them, painted by internationally renowned artists and advertised in tabloid Sunday magazines. But it's a far cry from a woodland vole to a dead mole, especially as the sketch hadn't even been performed or recorded yet, let alone transmitted.

So it was not until John Kett asked whether I still retained a keen interest in moles or if I had found any dead ones lately that the threads of memory pulled themselves together and I realised at last what everyone had been talking about. Not that they had kept mentioning this bloody mole because it was the most exciting animal to have hit Cawston since the Black Death, nor because it was the hero of an anecdote of any especial weight or interest in the life of the village. I realise now what I couldn't have known then – that they mentioned it because they had a little surprise planned for me and it would have been embarrassing for everyone, myself included, if I had forgotten the whole affair and reacted to their presentation ceremony with dumb puzzlement.

'Fancy you remembering the mole,' I said to John Kett as he led me up to meet the man in charge of the sound system (every village has one microphone and tape-recording expert). Once the PA had been explained and I had been shown twice where the switch on the microphone was, I asked John Kett if he in turn ever remembered an occasion when I had not dared to go into his classroom to give him some test results from Miss Meddlar.

He thought for a while and pulled an apologetic smile. 'No, I'm afraid not,' he said.

In John Kett's past the sun shines and birds sing, in mine there are banks of black thundercloud eternally forming over my head.

I have on my lap as I type a rectangle of varnished wood, four holes neatly drilled into each corner for convenient hanging and display. It was the little surprise, my present from Cawston Village School, their thank-you to me for opening their fete.

In neat Olde English lettering, the following is written:

ᚭᛞe to a mole

I didn't ask to come here
I didn't ask to go
But here I was
And off I went
With only a star for show   Cawston '89
Grand Summer Fair

3

I left Cawston Village School in the March of 1965 and arrived at Stouts Hill the following month, the only new boy of that summer term.

Now it is September. Samuel Anthony Farlowe Bunce and a handful of others are the squits and the Stephen Fry who shouted 'Miss, Miss!' and giggled with the girls by the hopscotch court has died and in his place stands Fry, Fry, S. J., Young Fry, Fry Minor, Fry the Younger, Fry Secundus, Fry Junior or, worst of all, Small Fry.

Stouts Hill, as I have described, was a mock castle, its stone turrets and battlements standing on a mound that rose up from the village of Uley in the shelter of the Bury.

The school's coat of arms sported a kingfisher, (reflecting perhaps both the school lake and the headmaster Robert Angus's commitment to creating a halcyon youth for his young charges) beneath which on a scroll was written the school motto, Τοις μελλουσι – to the future. The *corpus studenti* (since we've gone all classical) numbered just over a hundred, boys being divided into four Houses: Kingfishers, Otters, Wasps and Panthers. The dormitories were named after trees – Elm, Oak, Beech, Sycamore and Cypress.

A nightly spoonful of Radio Malt, a halibut liver oil capsule on the breakfast spoon (later replaced by the more palatable sugar-coated Haliborange), tuition in a musical instrument, riding, sailing, gliding, cubbing, elocution lessons, scouting, shooting and photography all counted as Extras and were surcharged on the termly bill in guineas. Stouts Hill accepted no day boys and the exceptionally grand uniform, which included the most wondrous herringbone winter coat (as worn by my brother, and perched upon by a monkey, in the photograph section in the middle of this book), Aertex shirts for summer, Clydella for winter, a cap, a boater, a grey suit for High Days and Church, blazers, V-necks, ties, games shirts, games pullovers, shorts, snake belt in school colours (optional long trousers for those aged ten and over) and the most fantastical numbers of games socks, uniform socks and regulation elastic garters for the upkeep of same socks, was to be ordered by parents exclusively from Daniel Neale's in Hanover Square and latterly, when Daniel Neale went out of business, from Gorringe's in Kensington High Street. All clothing was to be clearly marked with the owner's name – good business for Messrs Cash and Company who had cornered the market in name-tapes in those days. The other essential item, naturally, was the tuck-box, the boy's surname and initials to be printed in black upon the lid.

Aside from the Angus girls, the female presence included Sister Pinder who had a Royal Naval husband, a magnificent wimple, starched cuffs and an upside-down watch of the kind included in the nurse's outfits little girls always want for Christmas. Her preferred method of punishment when roused was a sharp slap with a metal ruler on the hand – far less painful than it sounds. Her son John was about my age and bound, if I remember rightly, for Pangbourne Naval College. For all I know he is an Admiral of the Fleet today, although if most of my school contemporaries are anything to go by he works in the City, in advertising, commercial property, the film business or as a happily indigent carpenter (at a pinch ceramic artist) in Cornwall. Such is my generation. As in the Carry On films there was a Matron as well as a Sister; on my arrival the incumbent was a Mrs Waterston, called Matey or Matey Bubbles after a nursery bath-foam of the same name. She also had a nephew at the school, though I fear I remember very little about him. Assistant Matrons came and went on the summer breeze and the only one I recall with any vividness was a bespectacled blonde girl called Marilyn (in my entirely unreliable memory an evangelical Christian) who played the guitar and would, when begged, lullaby my dormitory to sleep with a song inexplicably about (unless I have gone entirely mad) El Paso. Marilyn won the heart of my brother Roger on a walking tour in the Isle of Wight one summer holiday: he returned with a glass lighthouse filled with layers of different coloured sand from Ryde and a much larger Adam's apple than he had left with. The symbolism of the lighthouse is the kind of hackneyed detail that only real life has the impertinence to throw up. The school secretary, Mrs Wall, wore nice tweed suits and had a pleasantly citrus and peppery smell. I believe she went by the name of Enid. The school Chef was called Ken Hunt and his egg or chicken dishes were the consequent victim of endless spooneristic jokes, which I am sure you don't need to have spelled out for you. He had two kitchen porters, Celia, hugely fat, hairy and Spanish, by whom I was overwhelming mothered throughout my time at Stouts Hill and her husband Abiel, almost as hugely fat, Spanish and hairy as his wife and quite as generous to me.

There was a butler called Mr Dealey, of whom I was greatly in awe. He wore trousers of the kind known as spongebag and seemed to have no other thing to say to me whenever we encountered each other than, 'Now then, Master Fry, now then.' I hear his *almost* spivvy tones again whenever I watch films like *Hue and Cry* and *Laughter in Paradise*, lying as they do somewhere between Jack Warner and Guy Middleton. He in turn had a brylcreemed son called Colin with hair arranged in what I guess now was known as a rockabilly quiff. Colin helped about the place, could blow smoke-rings and whistle through his teeth to make a sound like a kazoo. He also held the tuck-shop key which made him greatly important. The school barber, John Owen, visited once a week and found my name amusing since it put him in mind of a famous auctioneer (famous auctioneer? Well, apparently so) called Frederick Fry.

As he snipped away at my hair, Owen would repeat, again and again, 'Frederick Fry FAI, Frederick Fry FAI. Fellow of the Auctioneers' Institute, Frederick Fry, FAI.'

The Angus love of animals was reflected out of doors by a profusion of ponies and horses and an aviary which housed, amongst other exotic bird life, a most exquisite golden pheasant. Within doors there were birdcages too: these were actually built into the walls near the headmaster's study. They contained a pair of amiable parrots and my most particular friend, a mynah bird. This was a very prodigious animal which could imitate the school bell, Dealey mumbling to himself as he polished the candlesticks in the grand dining room the other side of the cages, the dull bang of the cane being thwacked on to tight trouser seats in the headmaster's study and the voices of most of the staff; the bird was even capable of rendering exactly the sound of four crates of third-pint milk bottles being banged on to a Formica-topped trestle table, a sound it heard every day at morning break. It sounds an unlikely feat but I assure you I do not exaggerate. As a matter of fact I heard the broadcaster and naturalist Johnny Morris on the radio not so long ago talking about his mynah bird who could precisely mimic three pints being placed on a doorstep. The aural replication of milk delivery is clearly a common (if evolutionarily bewildering) gift amongst the domesticated mynahs of the West Country and a phenomenon into which more research cries out to be done.

The Angus family owned dogs too of course. There was a large number of perpetually furious Boston terriers, a boxer called Brutus, something fluffy and loud called Caesar and a squadron of others, all belonging to old Mrs Angus who was warm and powdery and of whom I find it impossible to think without there coming into my head the image of Her Majesty Queen Elizabeth the Queen Mother. It was into her presence that my brother and I were ushered to be told of the death of our step-grandmother. I shall never forget the precise intonation she used when she told us.

My grandfather's third wife was Viennese and Jewish, like my real grandmother whom I never knew. She had been a friend of Stefan Zweig and Gustav Klimt and Arnold Schoenberg and all those grand Viennese café intellectuals. She used to let me use her typewriter whenever I visited her, which to me was the greatest joy in the world. I have been able to type proficiently since I was ten. Her maiden name was Grabscheidt, pronounced, I fear, grab-shite. There is a still a huge cabin trunk somewhere in my parents' house on which is painted that wonderful name in great white letters. My brother and I had been to visit her in hospital when she was ill and she had been kind and told us not to be frightened by the tubes running into her nose.

Later on, back at school, we had been summoned to see Mrs Angus.

'You knew that your step-grandmother had been very ill,' she said, stroking one of her dogs.

My brother and I nodded.

'I'm afraid I have just heard from your mother that she *did* die . . .'

I don't know why the emphasis of that intonation is with me still. Whenever I think of Auntie Claire, as we called her, (although I suppose her name must have been Klara or Klära or something similar) I remember that she *did* die.

In the Easter holidays which fell between the end of my term at Cawston and the start of life away at what I thought of as Roger's School, I had read from cover to cover, over and over again, the Stouts Hill School Magazine, which included a section entitled:

LETTERS OF ENCOURAGEMENT
TO A POSSIBLE NEW BOY

I have that magazine in front of me now and reproduce the articles without amendment of any kind. Some of them I found I still knew almost by heart.

Tim Sangster
We play cars down a little sort of dip.

Jimmy King

We have lots of fun playing cricket, tennis, rounders and swimming in the summer. In the winter we play football and rugger. On Sundays we usually watch television. We go to bed at six o'clock. You have lots of free time – the work is not to difficult. You can get gardens to grow things if you want to. You can sail too, if you want to join the sailing club.

Anthony Macwhirter

If you are in fourth game you sometimes go boating on the lake and swim every day in the summer if it is warm. On Sundays you may have three swims if you don't go out.

Edmund Wilkins

It is very nice here because if you are in the country you have no one to play with, though at Stouts Hill there are lots of boys. In the summer we have swimming and boating and there is a half term holiday after the sports. If you are quite young you will go into the small form where you have potty work. We played Latin Football on Saturday which is great fun.

Richard Coley

There is a tuck shop only you are not allowed to bring tuck back. There are lots of butterflies to catch. There is a big lake with boats and oysters that clamp down on your fingers.

Charles Matthews

We have Cubs on Fridays, you wear your games clothes, its very hilly so we can do all sorts of things. When there is enough snow in winter we can go tobagganing which is super fun.

Malcolm Black

You can catch fish and row a boat if you want. Some boys like playing games like 'Man Hunt' or 'Tip and Run.' Most boys have a garden. In the summer baby frogs jump about. Sometimes there are Treasure Hunts up on the Bury. The Cubs go up into the woods and round about. They have their dens up in the woods.

Donald Laing

We have a museum and a model club as well. We have cellars, a changingroom and three dining-rooms. In the school we have five dormitories and two dormitories not in the school.

The sentence in Edmund Wilkins's article, 'If you are quite young you will go into the small form where you have potty work', haunted me for weeks before my arrival. The idea that I might be considered, willy nilly, in need of 'potty work' simply terrified me. It is true that from time to time I wetted the bed at home – 'It's not that I *mind*, darling. If only you would *tell* me. But when you pretend it never happened it just makes me so *cross* . . .' – it was just that, in my fevered imagination 'potty work' meant grimmer, darker business than preventing piddling in the bed and I spent much of the holidays begging my mother to write letters to the school excusing me from this humiliation, which I saw as taking place on a grand daïs in front of the whole school.

Nor was the next section in the magazine, some of which was the work of the same hands, calculated to set my mind entirely at ease.

OUR FIRST DAYS AT STOUTS HILL

J. Wynn

When we got into the car to go to Stouts Hill for the first time I was very excited. They dropped me and drove away I was not homesick. The very first day I felt rather lost. We had our first ice-cream day and I thou,;ht we had to have the money on us. I bou,;ht two and put one in the waste-paper basket. I did not realise that I could have given it to someone else.

A. McKane

I had been ill in bed for about two weeks when I heard my parents were coming, this was on a Sunday. I was only just six years old. My parents and brothers came up to see me also my sister. When they left me I started to cry, so my sister stayed with me but later on, she went. My mother and father went to the school service to hear my brothers sing in the choir. By the side of my bed there was a bell which I could ring when I wanted something. At this time I was feeling very homesick, so I rang the bell as loudly as I could. I rang it for some time until I heard footsteps coming up the stairs and in rushed Jane. The whole school had heard it and I was rather ashamed.

R. Maidlow

At night time when I got into bed it was horrible because the bed was uncomfortable and the springs were to tight for me. The breakfast was a nice breakfast. The eggs were not to hard for me. My first game of cricket was a nice game of cricket and I hit some runs on my first game of cricket.

T. Sangster

When mummy had gone home in the car I met Doland and we explored and looked around. We went and looked in a shed beside the third game pavilion and then went and peered into the empty swimming pool. A bell rang and we wondered what it was for so we went up to the dormitory. Then somebody asked whether we had had tea. So we said 'no' and somebody brought us milk and buns. When we had eaten we all talked and read until Matron came in and said 'No more talking'. And we went to sleep. Next day we went down to breakfast – I thought I was in IIB I stayed there for a lesson and then had to move into IIIB. In the middle of the lesson I arrived and sat down in the front row – I learned very little on the first morning. Then I went down to fourth game pitch and I was playing rounders – our side won by seven rounders. I was chosen about third but I did not do very well. My first day in third cricket I was put as square leg but I could not stop a ball. I did not have an innings.

Ian Hicks

I was worried about the lessons and wondered if I would be hacked playing football and what the food would be like and whether I would get indigestion like I always did at home. Then how was mum in the car and had she got back allright. I went to bed and everybody asked me my name. Then the next morning the master came into lessons and said "Hicks, have you learnt to do History yet?" "Yes, a bit" came the reply. By lunch I had settled down.

R. Coley

My first night at school the thing I dreaded most was seeing mummy and daddy go down the drive. However I found another new boy named Povey. We walked around a bit till the tea bell rang and we went to tea. Everybody thought I was most peculiar because I had 3 cups of milk and 5 slices of bread and 3 buns.

M. Dolan

At bed time we go to wash and go to bed. We are allowed to talk until 7 o'clock and we talk all the

time. When we are closed down we talk lots of
times and get caught and have to stand out for
twenty minutes. Our legs get tired.

I found myself dreading this strange world of ice-cream days
and third game pavilions and being put as square leg. The idea
that I might be asked if I had learnt to do History yet also filled
me with horror. I knew plenty of history, thanks to my
mother, herself a historian, and the endless quizzes I pestered
her to give me as I followed her about the house, but I was
certain that I hadn't in any way 'learnt to do History'.

Another essay in the magazine puzzled me, puzzles me to
this day. I felt it was *getting* at something, something awful to
which it didn't dare put a name. Ironic, given its title.

" FEAR, " by S. Alexander

Fear is the basis of cowardice and cowardice is the
opposite to courage, but fear is not the opposite to
courage. In many cases, fear is even the basis of
courage and so it is an extraordinary thing.

It gets complicated after that – the author presses Socrates and
Douglas Bader into the argument and I get a trifle lost even
now.

I was more heartened by the following:

WINNIE

Winnie was a loveable little pony. She had a gentle
temperament and liked having a fuss made of her.
She was very old when she died. Everyone who
rode her will probably remember her for a long
time. She was very persevering and would tolerate
a tremendous amount of hitting around. I have
never known her to lose her temper, so I think if
there is a heaven, Winnie is there. Winnie passed

into the next world on the afternoon of the 30th January. May she find rest in the endless pastures of Paradise.

J. Bisset.

I think I remember this Bisset. I believe he came from Rhodesia and had a younger brother who arrived at Stouts Hill at about the same time as me. The younger Bisset quite suddenly and inexplicably announced one term that he had changed his name to Tilney, something we all rather envied and I, personally, decided to emulate at once. I informed the master on duty that from now on I was to be referred to as Whatenough, Peregrine Ainsley Whatenough, but was told not to be an arse, which struck me as unfair. Looking back, one assumes the Bisset/Tilney name change was something to do with step-fatherage, a broken home and other things that were kept from us.

Returning to the magazine, there follow endless pages cataloguing the achievements of old boys, with the usual depressing information as to their destinies.

We were delighted to hear from Ian who is doing very well at Price Waterhouse and still plays squash regularly.

John has done extremely well with an Agricultural firm dealing with machinery in Uganda.

Adam Carter wrote to us from Gibraltar where he is stationed with the Somerset and Cornwall Light Infantry.

No reunion or social gathering would be complete without Charles Hamilton. He looked splendid at the Berkeley Hunt Ball in his kilt.

We hear Martin Wood is very happy at Stowe and is now a keen Beagler.

Peter Presland goes up to London every day, where he is

with a firm of solicitors, Bracewell and Leaver, where he specialises in commercial work during the day and at night is a libel "Expert" for a daily newspaper.

I like the capitalised, double inverted-commas "Expert", lending it a properly disreputable air.

Of one old boy, later to become well known through marriage, we learn:

> **Mark Phillips (1957-1962) Marlborough**
> We were all delighted when Mark once again won at Badminton.

... the annual three-day eventing horse-trials, one assumes, not some ordinary game of shuttlecock and battledore ...

Stouts Hill was a *country* school, this is the point that seems to emerge most from the magazines. London and all things urban were miles away. Whenever I picture myself at prep school, I picture myself out of doors: walking, sliding, tumbling, den-building, boating, fishing and in winter, sliding across the thickly iced lake, tobogganing and rolling snowballs down slopes until they grew to be the size of small vans. I remember being taught the names of wildflowers and birds, climbing trees, penetrating the woods and scaling the Bury.

None of these activities came without pain. The pain began with bad luck over which I had no control but ended in a physical self-consciousness that has dominated my life ever since.

The bad luck was principally asthma, a congenital condition inherited, I suppose, from my father who had spent a year in hospital as a child.

I had joined the school's tree climbing club and found to my surprise that a dread of heights did not prevent me from climbing trees quickly and without fear. Then, when I was nine, I developed a terrible allergy to whatever it is that lime trees put out in the summer, that same stuff that deposits its layer of sticky goo on the roofs of cars that are foolish enough to park in lime avenues. The result was two days in bed with my lungs wheezing like mouse-nibbled organ bellows. A number of boys at Stouts Hill had asthma, the Gloucestershire air was said to be good for them. One boy came for that very reason but made no improvement. He left for Switzerland after only five weeks, a five weeks spent with an inhaler constantly at his lips. The following term at morning prayers the headmaster reported his death to us and everyone turned to look at me.

Later, at public school in particular, I became adept at using my asthma as an excuse for avoiding undesirable activities. I could induce attacks easily by burying my head inside dusty desks or in bushes and shrubs which I knew to be dangerous. I became intensely proud of my asthma, just as I was to become proud of my jewishness and proud of my sexuality. Taking an aggressively defiant stance on qualities in myself that others might judge to be weaknesses became one of my most distinctive character traits. Still is, I suppose.

Seesawing with a friend one afternoon, I fractured the humerus bone of my left arm and went about in a sling for the rest of the term. Two days later my brother broke his arm in *exactly* the same place, a genuine coincidence. He had broken it in the field of battle, at rugger. I was the fool who could have avoided it, he was the brave soldier. As it later turned out, Roger had actually broken his arm by trying to pinch some food from the kitchen under the eye of Abiel, who had hurled him up some steps. In those days, things like that were hushed up. Poor Abiel hadn't meant any harm, and a rugger injury looked better all round.

I can't separate out the connections, the causes and effects, but by my third year at Stouts Hill, after the onset of asthma and the breaking of my arm, I began to dread physical activity of almost any kind. I became prey to an acute sense of physical self-consciousness. This has sexual connections which we will come to later.

In a prep school set in the country, in love with the country, inspired by the country and dedicated to the country, the boy who fears the country, fears it in all its manifestations, naturally becomes something of a loner: if his home-life is also spent in even deeper country he has a problem. The terror of the rotting mole and of the insects that gorge on dead flesh had never left me. I was scared to distraction by the mere thought of silverfish and lice, maggots and blow-flies, puff-balls and exploding fungi. The malignancy and stench of death that hung over the forests, copses and lakeside woods at Stouts Hill expunged any pleasure I derived from the lively quickness of squirrels and badgers, from the gentle dignity of alders, larches, elms and oaks and from the delicate beauty of the herb robert, the campion, the harebell and the shepherd's purse.

More than that, the fearlessness of the other boys became itself something new to fear. That they could not see what was amiss with the world showed them to be strong and me to be weak.

I was at the time, I think, unaware of all this at any conscious level worth bothering with. Other boys, after all, were what we would call today wimps. Some were wimpier than me by far. Some wore absurd spectacles with lenses an inch thick, others had spazzy walks and possessed eye–hand co-ordination that made me feel positively athletic. One boy was so afraid of horses that he would break out into a sweat if he came within twenty yards of the smallest pony.

Two defects of mine did haunt me consciously however, and I cannot claim ever to have entirely exorcised myself of them.

Natation first. The school had an excellent lake, in which some supervised swimming was allowed. There was a swimming-pool too, a most extraordinary white oval affair which might have been designed by Gropius, with an elaborate gravel filter for the water, which showed itself in the form of an endlessly playing fountain beside the pool. At either end was a bowl filled with a deep purple liquid into which one had to dip one's feet before entry – something to do with verrucas I believe.

If a boy had been officially witnessed to have swum two full unassisted lengths of the pool he was a Swimmer and entitled to wear blue swimming trunks and enjoy access to the deep end and the diving board. Non Swimmers wore red trunks and had to paddle in the shallow end holding preposterous polystyrene swimming aids sculpted into the shape of tombstones or, worse still, have inflatable water-wings sealed about their skinny arms.

I was a non swimmer until my very last year.

All my life I have never since bought a pair of *red* swimming trunks.

At night, as others slept, I projected films in my head, films in which I swam like Johnny Weissmuller, Esther Williams and Captain Webb. Dipping, rolling and diving, head facing down into the surface of the water, I powered myself with easy, rhythmically pumping feet. I launched myself backwards and forwards, up and down the pool, head rising up to take one lungful of air for each length, while boys crowded round the pool, their mouths rounded in wonderment and admiration, watching me, praising me, cheering me on . . .

I could do it, I *knew* I could it do it then. It was clear to me that the achievement was all in the knowing. The only reason I couldn't swim was that I had been told that I was a non swimmer. But there, on my hard-sprung Vono bed, while the others slept, I knew that I was an otter, a sea-lion, a leaping dolphin, Poseidon's child, Marine Boy, the friend of Thetis and Triton, at one with water.

If only they would let me wear blue trunks, then I would show them.

The loud collision of detail, noise and hurry in the daytime confused everything and threw me off balance.

'Aren't you changed, Fry?'

'Right, in you get.'

'Come on, boy!'

'It's not *cold*, for God's sake . . .'

'Legs! Legs, legs, legs! Get those legs working!'

'Get your head *down*. It's water, it's not going to bite you . . .'

'What a *spazz* . . .'

The explosions of other boys laughing and bombing and bellyflopping at the deep end turned into a distant mocking echo as the blood and fear flooded into me.

'But I could do it last night!' I wanted to shout. 'You should have seen me last night. Like a salmon, I was . . . like a leaping salmon!'

Blue and shivering, I would push the polystyrene tombstone out before me, eyes screwed shut, head up so far that my neck bent backwards, thrashing myself forwards, my legs kicking up and down, panting and whooping with exertion and panic. Then I would rise, gasping and choking like a new born baby, twisted strings of snot streaming from my nose, chlorine burning my throat and eyes, sure that this time, *this time*, I had covered at least half the length of the pool.

'Congratulations, Fry. One and a half yards.'

Hurrying across the grass, I would wrap myself in a towel, shivering and gulping with shame and exhaustion.

The aching and the longing in me as I watched Laing silently glide underwater from end to end like a silver eel. He would break the surface without a ripple or a gasp, and then, laughing like a lord, backstroke, side-stroke and butterfly to the other end, rolling over and over as he swam, the water seeming to encase him in a silver envelope that glistened and pulsed like the birth sac of a gigantic insect.

With my towel Balinese tight about my waist, I would, in Adam's primal *pudeur*, perform the awkward ballet of swapping trunks for underpants, so absolutely, unconditionally and helplessly cast into black misery that nothing, not money, hugging, sweets, understanding, friendship or love, could have offered me the smallest sliver of joy or hope. The fierce knot of admiration, resentment, shame and fury that tightened in the pit of my stomach is one of those background sensations of childhood, like the taste of lemon sherbet or tomatoes on fried bread, flavours that can be blown back on the wind of memory or association to torture and now, of course, to amuse.

Swimming was for me the closest a human being could come to flight. The freedom of it, the ease, the elegance, the delirious escape. Every living creature but Fry could swim. The tiniest tadpole, the most reluctant cat, the most primitive amoeba and the simplest daphnia.

And I would never be able to do it, never. Never be able to

join in, splashing and laughing and ducking and grabbing and roaring with the others. Never. Save in my mind.

We talk of the callousness of the young. 'Children can be so cruel,' we say. But only those who are concerned with others can be cruel. Children are both careless and carefree in their connections with others. For one nine-year-old to think passingly about the non-swimming agonies of another would be ridiculous.

There were contemporaries of mine at prep school who laboured and tortured themselves over their absolute failure to understand the rudiments of sentence structure: the nominative and accusative in Latin and Greek, the concept of an indirect object, the ablative absolute and the sequence of tenses – these things kept *them* awake at night. There were others who tossed in insomniac misery because of their fatness, freckledness or squintedness. I don't remember, I don't remember because I didn't care. Only my own agony mattered.

Nothing prayed for – it is life's strictest and least graceful rule – comes to you at the time of praying. Good things always come too late. I can swim now.

I cannot recall how and when I passed my test and won those blue trunks. I know it did happen. I know that somehow I learned to doggy-paddle without the tombstone and the water-wings and that I completed my two compulsory lengths. I know too that I discovered how swimming was never going to be that fine, free soaring expansion of joy I had dreamt it would be.

The pain of the red trunks, however, was as a minor aggravation, a teasing itch when compared to the blistering agony of Cong Prac.

Stouts Hill never gave off an atmosphere of being any more or less religious than other schools I have known. It was with some surprise that I discovered not long ago that Robert Angus, the headmaster, had been a writer of deeply spiritual Christian poetry. Today, with the foul miasma of evangelism rising up to engulf us from every corner of God's poor earth it is hard to remember that good Christian lives were once lived

without words like 'outreach' and 'salvation' being dragged
into general conversation. God was a dignified, generous,
father and Christ his beautiful, liquid-eyed son: they loved you
even when they saw you on the lavatory or caught you stealing
sweets. That was Christianity, something quite unconnected to
hymns, psalms, anthems and the liturgy of the church.

In the 1960s Britain was just beginning to slither about in the
horrid mess made by sacred music written especially for
children – 'Jonah', 'The Lord of the Dance', 'Morning Has
Broken' and all that preposterous rubbish. New tunes for 'O
Jesus I have Promised' were being composed, as music masters
and idle, fatuous composers the length and breadth of the land
were bothering us all with new carols and new settings for the
Te Deum and *Nunc Dimittis*, some of them even ransacking
the rhetoric of negro spirituals and American gospel songs,
with results so nauseatingly embarrassing that I still blush to
recall them. White, well-nourished British children who
holidayed with their parents in old plantation houses in the
Bahamas and Jamaica, clapping their hands, thumping tam-
bourines and striking triangles to the lisped words of 'Let my
people go' and 'Nobody knows the trouble I see', to a clash of
cymbals and symbols that still harrows the imagination.

But there, the very thought of music masters clapping their
hands in rhythm and calling out 'And *one* and *two* and *three*
and ta-ta-ta-*tah*!!' will always send the blood simmering to my
head, never mind ethnic guilt and other associations.

Every morning after breakfast at Stouts Hill, a bell rang for
chapel, a service which involved no more than a perfunctory
clutch of prayers, a lesson read by a prefect (hitting hard, in
time honoured British fashion, the italicised words of the text
of the Authorised Version as if they had been put there for
emphasis) and a known hymn, but on Sundays there was held
a proper service, with collects, psalms, canticles, versicles,
responses, anthems and a sermon. The choir dressed up in blue
surplices and starched ruffs and processed with candles, the
masters added the appropriate ermine or scarlet hoods to their
gowns and we boys turned out in our best suits and tidiest hair,
all checked up in the dormitories by Sister Pinder, Matron and

a squad of sergeant-majorly prefects. Each Sunday service, according to litany and season, had its own psalm, and Mr Hemuss, the music master, liked also to use Sundays as an opportunity to introduce us to hymns we had never sung before. This meant they had to be learned. After morning prayers on Saturday therefore we stayed behind in the chapel (actually a gymnasium with an altar) and Cong Prac was held – an abbreviation, though it never ever crossed my mind as such at the time, for Congregational Practice. Here the setting for the morrow's psalm and the tunes for the morrow's unfamiliar hymns would be gone through, bar by bar. Saturday's breakfast was always boiled eggs, and there is nothing so unpleasant in all this world as a roomful of human beings who have just eaten boiled eggs. Every fart and burp sulphurises the room with the most odious humming guff, a smell I can never smell to this day without returning to the hell of Cong Prac.

I have just leaked all over you the feelings of longing and self-reproach that tortured me over my inability to swim. These feelings were as nothing, *are* as nothing, to what I felt and still feel about God's cruelty, God's malice, God's unforgivable cruelty in denying me the gift of music.

Music is the deepest of the arts and deep beneath all arts. So E. M. Forster wrote somewhere. If swimming suggested to me the idea of physical flight, then music suggested something much more. Music was a kind of penetration. Perhaps *absorption* is a less freighted word. The penetration or absorption of everything into itself. I don't know if you have ever taken LSD, but when you do so the doors of perception, as Aldous Huxley, Jim Morrison and their adherents ceaselessly remind us, swing open wide. That is actually the sort of phrase, unless you are William Blake, that only makes sense when there is some LSD actually swimming about inside you. In the cold light of the cup of coffee and banana sandwich that are beside me now it appears to be nonsense, but I expect you know what it is taken to mean. LSD reveals the *whatness* of things, their quiddity, their essence. The wateriness of water is suddenly revealed to you, the carpetness of carpets, the woodness of wood, the yellowness of yellow, the fingernailness of fingernails, the allness of all, the nothingness of all, the allness of nothing. For me music gives access to every one of these essences of existence, but at a fraction of the social or financial cost of a drug and without the need to cry 'Wow!' all the time, which is one of LSD's most distressing and least endearing side-effects.

Other arts do this too, but other arts are for ever confined and anchored by reference. Sculptures are either figuratively representative or physically limited by their material, which is actual and palpable. The words in poems are referential, they breathe with denotation and connotation, suggestion and semantics, coding and signing. Paint is real stuff and the matter of painting contains itself in a frame. Music, in the precision of its form and the mathematical tyranny of its laws, escapes into an eternity of abstraction and an absurd sublime that is everywhere and nowhere at once. The grunt of rosin-rubbed catgut, the saliva-bubble blast of a brass tube, the sweaty-fingered squeak on a guitar fret, all that physicality, all that clumsy 'music-making', all that grain of human performance, so much messier than the artfully patinated pentimenti or self-conscious painterly mannerism of the sister arts, transcends itself at the moment of its happening, that moment when music actually *becomes*, as it makes the journey from the vibrating instrument, the vibrating hi-fi speaker, as it sends those vibrations across to the human tympanum and through to the inner ear and into the brain, where the mind is set to vibrate to frequencies of its own making.

The nothingness of music can be moulded by the mood of the listener into the most precise shapes or allowed to float as free as thought; music can follow the academic and theoretical pattern of its own modality or adhere to some narrative or dialectical programme imposed by a friend, a scholar or the composer himself. Music is everything and nothing. It is useless and no limit can be set on its use. Music takes me to places of illimitable sensual and insensate joy, accessing points of ecstasy that no angelic lover could ever locate, or plunging me into gibbering weeping hells of pain that no torturer could ever devise. Music makes me write this sort of maundering adolescent nonsense without embarrassment. Music is in fact the dog's bollocks. Nothing else comes close.

AND I CAN'T FUCKING DO IT

I can't so much as hum 'Three Blind Mice' without going off key. I can't stick to the rhythm of 'Onward Christian Soldiers' without speeding up. I can't *fucking do it*.

Bollocks to Salieri and his precious, petulant whining. Maybe it *is* worse to be able to make music *just a bit*, but not as well as you would like to. I'd *love* to find out. But I can't fucking do it *at all*.

To see friends gathering round a piano and singing 'Always Look on the Bright Side of Life', 'Anything Goes', 'Yellow Submarine', 'Summertime', 'Der Erlkönig', 'She'll Be Coming Round the Mountain', 'Edelweiss', 'Non Più Andrai' – it doesn't fucking matter *what* bloody song it is . . .

I CAN'T FUCKING JOIN IN

I have to mime at parties when everyone sings Happy Birthday . . . mime or mumble and rumble and growl and grunt so deep that only moles, manta rays and mushrooms can hear me.

I'm not even tone deaf, that's the arse-mothering, fuck-nosed, bugger-sucking *wank* of the thing.

I'M NOT EVEN TONE
FUCKING DEAF

I'm tone DUMB.

The tunes are there in my head. There they are all right, perfect to the last quarter-tone of pitch and the last hemi-demi-semiquaver of time. The 'Haffner', 'Fernando', the Siegfried motif, 'Whole Lotta Love', 'Marche Militaire', 'Night and Day', 'The Dance of the Sugar Plum Fairy', 'I Heard it Through the Grapevine', 'The Great Gate of Kiev', 'Lara's Theme', 'Now Voyager', 'Remember You're a Womble', even the opening bars of *Till* bloody *Eulenspiegel*, I can play them all effortlessly in my head.

Not just the tunes, but the harmonies too, the rhythmic patterns, *everything*. I find I can usually tell if a tune is in the keys of C minor, D major or E flat major, they are like recognisable colours to me, not a stunning gift, but proof surely that I am *not* tone deaf. But between what is there in my head and what I can express with my voice or my fingers . . . there falls a mighty and substantial shadow.

'Oh, how does that tune from *Bonanza* go?' someone will ask, and everybody will clutch their foreheads and screw up their faces as they try to force their memories.

But there it is, the whole *Bonanza* theme in my head, fully armed, orchestrated entire, perfect to the last trill and triplet, every element complete and perfect, as if played inside me by the Vienna Philharmonic, led by Isaac Stern and conducted by Furtwängler. I can hear it as clearly in my head now as I can hear the mighty roar of King's Lynn's rush-minute traffic heading for Swaffham along the A47.

'Go on, then, Stephen. If you can hear it, *hum* it . . .'

Ha! That's a joke. Hum it. I might as well try to make a car engine out of spaghetti or a well-dressed man out of Martyn Lewis.

If I try, if I really try to render it, to reproduce the concord of sweet sound that moves so perfectly in my head, the sound that emerges will shock and embarrass. I am looked at with reproach and faint disgust as if I've done something unpardonably tasteless and unbritish, like farting at the Queen Mother or kicking Alan Bennett in the balls.

I've got a voice, haven't I? A voice that can mimic accents, a voice with a fair repertoire of impressions and impersonations. Why can't it express musical sounds as I hear them? Why this musical constipation? Why, oh Lord, *why*?

And why so *cross* about it? I've covered a page with the most intemperate profanities and the most ungovernable rages on this subject, why does it upset me so much? Some people can't *walk*, for Christ's sake. Some people have severe dyslexia or cerebral palsy, and I'm whining about not having a gift for music. After all, what's so bad about not being able to render a tune?

'Come on, old fellow,' the reasonable person might say, '*we* all know what the Mona Lisa looks like. We can all picture her in our heads, right down to the crazing on the varnish and the smokily shaded dimples at the side of her mouth. But which of us can doodle her? We don't complain, we just shrug and say that we're hopeless at drawing . . . why can't you say that about not being able to sing?'

Yeah, that's all very well. But you see music is more than that. Music is *social*, music begins in *dance*. Music is actually about *joining in*. When I moan about swimming or about singing, I'm really moaning about not being able to join in. And I'm not really moaning, either. I'm trying to recapture an old misery and unravel it.

There is a scene in one of my favourite films, Sidney Lumet's 1988 *Running On Empty*, where River Phoenix (at his absolute coltish best) arrives at a new school with a new name (Manfield), a new history (made up) and hair dyed newly blond (dreamy). He and his family have spent their life running from the FBI – 'on the lam' as they say in America. We the film audience know, but Ed Crowley who plays the music teacher at this new school does not, that Phoenix's character is an exceptionally gifted pianist. As Phoenix is welcomed into the music class, he sinks down into his seat and Crowley plays excerpts from two musical tapes, one a Madonna dance track, the other a classical string piece.

'What's the difference between these two pieces of music?' asks Crowley.

The class giggles. The difference is surely so obvious.

'One is good and the other is bad?' suggests a student.

What a sycophantic creep. We can see that most of the class find the Madonna much more fun than the classical.

'That's a matter of opinion surely,' Crowley says to the sycophant.

Phoenix, trained his whole life not to draw attention to himself, looks around the classroom. We *know* that he has an answer, but what can it be?

What answer would *you* give, come to that, if asked to describe the difference between a Madonna track and a classical string quartet?

Ed Crowley turns to this new student.

'Mr Manfield?' he asks. 'Help us out. What do *you* think?'

There is a fraction of a pause as Phoenix twiddles shyly with his pencil before giving this reply.

'You can't dance to Beethoven?'

I like that.

You can't dance to Beethoven.

And if you can't dance, you can't *join in*.

Music from the 'ragtime and jazz tradition' (why do I feel that the word Tradition is taking on the greasiness of the word Community? The 'gay community', 'the divided communities of Northern Ireland' – the 'Gospel tradition', the 'folk tradition') all the way through to blues, R&B, rock and roll, soul, funk, reggae, pop, ska, disco, rap, hip-hop, techno, acid-house, jungle, Tesco, handbag, trance, hypno and the rest, always keeps its back-beat and its dance roots; its proper home is still the dance floor and the shared experience of adolescents swapping records in their bedrooms. It is public music, it publicly defines an age, it is still *dance*, now in fact, since the high days of folk-rock and hard rock, it is more than ever *dance*.

When two or three gather together and hear 'Blockbuster', 'Blowin in the Wind', 'The Piper at the Gates of Dawn', 'Maxwell's Silver Hammer', 'Come on Eileen' or 'Relax', there is that other dance to be danced, the generational dance in which listeners are united in their decade, the age they were at the time of the music's release, the ridiculous trousers they wore, the television programmes they watched, the sweets they bought, the hi-fi set-up they spent weeks arranging and rearranging in their bedroom, the girls and boys they thought of as the love-lyrics and guitar licks pounded into them.

To earlier generations 'Are You Lonesome Tonight?', 'A-tisket, a-tasket', 'We'll Meet Again' and Glenn Miller's 'Moonlight Serenade' might perform the same office. Those same people who, listening to the Andrews Sisters' 'Boogie-Woogie Bugle Boy' will shriek, 'Oh, that takes me back to my very first dance! My very first nylons! My very first Alvis motorcar!' will have been young and bouncy when Britten wrote *The Turn of the Screw* or when Walton produced *Belshazzar's Feast*, but you won't hear them squeal with the delight of public reminiscence and the memory of first snogs and first lipsticks when the 'Sea Interlude' from *Peter Grimes* floats over the airwaves. Classical music is private art, stripped of that kind of association.

That, partly, is why classical music is also very nerdy. Its decontextualised abstractions take the classical music lover and the classical music practitioner out of the social stream and into their own heads, as do chess and maths and other nerdile pursuits. Mussorgsky's 'Night on the Bare Mountain' is *not* nerdy however, when it makes everyone brighten up and do their whispering impression of the slogan for that cassette tape TV commercial: 'Maxell! Break the sound barrier . . .'

Classical music can be 'rescued' therefore from the void of abstract nerdaciousness by association with film, television and advertising, so that Beethoven can make you think of power generation companies, Mozart of *Elvira Madigan* and *Trading Places*, Carl Orff of Old Spice aftershave and so on, and no doubt our own contemporary composers Philip Glass, Gorecki, and, God help us all, Michael Nyman, will be similarly pressed into service by Laboratoires Garnier and Kellogg's Frosties before the century is out. It is customary for those who like classical music to damn the advertising industry and the producers of commercials and TV programmes for vulgarising their beloved music. If you can't hear 'Eine Kleine Nachtmusik', they say, without thinking of Robert Robinson and *Brain of Britain*, or Mozart's 'Musical Joke' without Hickstead and the Horse of the Year Show galloping through your head, then you're a philistine. Well that's just the arse's arse. The same snobbery is being applied now to pop music and we are starting to hear complaints about the Kinks being yoked to the Yellow Pages and John Lee Hooker turning into a lager salesman.

There is simply no limit to the tyrannical snobbery that otherwise decent people can descend into when it comes to music.

Hugh Laurie made me laugh for a week early on in our friendship when he re-enacted the youthful party scene in which some nameless figure will approach a stack of records next to the hi-fi, go through them one by one and then say, his brow wrinkled with cool, sour disfavour, 'Haven't you got any *decent* music then?'

The mirror-shaded *NME* journalists have no idea how close they are to the opera queen, the balletomane and the symphonic reviewer for *Gramophone* magazine. They are sisters under the skin. Cysts under the skin more like.

The tribal belonging, the sexual association, the sense of *party* – these are what popular music offer, and they have always been exclusion zones for me. Partly because of my musical constipation – can't dance, can't join in the chorus – partly because of my sense of physical self, feeling a fool, tall, unco-ordinated and gangly.

On the other hand I'm not Bernard Levin. I am not in love with the *world* of classical music or set upon the intellectual, personal or aesthetic path of a private relationship with Schubert, Wagner, Brahms or Berg. Nor am I a Ned Sherrin, devoted to the musical, to Tin Pan Alley and twentieth-century song. I did well professionally first crack out of the box with a stage musical, but musicals don't mean much to me. I am not a show girl I fear.

There is no proper way for me to express what music does to me without my sounding precious, pretentious, over-emotional, sentimental, self-indulgent and absurd. No proper way therefore to express either what it has done to me over the years to know that I would never be able to make music of even the most basic kind.

I *would* like to dance. Not professionally, just when everyone else does.

I *would* like to sing. Not professionally, just when everyone else does.

I'd like to *join in*, you see.

Guilty feet, as George Michael tells us, have got no rhythm.

I can *play* . . . I mean, as an effort of will I can sit down and learn a piece at the piano and reproduce it, so that those who hear will not necessarily move away with their hands clutched to their mouths, vomit leaking through fingers, blood dripping from ears. Then of course, a piano needs no real-time tuning. I strike middle C and I know that middle C will come out. Were I to try and learn a stringed or brass instrument that needed me to *make* the notes *as* I played, then I hate to think what might be the result. Playing the piano is not the same as making music.

None of this is important in itself, but I feel somewhere that it has a lot to do with why I have always felt separate, why I have always felt unable to join in, to let go, to become part of the tribe, why I have always sniped or joked from the sidelines, why I have never, ever, lost my overwhelmingly self-conscious self-consciousness.

It's not all bad. Heightened self-consciousness, apartness, an inability to join in, physical shame and self-loathing – they are not all bad. Those devils have also been my angels. Without them I would never have disappeared into language, literature, the mind, laughter and all the mad intensities that made and unmade me.

Singing began for me, as it does for most of us, in a communal form. Whether it is 'All Things Bright and Beautiful', 'Little Bo-Peep', 'Away in a Manger' or 'Thank You For the Food We Eat' that is how children first raise their voices in music. I joined in like every other child and never thought much about it until prep school and Congregational Practice.

It was the custom of prefects to patrol the pews during Cong Prac and make sure that everyone was paying attention and doing his best to join in.

One Saturday, perhaps my third or fourth week at Stouts Hill, Hemuss the music master had selected the hymn

'Jerusalem the Golden' for the next day's service. We had never sung it before. Don't know if you're familiar with it – it's very beautiful, but not easy. Lots of unusually flattened notes and set in a subtle rhythm that seems a world away from the simple tumpty-tum of 'Onward Christian Soldiers' which is a hymn any old fool can speak-sing without drawing too much attention to himself.

We listened to Hemuss playing this new tune through on the piano a few times then as usual, the choir had a stab on their own. Next came our turn.

I wasn't really thinking of much, just joining in aimlessly, when I became aware of a prefect, Kirk, standing next to me. He pushed his face right up to mine, his ear against my mouth and then called out in a loud voice.

'Sir, Fry's mucking about!'

The boiling flood that rose to my face then is rising again now. It is of that heat and fever that can only be caused by injustice – rank, wicked, obscene, unpardonable injustice.

Hemuss stopped playing, a hundred voices trailed off into silence, a hundred faces turned to look at me.

'On your own then, Fry,' said Hemuss, 'and *two* and *three* and . . .'

And . . .

. . . silence.

My mouth rounded in the shape of the words, a small husky breath may or may not have hissed from my throat, but the school heard nothing and saw nothing, save a crimson straining face and eyes screwed shut in shame.

'This isn't a *game*, Fry! *And* two, three *and* . . .'

This time I tried. I really tried. Words did emerge.

I had got no further than '. . . with milk and honey blest' before, within seconds of each other, Hemuss stopped playing, Kirk hissed, 'God you're *completely flat*!' and the whole hall exploded with hooting, braying laughter.

Since that time I have been to weddings and to the funerals of deeply loved friends and been entirely unable to do anything but mime the words of the hymns I have so desperately wanted to sing. I have felt guilty for paying nothing but literal lip service to those for whom I care. Since I have a certain facility with words and with performance I am often asked to give speeches on such occasions and this I can manage. But I don't want that. All I have ever wanted is to be part of the chorus, to be able to join in.

Is that true?

I've just written it, but is it true?

An odd thing is this. I had no memory at all of the Cong Prac hooting braying incident until I went to see a hypnotist nearly twenty years later.

Oh, hello . . . a hypnotist now, is it?

Actually, this was a completely practical visit to a hypnotist.

Hugh Laurie and I used to write and perform material of a more or less comedic nature in a 1980s Channel 4 comedy and music show called *Saturday Live*. It was the programme that notably launched Ben Elton and Harry Enfield into public fame.

One week Hugh and I had some sketch or other which involved an ending in which I needed to sing. Not a complicated song, some sort of R&B verse, nothing more. Harry Enfield was to conduct a band wearing amusing headphones and a pleasing Ronnie Hazlehurst grin and Hugh, I suppose, was to play the guitar or piano. I can't remember why I had to sing and why Hugh couldn't have looked after the vocal department as he usually did. Perhaps he had a mouth organ to deal with too. Hugh can sing splendidly, and play any musical instrument you throw at him, the son of a son of a son of a son of a *son* of a bitch.

I said to Hugh, as I say to everyone who will listen, 'But this is mad! You *know* I can't sing . . .'

Hugh, either out of exasperation or a cunningly laid plan to force me to wrestle my musical demons to the ground, said that I would just plain *have* to and that was that. I suppose this would have been a Wednesday: the programme, as the title suggested, was transmitted live on Saturday evenings.

By Thursday morning I was all but a puddle on the floor.

How could I possibly sing live on television?

The problem was, even if I *spoke* the lines, I wouldn't be able to do so in rhythm. The musical intro would begin and I would be unable to come in on the right beat of the right bar. The very oddity of my performance would detract from the point of the sketch. The whole thing would become a number about a person making an appalling noise for no apparent reason.

Many people get stage fright: the moment they have to speak or act in public their voices tighten, their legs wobble and the saliva turns to alum powder in their mouths. That doesn't happen to me with speech, only with music. Alone or in the shower, I can soap myself in strict tempo if there is music playing on my Sony Bathmaster. But if I think so much as a house-fly is eavesdropping, everything goes hot, bothered and bastardly: I lose the ability even to count the number of beats to a bar.

It occurred to me, therefore, the Thursday prior to this programme, that a hypnotist might perhaps be able somehow to cure me of this self-consciousness and allow me to kid myself, when the moment came round on Saturday in front of cameras and studio audience, that I was alone and unwitnessed.

The more I thought about it, the more logical it seemed. A hypnotist couldn't turn me into Mozart or Muddy Waters, but he might be able to remove the psychological obstacles that froze me whenever music and I met in public.

I let my fingers to do the initial walking and then followed them all the way to Maddox Street, W1 where a hypnotherapist calling himself Michael Joseph had a little surgery. He came complete with a soothing manner and a most reassuring Hungarian voice. The matey, disc-jockey tones of a Paul McKenna would have sent me scuttling, but a rich middle-European accent seemed just what was required. Aside from anything else, it reminded me of my grandfather.

I explained the nature of my problem.

'I see,' said Mr Joseph, folding his hands together, like Sherlock Holmes at the commencement of a consultancy. 'And what is dee . . . how you say? . . . dee *cue* that comes before you must start singing for diss programme?'

I had to explain that the words that immediately preceded my singing were in fact 'Hit it, bitch . . .'

'So. Your friend, he is saying "Hit it, bitch" ... and next music is starting and you must be singing? Yes?'

'Yes.'

The business of being put in a trance seemed childishly simple and disappointingly banal. No pocket watches were swung before me, no mood music or whale song played in the background, no mesmeric eyes bored into my soul. I was simply told to put my hands on my knees and to feel the palms melt down into the flesh of the knees. After a short time it became impossible to feel what was hand and what was knee, while miles away in the distance rich, sonorous Hungarian tones told me how pleasantly relaxed I was beginning to feel and how leaden and heavy my eyelids had become. It was a little like being lowered down a well, with the hypnotist's voice as the rope that kept me from any feeling of abandonment or panic.

Once I was in what I might as well call a trance, I was asked for all memories and thoughts connected to singing. It was at this point that every detail of Kirk and the humiliation that attended my attempt at a solo 'Jerusalem the Golden' flooded unbidden into my mind.

So that was it! That was what had been holding me back all these years. A memory of childish public humiliation that had convinced me that I never could and never would sing in public.

The hypnotist's voice, at once both far away and incredibly close, made the suggestion that when I heard the words 'Hit it, bitch ...' I would feel totally relaxed and confident, as if alone in the bath, unjudged, unselfconscious and unembarrassed. I would sing the verse I had to sing on Saturday lustily, forcefully, amusingly and with all the relish, gusto and self-pleasure of a group of Welshmen in the back seat of a rugby coach. Not his simile, but that is what he meant.

I assimilated this suggestion and made a strange, echoey interior note to myself that it was all quite true and that it was absurd that Saturday's gig had ever held any terrors for me, while my voice murmured assent.

After counting me backwards into consciousness and telling

me how refreshed and splendid I would feel for the rest of the day, the hypnotist tried to sell me the inevitable Smoking, Dieting and Insomnia tapes that lined his bookshelves and sent me on my way, my wallet lighter by fifty or so pounds and my heart by a million kilos.

My performance that Saturday will never be counted alongside Marilyn Horne's début at the Met or the release of *Imagine*, but I did get through it without a blush of self-consciousness or a tinge of fear.

It was only afterwards, winding down as usual in the Zanzibar, the early pre-Groucho watering-hole of choice amongst 1980s comedians, photographers, artists and the like, that it occurred to me that the bloody man had only released me from my singing burden for that one *single* occasion.

'Hit it, bitch . . .' had been my trigger and this one Saturday night the moment of its activation. He had not freed me of my musical inhibitions permanently. The talisman's power had been all used up and if I wanted to sing again in public I would have to make another sodding appointment. There and then, in the vodka and cocaine fuelled passion of the moment, I made a vow never to do so.

Singing and Stephen were not meant to be.

I am grateful to him for allowing me access to a forgotten memory, but it is not a path I have any desire to travel down again. I dare say there are other memories hidden away in the tangled briar-bush of my head, but I see no earthly reason to start hacking away there.

Music matters to me desperately, I've made that clear, and I could cover pages and pages with my thoughts about Wagner and Mozart and Schubert and Strauss and all the rest of it, but in this book my passion for music and my inability to express it in musical terms stand really as symbols for the sense of separateness and apartness I have always felt. In fact they stand too as a symbol of love and my inability to express love as it should be expressed.

I have always wanted to be able to express music and love and the things that I have felt in their own proper language –

not like this, *not* like this with the procession of particular English verbs, adjectives, adverbs, nouns and prepositions that rolls before you now towards this full-stop and the coming paragraph of yet more words.

You see, when it comes down to it, I sometimes believe that words are all I have. I am not actually sure that I am capable of thought, let alone feeling, except through language. There is an old complaint:

> *How can I tell you what I think*
> *until I've heard what I'm going to say?*

It might have been designed for me, that question. It was years before Oscar Wilde was to shake me out of a feeling that this was a failure in me, when I read his essay, written in the form of a Platonic dialogue, *The Critic As Artist:*

ERNEST: Even you must admit that it is much more difficult to do a thing than to talk about it.

GILBERT: More difficult to do a thing than to talk about it? Not at all. That is a gross popular error. It is very much more difficult to talk about a thing than to do it. In the sphere of actual life that is of course obvious. Anybody can make history. Only a great man can write it. There is no mode of action, no form of emotion, that we do not share with the lower animals. It is only by language that we rise above them, or above each other – by *language, which is the parent, not the child, of thought.* (My italics, Mrs Edwards, my italics)

Language was all that I could do, but it never, I felt, came close to a dance or a song or a gliding through water. Language could serve as a weapon, a shield and a disguise, it had many strengths. It could bully, cajole, deceive, wheedle and intimidate. Sometimes it could even delight, amuse, charm, seduce and endear, but always as a solo turn, never a dance.

Swimming, turned out when I did it, to be simply the ability to move forwards in water. When I did learn to play pieces on the piano, I discovered that I did not fly or approach any penetration of the cosmos. Language, I had to confess to myself, *did* get me places. It got me academic success, and later financial and worldly rewards that I could never have dreamed of. I learned to use it to save me from bullying, mockery and rejection. Language went on to give me the chance to do things that I am pleased to have done. I have no reason to complain about language.

Others, however, had much to complain about in me, so far as my language was concerned.

They could not understand it.

During my first term at Stouts Hill I found it almost impossible to make myself understood. It drove me insane: I would say things perfectly plainly and always receive the same reply –

'What? Hng? What's the boy saying?'

Was everybody *deaf*?

My problem was eventually diagnosed by a keen-eared master. I was speaking too quickly, far too quickly; I talked at a rate that made me unintelligible to all but myself. The words and thoughts tumbled from my mouth in an entirely pauseless profusion.

For example, 'Sir, is it really true that there are no snakes in Ireland, sir?' would emerge as something like 'Sriseeltroosnayxironss?'

I heard myself plainly and was most hurt and offended when the same insulting word was thrown back at me again and again.

'Don't *gabble*, boy.'

A solution was found by the school in the endearingly Margaret Rutherford form of an extraordinary old lady bedecked with amber beads, lavender water, wispy hair and a Diploma in the Science of Elocution. Every Wednesday and Friday she drove from Cheltenham to Uley in a car that looked like a gigantic Bayswater pram and trained me for an hour in the art of Diction.

She would sit patiently at a table and say to me, dipping her head up from the table and blinking her eyelids with astonishing rapidity as she did so: 'And turn it down! And turn it down!'

I would obediently repeat, 'Annidern, annidern.'

'No, dear. "And-ah, turn-ah, it-ah, down-nn!" You see?'

'And-ah, turn-ah, it-ah, down-nn?'

'I do not want you to say "and-ah, turn-ah", my dear. I want you to be aware that the "d" at the end of the "and" must not run into the "t" at the beginning of "turn", do you see? And. Say "and" for me.'

'And.'

Did she think I was a *baby*?

'Good. Now "Turn".'

'Turn.'

'And turn.'

'Anturn.'

'And-ah turn!'

'And-ah turn!'

Poor woman, she did get there in the end. She introduced me to the pleasure of hearing a progression of plosive and dental consonants – the sheer physical delight to be derived from the sounds and the sensations of the tongue on the teeth – by teaching me the tale of that extraordinarily persevering and stupid woman called Elizabeth, whose Shrove Tuesday misadventures with rancid butter teach us all how by striving, we might turn disaster into triumph. The story went like this.

'Betty had a bit of bitter butter and put it in her batter and made her batter bitter. Then Betty put a bit of better butter in her bitter batter and made her bitter batter better.'

From there we moved on to 'She stood at the door of Burgess's fish sauce shop, welcoming them in.'

The standing at the door was fine – piece of piss – but the welcoming of them in nearly turned my tonsils inside out.

'Yes, perhaps that one is too difficult for you, dear.'

Too difficult? For *me*? Ha! I'd show *her*.

Hours I spent one weekend mastering the art of welcoming them in. At the next lesson I enunciated it like Leslie Howard on benzedrine.

'*Very* nice, dear. Now I should like you to say: "She stood at the door of Burgess's fish sauce shop, welcoming *him* in."'

Aaaaagh! Disaster. I made a great run for it and fell to the ground in a welter of 'mimming' and 'innimming', my larynx as tangled as a plate of spaghetti.

'You see, my dear, I am not interested in you learning these sentences as if they were tongue twisters. I want you to try and *feel* how to talk. I want you to allow the words to come one after the other. I think you like to compress them all into one bunch. Your mind races ahead of your tongue. I would like your tongue to see the words ahead, each one a little flower on the wayside, that can only be picked up as you pass. Don't try to snatch at a flower before you have reached it.'

I wriggled in my seat at the soppiness of the image, but it did clarify things for me. Before long I was even able to tell the strange story of the blacksmith's mother who wants to know just what her son thinks he's up to with that set of saucepans:

'Are you copper-bottoming 'em, my man?'

'No. I'm aluminiuming 'em, mum.'

I was able to say: the seething sea ceaseth, and thus sufficeth us, and able to imagine an imaginary menagerie manager, managing an imaginary menagerie.

But many an anemone has an enemy, and her enemy was pace.

'This is not a fifty-yard dash, my dear. I want you to *love* every single movement of your tongue and lips and teeth. Every single movement of your tongue and lips and teeth. What is it that I want you to love?'

'Ev-ery single movement of my tongue and lips and teeth.'

'Ev'ry, dear, not ev-ery. We do not wish, after all, to sound foreign. But you said there "tongue and lips and teeth". A few weeks ago you would have said "tung-nips-n-teeth", wouldn't you?'

I nodded.

'And now you know our wonderful secret. How beautiful it is to hear every single movement of your tongue and lips and teeth.'

We moved on from John Masefield's 'Cargoes' to Alfred

Tennyson's 'Blow Bugle Blow' and within a term I was comprehensible to all. Like those foreigners in adventure stories who would come out with *Caramba! Zut!* and *Himmel!* when excited, I was still likely to revert to rushing streams of Stephenese at moments of high passion, but essentially I was cured. But something wonderful and new had happened to me, something much more glorious than simply being understood. I had discovered the beauty of speech. Suddenly I had an endless supply of toys: words. Meaningless phatic utterance for its own sake would become my equivalent of a Winnie the Pooh hum, my *music*. In the holidays I would torment my poor mother for hours in the car by saying over and over again 'My name is Gwendoline Bruce Snetterton. Gwendoline Bruce Snetterton. Snetterton. Snetterton. Snetterton.' Ignoring the gender implications of such a name choice, which are not our concern just now, these were the only songs that I could sing. It was the journey from consonant to vowel, the tripping rhythm, the *texture* that delighted me. As others get tunes on their brain, I get words or phrases on the brain. I will awaken, for example, with the sentence, 'Hoversmack tender estimate' on my lips. I will say it in the shower, while I wait for the kettle to boil, and as I open the morning post. Sometimes it will be with me all day.

I was immensely put out, incidentally, when a few years later *Monty Python* used the name Vince Snetterton in one of their sketches. Snetterton is a village in Norfolk, and I felt that they had stolen it from me. From that day forward, Gwendoline Bruce Snetterton ceased to be.

Language was something more than power then, it was more than my only resource in a world of tribal shouts and athleticism and *them*, the swimmers and singers, it was also a private gem collection, a sweet shop, a treasure chest.

But in a culture like ours, language is exclusive, not inclusive. Those on easy terms with words are distrusted. I was always encouraged to believe that cleverness and elegance with words obscured and twisted decent truth: Britain's idea of a golden mean was (and still is) healthy inarticulacy. Mean, certainly – but golden? Leaden, I think. To the healthy English mind (a phenomenon we will dwell on later) there is something intellectually spivvy, something flash, something *jewy* about verbal facility. George Steiner, Jonathan Miller, Frederic Raphael, Will Self, Ben Elton even . . . how often that damning word *clever* is attached to them, hurled at them like an inky dart by the snowy-haired, lobster-faced, Garrick Club buffoons of the *Sunday Telegraph* and the *Spectator*.

As usual, I scamper ahead of myself.

4

When I was a prep-school master at Cundall Manor School in North Yorkshire, eleven or twelve years after arriving at Stouts Hill (note the dashing blazer in the photograph and wonder that this man was allowed to live) the boys at my breakfast table liked me to tell them over and over again the story of Bunce and the Village Shop. I think it gave them a kick to know that a teacher could once have been Bad – not just naughty, but Bad, really Bad.

Discipline at Stouts Hill, for all that I have correctly described the place as familial, friendly and warm, was tough, or what would be called tough today. It centred more or less entirely around the cane: the whack as it was called by masters, matrons and boys.

'You get caught doing that, you'll get the whack . . .' a friend might say with lip-smacking relish.

'Right, Fry, if you're not in bed in ten seconds flat, it'll be the whack for you,' the master-on-duty would warn.

'How many times have you had the whack this week, Fry?' I would be asked in wonderment.

The headmaster when I arrived at Stouts Hill was still the school's founder, Robert Angus. He kept a collection of whippy bamboo canes behind the shutters of his study and they were used with great regularity, most especially during the feared Health Week, a time when he made it plain that his

arms and shoulders craved exercise and would look for the
slenderest excuses to find it. During Health Week an infraction
of the rules that would usually have resulted in lines or detention would be upgraded to the whack. A crime ordinarily pun-
ishable by three strokes would be dealt with by six, and so on.

If Health Week was to be feared, far more terrifying were
those occasions when Angus was unwell or away and the
deputy headmaster, Mid Kemp, took over the running of the
school and the administration of physical punishment.

Mid, I was disconsolate to find out while researching for this
book, was short for Middleton. I had spent the whole of my life
up until now convinced that it was an abbreviation for
Midfred, which would have suited the man better.

In my memory Mid Kemp's hands, his patched tweed
jackets, his moustache and his hair were all yellowed with
nicotine. I don't know what it is about modern cigarettes, but
no longer does one see the great stained smoking fingers and
egg-yolk streaked white hair of old. Mid Kemp looked and
talked like C. Aubrey Smith in *The Four Feathers*. His
favourite word, one for which I have a great deal of time myself
as a matter of fact, was Arse. Everyone was a more or less an
arse most of the time, but I was arsier than just about everyone
else in the school. In fact, in my case he would often go further
– I was on many occasions a *bumptious* arse. Before I learned
what bumptious actually meant I assumed that it derived from
'bum' and believed therefore with great pride that as a
bumptious arse I was doubly arsey – twice the arse of ordinary
arses.

When umpiring cricket matches, Mid Kemp treated his own
arse to the bracing leather comforts of a shooting stick and
would perch at square leg in a yellow haze of nicotine that
spread from short midwicket to deep fine leg.

Mid Kemp treated boys' arses, on those occasions when
Angus was away, to the most ferocious cuts of the cane.
Instead of the straightforward thwack, his speciality was the
bacon-slicer, a vertical downwards slash requiring far less
effort and inflicting infinitely more pain than the conventional
horizontal swat.

Early in my time at Stouts Hill he was replaced as deputy
headmaster by Angus's son-in-law, A. J. Cromie, an alumnus
of Trinity College Dublin who bore a ferocious moustache and
terrified me more than he could ever have known. Cromie
drove a spectacularly beautiful blue Rolls Royce, wore (in my
memory at least) green Irish thornproof tweeds and taught me
French in an accent which, young as I may have been, I
suspected to be far from authentically Gallic.

Angus in his day beat me many times, always with gentle
sorrow. Mid Kemp sliced me from time to time with a rather
mad, rather frightening glazed boredom. Cromie beat me more
than anyone since his reign as proper headmaster coincided
with my rise from infancy to boyhood, from naughtiness to
wickedness. When he beat me it was always with a glum
resignation.

'Oh God, it's you again . . .' he would bark when he arrived
at his study to find me waiting outside the door, the approved
station for those who had been sent for a thrashing. 'And what
is it *this* time?'

Did it do me any harm being beaten? Did it do me any good?
I really don't know. *Autres temps, autres mœurs* – it is now
considered barbaric, sadistic, harmful, disgraceful, perverted
and unpardonable. As far as I was concerned it had at least the
virtue of being over quickly, unlike detention, lines or the
wearisome cleaning and sweeping errands that stood as lesser
penalties. Often, in fact, one was given a choice of punishments
and I always chose the cane.

I never got any *pleasure* out of it, mind you. My sexual
fantasies are, I trust, as weird, frightening and grotesque as
yours and the next person's and the person next to them, but
flagellation, spanking, birching and the infliction of even the
mildest pain have never been anything for me other than
absolute turn-offs.

There *was* pleasure in going straight to the school lavs after
a beating, pulling down one's shorts and pants and flushing the
loo, to the accompaniment of a great hissing sigh – like Tom
sitting himself in a bucket of water after Jerry has set light to
his tail – that I did enjoy. There was too the talismanic pride of

showing one's stripes to the dormitory, like a Prussian Junker displaying his duelling scars.

'Wow, that one bit . . .'

'Nice *grouping* . . .'

'Actually Fry, if it breaks the skin and you bleed you can complain to the government and he'll go to prison, that's what I heard.'

'Apparently, if he raises his arm above shoulder height, it's illegal . . .'

Maybe some of you reading this will think that men who can beat children like that are swine.

I feel terrible about that because the men who beat me were not swine.

Maybe now you'll think people like me who can forgive their childhood beatings – or claim even that there is nothing *to* forgive – are victims of some sort of 'cycle of abuse'. Maybe you think I should be angry, that I should damn the schoolmasters who beat me and damn my parents and damn the men and women who allowed it.

Maybe you think there is nothing more pathetic, nothing that more perfectly illustrates all the vices and impediments of Old England than the spectacle of the Old Boy trying to defend the system that chastised him with strokes of the cane.

Maybe you are right. Maybe I *am* a woeful and pathetic specimen. Maybe I do suffer without knowing it the disastrous consequences of a barbaric and outdated education. Maybe it has disturbed the balance of my mind. Maybe it has warped and thwarted me. Fuck knows. *I* don't and, without wishing to be rude, *you* most certainly can't know either. We are living in a statistically rare and improbable period of British life. The last twenty years are the only twenty years of our history in which children have *not* been beaten for misbehaviour. Every Briton you can think of, from Chaucer to Churchill, from Shakespeare to Shilton, was beaten as a child. If you are under thirty, then you are the exception. Maybe we are on the threshold of a brave new world of balanced and beautiful Britons. I hope so.

You won't find me offering the opinion that beating is a *good* thing or recommending the return of the birch. I frankly regard corporal punishment as of no greater significance in the life of most human beings than bustles, hula-hoops, flared trousers, side-whiskers or any other fad. *Until*, that is, one says that it isn't. Which is to say, the moment mankind *decides* that a practice like beating is of significance then it becomes of significance. I should imagine that were I a child *now* and found myself being beaten by schoolmasters I would be highly traumatised by the experience, for every cultural signal would tell me that beating is, to use the American description, a 'cruel and unusual punishment' and I would feel singled out for injustice and smart and wail accordingly.

Let's try – and God knows it's hard – to be logical about this. If we object to corporal punishment, and I assume we do, on what grounds is this objection based? On the grounds that it is wrong to cause a child pain? Well I don't know about you, but when I recall childhood pain, I don't recall the pains of toothache, a thrashed backside, broken bones, stubbed toes, gashed knees or twisted ankles – I recall the pains of loneliness, boredom, abandonment, humiliation, rejection and fear. *Those* are the pains on which I might and, still sometimes do, dwell, and *those* pains, almost without exception, were inflicted on me by other children and by myself.

I have paused on this subject of corporal punishment because the issue is so culturally loaded today as to be almost impossible to inspect. It comes in so many people's minds very close to the idea of 'abuse', a word which when used within ten spaces of the word 'child' causes hysteria, madness and stupidity in almost everybody.

I know that had I dispassionately described to you the use of the cane without any comment, without summoning counsel for a conference in chambers, then many of you would have wondered what I was up to and whether I was entirely balanced. You will have to form your own judgements, but try to understand that when I think about being caned for repeatedly talking after lights out, or for Mobbing About In The Malt Queue, and other such mad prep-schooly infractions, I feel far less passion and distress than I do when I think about the times I was put into detention for crimes of which I was innocent. If it should so happen that you could prove to me that one of the masters who beat me may have derived sexual gratification from the practice, I would shrug my shoulders and say, 'Poor old soul, at least he never harmed me.' Abuse is exploitation of trust and exploitation of authority and I was lucky enough never to suffer from that or from any violation or cruelty, real or imagined.

It is a cliché that most clichés are true, but then like most clichés, that cliché is untrue.

Sticks and stones may break my bones, but words will always hurt me.

Bones mend and become actually stronger in the very place they were broken and where they have knitted up; mental wounds can grind and ooze for decades and be re-opened by the quietest whisper. Kirk drawing attention to my singing, *that* was abuse, and he was just a silly child who knew no better. Mid Kemp and his mad bacon-slicers, that was the Game and it amuses me.

Sidebar over.

Of all the school rules I liked most to flout, the breaking of bounds gave me the greatest pleasure. Perhaps there's a metaphor there, I do hope not, all this psychology grows wearisome.

The school grounds were extensive. I've made glancing mention of the lake, woods and pony-paddocks. Uley itself lay out of bounds and beyond legal reach. We crocodiled to the church there on special Sundays – the Christmas Carol service, for example, when Easter Day fell in term time, or when the school play was performed in the village hall ('Stephen Fry's Mrs Higgins would grace any drawing-room', my first review) – but at all other times Uley was *verboten*, off limits, here be dragons, don't you bloody *dare*.

Uley had a village shop-cum-post-office crammed with Sherbet Fountains, Everlasting Strips, and two types of penny chew – Fruit Salads and Blackjacks. I don't know why they were called penny chews, they should really have been called farthing chews because you could buy four of these little wrapped squares of deliciously sticky tooth-decay for just one penny. The village shop also sold a brown, shredded confection that was packaged to look like rolling tobacco and tasted I think of coconut. It came wrapped in waxed paper and had a picture of a Spanish Galleon on the front. That and the endless varieties of other pretend smoking materials – candied cigarettes with red dyed ends, chocolate cigarettes wrapped in real paper and liquorice pipes – must now seem almost as wicked to the modern puritan sensibility as child-beating and fox-hunting. The most important thing about these sweets however is that *they could not be bought at the school tuck-shop.* The tuck-shop had its Fry's Turkish Delight (bane of my life, that and all the other nicknaming possibilities around it), Crunchie and Picnic bars, but only the village shop had rice-paper flying saucers filled with sherbet, pink foamy shrimps, rubbery little milk bottles and chocolate buttons sprinkled with hundreds and thousands.

The ownership and sly proffering of paper bags filled with those forbidden fruits became almost as great a totem of heroism as the possession of pubic hair, and was shared with friends in just the same shifty but giggling, shy but boastful manner. Since no amount of pinching, teasing, soaping, threatening and cajoling could cause even the blondest silken millimetre of pubic hair to sprout from me, sweets became my testament of manliness.

Aside from all that, the very act of slipping and sliding around the lake's edge, cutting down past the boathouse, across the gymkhana field with its dressage poles and tatty jumps, over the second games field, across the lane and into Out of Bounds territory had its own thrill. At this time too, nature's best side, the side that didn't creep and crawl and ooze, was beginning to open itself up to me. *Cider With Rosie*, in literary terms, was just about an item of school uniform to us; many of the boys knew Laurie Lee as a friend, he sometimes drank his beer in Uley's pub and on special occasions came to read to us. A killer Cyborg from Vark would fall in love with the countryside if he heard Laurie Lee reading about it.

The walk from the school to the shop was I reckon, a little over a country mile, but I liked to linger. I picture myself, eyes streaming and face blotched with hayfever, sitting under elm trees, firing plantain buds, blowing grassblade fanfares through my thumbs and rubbing nettled shins with dock. The overpowering breath of watermint from the skirting of the lake margin would stay with me until one of my sandals had broken the crisp leathery surface of a cowpat and from then on I would carry with me the decent tang of sun-cured dung. There was a curious pleasure to be gained too, perhaps a hangover from playing rudies with Timothy in Chesham, from pulling down my shorts and crapping in the grass unseen by all but cattle. Maybe that's a primal thing, maybe it's just that I am weird.

I never liked to be accompanied on these trips. I once tried going with someone else, but it felt wrong. He was too scared to dwell on the journey itself, too keen to eat all the sweets before getting back to school, too frightened, in short, of getting caught. Getting caught, I think now, is what it was all about to me.

People sometimes say to me these days, 'You know, I was just as bad as you at school, Stephen. Thing is, I never got found out.'

Well, where's the fun in *that*? I always want to reply. That's a *boast*? 'I never got found out, clever, clever me.'

I am quite aware, by the way, that I am the exception and they are the rule. I'm the freak in this equation, I know that. Not that I actively, consciously *knew* that I wanted to be caught.

I did love sweets, God how I loved them. The mouthful of fillings today and the gaps where grinders should be show that I loved sweets long past the proper age.

One afternoon, perhaps I was eleven years old and moving towards a kind of seniority within the school, I came across a joke shop catalogue lying about in one of the dormitories. I suppose the rest of the school was playing cricket and I had managed as usual to get myself Off Games by inducing an asthma attack. I loved the feeling of having the school to myself, the distant shouts and echoes without and the absolute stillness within. My heart always sank when the final whistles went, the school noises drew closer and I knew that I was no longer the master of the lost domain.

A voice is whispering in my ear that this joke shop catalogue belonged to a boy called Nick Charles-Jones, but this is of minor importance. For a half-crown postal order, it seemed, a fellow could have dispatched to him:

- chattering false teeth
- a small round membrane of cloth and tin which allowed one to throstle, warble and apparently throw one's voice like a ventriloquist
- a bar of soap that turned the user soot black
- itching powder
- a sugar cube that melted and left a realistic looking spider floating on the surface of the victim's tea-cup
- a finger-ring buzzer
- a lookalike chewing gum pack that snapped like a mouse-trap.

Trouble was, I had no postal order, nor any access to such a thing. Unlike Billy Bunter, the Winslow Boy and other famous schoolchildren, I didn't even really know what a postal order *was*. To be perfectly frank with you I'm still not that sure today.

However. It occurred to me that if I mustered up two shillings and sixpence in loose change and then stuck all the coins together with sticky tape and sent them off for 'The most hilarious collection of jokes and gags EVER assembled' with a note of apology accompanying, then only the flintiest-hearted mail-order joke shop would refuse to honour my order.

I had about a shilling on me, which left one and sixpence to go. One and six (seven and a half pence in today's currency) was not a *great* deal of money, but any sum that you do not have when you are eleven years old seems a fortune. I expect today schoolchildren get sent four credit card application forms every day through the post like everybody else, but things were different then. The sand gold and navy blue of a

Barclaycard had only just been introduced and was at first taken up by rather dodgy characters – the sort of people who smoked Rothmans, drove E-Types and swanked about the place with BEA bags over their shoulders and were best played by Leslie Phillips or Guy Middleton.

Stealing had become second nature to me by this time and the boys' changing room was the place to start. Up and down the pegs I would go, lightly tapping the trousers and blazers until I heard the chink of coins.

You can steal from the school, you can steal from a shop, you can steal from a bank. Stealing money from the clothing of friends is . . . what is it? It is not naughty or unstable or unmanageable or *difficult*: it is as bad as bad can be. It is wicked, it is *evil*. It makes you a . . .

THIEF

. . . and nobody loves a thief.

I still blush and shiver when I hear the word used aggressively. It crops up in films on television.

Gentlemen, I am sorry to say that we appear to have a thief among us.

Stop thief!

You thieving little rat . . .

Why, you're nothing but a cheating, lying thief . . .

It's still doing it to me, that word.

The changing rooms. The clink of money. Breathing hard. Mouth parted. Heart hammering. *They* are all outside playing games. Coast is clear.

I am trying hard, even now, to forgive myself for these years of stealing. The shoplifting, the more glamorous insanity with credit cards later on, all that can be laughed or shrugged off. Perhaps.

But this, this was *nasty*, this was *sly*.

'There always was something *sly* about you, Fry.'

There was a way some masters and prefects had of pronouncing my surname that seemed to me, in my guilt, to mean cunning and unclean and ratty and foxy and devious and unhealthy and deceitful and duplicitous and *sly*. Sly Fry.

I could argue in my defence that I spread the load that afternoon. I could say that I needed (*needed?*) one and sixpence, so I took just small quantities of three-penny bits and pennies to make up the sum, rather than cleaning out and impoverishing one particular victim.

But that's not right.

I took small amounts from several people to lessen the chance of there being a fuss.

'Bloody hell. I had a bob here at lunchtime . . .' would have been the cry of any boy robbed of a whole shilling.

Whereas, 'Tsh, I'm *sure* had tuppence somewhere . . .' was less likely to raise a hue and cry.

Those changing rooms at Stouts Hill, then later at Uppingham. From Mary Hench's boot to the regular, almost daily ransacking of boys' pockets for cash, changing rooms have been my killing fields.

I'm still trying to find excuses for myself. I'm wondering whether it was some kind of vengeance. I hated games so much, hated so much those who loved them and excelled at them. Was that why the preferred locus of theft for me was always the changing room, with its casually dropped jock-straps, muddy laces and stink of stale sweat?

Did I hate games because I was so shite at them, or was I so shite at them because I hated them and did I hate them because of . . .

THE BATHS
&
THE SHOWERS?

Is *that* where it all begins? With the cock-shy terror of the showers?

It did consume me, the thought of undressing in front of

others. It ate at me like acid throughout my schooldays and beyond.

There's more on this theme coming later. Let's just say for the time being that I was wicked. When I wanted money or sweets, I stole them and I didn't care from whom. From my mother's handbag at home or from the desks and hanging clothes of my fellow pupils. For the moment, we'll call me a weasley cunt and have done with it.

So, there we are. I'm back in the dormitory sellotaping together nine or ten coins. With a neatly filled-in order-form they are slipped into an envelope which I stuff with a handkerchief to make an innocent package – after all, perhaps the postman may be an awful *thief* and if he felt the coins he might just *steal* them, and wouldn't that be too *dreadful*...

It was Julian Mather's handkerchief that did the stuffing as it happens, the nametape lovingly stitched by a sister, a nanny or an *au pair* perhaps. Myself, to the great aggravation of my mother, I could never keep a handkerchief for longer than a week.

'What do you *do* with them, darling? Eat them?'

And I would repeat the eternal schoolboy lie.

'Oh, *everybody* loses their handkerchiefs, Mummy.'

Or perhaps I would blame the school laundry. 'Nobody's handkerchief comes back. *Everyone* knows that...'

So, down the stairs I crept, on the hunt now for postage stamps.

I knew that Cromie was umpiring a cricket match and that his study was likely to be unlocked.

It was an intensely exciting pleasure to be illicitly alone in the headmaster's study. On one occasion when I had been there before, rifling though his papers, I had come across a report on myself. It concerned my Eleven Plus results.

We had taken the Eleven Plus at Stouts Hill without ever knowing what it was or what it meant. My form master, Major Dobson, had simply come in one day with a pile of papers and said, 'You're all getting rather lazy, so I've decided you can keep yourselves busy with these.'

He had handed out some strangely printed papers and told

us we had half an hour or fifty minutes or whatever it was to answer all the questions.

We were never told that this was the notorious Eleven Plus, the national compulsory test that separated the children of the land into Grammar School children and Secondary Modern children, dummies and smart-arses, failures and achievers, smarmy gits and sad no-hopers, greasy clever-clogses and rejected thickies. A stupider and more divisive nonsense has rarely been imposed upon a democratic nation. Many lives were trashed, many hopes blighted, many prides permanently dented on account of this foolish, fanatical and irrational attempt at social engineering.

Since all of us at prep school were bound for independent public schools who took no notice of such drivel anyway, the whole thing was considered by the Stouts Hill staff to be a massive irrelevance, a tedious and impertinent piece of bureaucracy to be got through with as little fuss as possible and certainly without the boys needing to be told anything about it.

The examination itself took the form of one of those fatuous Eynsecky IQ tests, mostly to do with shape-recognition and seeing what new word could be slipped between two existing words to make two phrases, that sort of hum-dudgeon . . .

BLOW . . . LOT

. . . for example, to which the answer would be JOB, as in 'blow job' and 'job lot' – though I've a feeling that may not have been one of the actual questions set for us on the day. I remember questions like:

'HEAR is to LISTEN as SEE is to . . .?' or

'Complete this numerical sequence 1,3,5,7,11 . . .?'

And so on.

So, foraging through the headmaster's desk one afternoon I had happened upon a list which called itself Eleven Plus results, listing Intelligence Quotient Results or some such guff. I noticed it because my name was at the top with an asterisk typed next to it and the words 'Approaching genius' added in brackets. Cromie, the headmaster had underlined it in his blue-black ink and scrawled, 'Well that bloody explains *everything . . .*'

It will seem boasting wherever I go with this, but I was not in the least pleased to learn that I had a high IQ. For a start I didn't like the 'approaching' part of the phrase 'approaching genius' (if you're going to be a freak, be a complete freak, no point at all in going at it half-cock) and secondly I wriggled in discomfort at the idea of being singled out for something over which I felt I had no control. They might as well have exclaimed at my height or hair colour for all that I felt it had anything to do with me as a person.

Years later as an adolescent, when I fell into the error of confusing my brain with my self, I actually went so tragically far as to send off for and complete the Mensa application test and proved to myself that I was more than 'approaching' genius and felt extremely self-satisfied. It was only when I realised that the kind of intelligence that *wants* to get into Mensa, *succeeds* in getting into Mensa and then *runs* Mensa and the kind of intelligence that I thought worth possessing were so astronomically distant from each other, that the icing fell off the cake with a great squelch. It is on occasions like this that I praise God for my criminal tendencies, my homosexuality, my jewishness and the loathing of the bourgeois, the conventional and the respectable that these seem to have inculcated in me. I could so easily, given the smallest twist to the least gene on the outermost strand of my string of DNA, have turned into one of those awful McWhirterish ticks, one of those asocial right-wing libertarian freaks who think their ability to find anagrams and solve Rubik's cubes is a serious index of mental value. Having said which, I was determined to solve Rubik's Cube myself and pride myself on my ability to do the *Times* crossword quickly. I square this rather vile vanity with myself by claiming that I do these things to show that it is possible to have a knack with such games and *not* be a graceless Freedom Association beardie or a Clive Sinclair style loon. Also, if I'm honest, I submit myself to these forms of mental masturbation from time to time to prove to myself that my brain hasn't yet been rotted away by drugs and alcohol. My great Cambridge friend, Kim Harris, the friend to whom I dedicated my second novel, *The Hippopotamus*, is a superb chess player, attaining a Master level at a young age: he takes a wicked delight in drinking at the chess board and being wholly unlike the scurfy, bottle-end spectacled schlemiels whom he faces over the board. I think we are both honest enough to admit that we are each in our own way guilty of snobbery of a quite dreadful kind.

While on the subject of intelligence, I have to say that I have never found it an appealing quality in anyone and therefore have never expected anyone to find it appealing in me. It grieves me deeply that many people who think me intelligent or believe that *I* fancy myself intelligent or have read some-where that some journalist has described me as such, expect me to judge others by intelligence. The number of times strangers have opened conversations with me in this manner . . .

'Of course, I'm no brain box like you . . .'

'I know I'm only stupid, but . . .'

Or worse still, 'Don't you find it rather dull being surrounded by actors for so much of the time? I mean let's face it, most of them are thick as two short planks.'

I just don't know where to begin with this kind of talk.

Even if it were true that most actors are stupid, and it isn't, the idea that I might project myself as the kind of person who looks for intelligence in others as an index of value sends the creepiest of shivers down my spine. I might use long words from time to time and talk rapidly or name-drop culturally here and there and display any number of other silly donnish affectations, but if this gives the impression that I might admire a similar manner or nature in others, then it makes me just want to go 'bibbly-bobbly-bubbly-snibbly wib-wib floppit' for the rest of my life, read nothing but Georgette Heyer, watch nothing but Emmerdale, do nothing but play snooker, take coke and get drunk and use no words longer than 'wanker' and 'cunt'.

I don't know many people who can do the *Times* crossword more quickly than me. There again I do know dozens and dozens of people vastly more intelligent than me for whom the simplest cryptic clue is a mystery – and one they are not in the least interested in penetrating.

Also, it must be said, I don't know many people as capable of my kinds of supreme dumbness.

I'm the last person on earth to bear with equanimity that kind of Bernard Inghamy, Fred Truemany Yorkshireman who blathers on about nous, gumption, common sense and the University of Life – 'you see, they're all very well these Oxbridge-educated so-called intellectuals but have you ever seen them trying to boil a tyre or change an egg . . .?' and all that pompous bum-wash, but, awful as such attitudes are they are no worse than the eugenic snobbery of those who believe that the ability to see the word 'carthorse' scrambled in the word 'orchestra' or to name every American state in alphabetical order raises them above the level of the average twitcher, trainspotter or Gyles Brandreth style word-game funster.

The discovery of Cromie's scrawled 'Well that bloody explains *everything* . . .' next to my name determined me to investigate his study on every available occasion. I did not like the idea that things were being written about me without my knowing it.

So, back to our main time-line again. I'm in the study alone. This time I'm looking for stamps.

Cromie had one of those elegant polished desks, with lots of knobs and sliders and fluted volutes and secret drawers – the kind of desk a sly fox like me loved to play with.

I succeeded in pressing a wooden stud under the desk: a section flew back on a spring and what did I see?

Sweets.

Bags and bags of sweets.

Confiscated sweets. Foam shrimps, fruit salads, blackjacks, flying-saucers, red-liquorice bootlaces, every desirable item of Uley village shop bounty that could be imagined.

In that lips-parted, heart-pounding, face-flushed state that can signify sexual ecstasy or the thrill of guilt and fear, I grabbed from each bag four, five, six or seven sweets, stuffing them into my pockets, unable to believe that such good fortune could have come my way. You set out to steal a few postage stamps and there before you is a drawer filled with all the treasure you have ever dreamed of.

Granddaddy was watching, that I knew. It was the one great worm in every delicious apple I ever stole. My mother's father had only recently died and he had become my *figura rerum*, my familiar. I knew whenever I stalked about my bedroom naked, sitting on mirrors, sticking a finger up my bum or doing any of those other mad, guilty childish things that constitute infantile sexual play to the psychologist, that Granddaddy Was Watching. Whenever I did truly bad things too, like stealing, lying and cheating, Granddaddy Was Watching then. I had learned to ignore him, of course, and the disappointed look in his eyes as he turned away in disgust. He expected so much better of his grandson than this. But then I had learned to ignore the sad, sweet expectations of the soft-eyed Jesus who also watched me whenever I was bad. At that time I never thought of myself as Jewish, which is perhaps as well, or those two Jews, one recently dead, the other fluttering like a dove over the altar every morning at chapel, might have driven me to a wilder state of madness and self-loathing than I was already in.

Just as I crammed a few final penny chews into my last spare pocket I heard, not too far distant, the creak of a footstep upon a wooden plank.

I pushed the secret drawer shut and peered through the study door.

I could see no one there, just the deserted hallway and the birdcages. Perhaps the mynah bird had been practising new sounds.

I edged myself out of the study, closed the door quietly and turned, just in time to see Mr Dealey, the school butler, emerge from the dining room, bearing silver candlesticks and a vast epergne.

'Ah, now then, Master Fry,' he said in his Jack-Warner-I've-been-about-the-world-a-bit-and-have-got-*your*-number kind of a way.

I was sure that he had no idea that I had been *inside* the

study. Surely he had seen me at the door and thought I was
waiting outside?

'You won't find the Headmaster inside on a fine afternoon
like this, young Fry,' he said, confirming the thought. 'You
shouldn't be inside yourself. Young lad. Sunny day. It's not
healthy.'

I started to pant a little, and pointed to my chest. 'Off
games,' I said with a brave, shoulder-heaving wheeze.

'Ho,' said Dealey. 'Then perhaps you should come with me
and learn how to polish silver.'

'No fear!' I said and scuttled away.

Close calls of that nature always charged me up into a state
of mania. My passion at the time for the prison-of-war genre in
books and films derived, I suppose, from an identification with
the POWs and the edge of discovery and detection on which
they permanently lived . . . replacing the stove over the tunnel's
hiding-place *just* before the entrance of the Commandant,
popping their heads down *seconds* before the searchlight
revealed them. Books like *The Wooden Horse* and *Reach for
the Sky* were full of these moments and I consumed them with
a passionate fever.

This time, I was away and free, a whole pocketful of sweets
to the good, not a Jerry in sight and the Swiss border only a few
miles hence.

I slipped out into the garden and made my way towards the
lake. The boathouse there was a good place to sit and eat
sweets.

On the way however, I encountered Donaldson, who was
also off games and he had a new game to show me.

An electric fence had just been erected around a section of
one of the fields. This area was to be turned into a fourth eleven
cricket pitch or something similar, and the fence was needed to
stop the ponies from going near. An announcement had been
made about it and how we were not to touch it.

'But how about this,' said Donaldson, taking me towards the
fence.

I followed him in some trepidation, he was no particular
friend of mine, Donaldson. He was big and beefy, only off

games because he was injured, not because he was cowardly or a weed. He had never bullied me, nor ever tried to, but I feared some practical joke which would end with me being pushed against the electric fence and being given an electric shock. Growing up in a house with Victorian wiring, I had got to know enough about electric shocks to dread their sullen thumping kicks.

Donaldson stood by the fence, motioned me to be quiet and then suddenly leaned out and grabbed the wire with one hand before letting go of it again just as suddenly. His body hadn't jolted or jumped at all.

'Is it switched off then?' I asked.

'There's a ticker,' he said. 'Listen.'

Sure enough, from some control device on one of the corner fence-posts came a regular ticking sound.

'Every time it ticks,' said Donaldson, 'it sends a charge. But if you grab it in between ticks, you're okay. Go on. Have a go.'

Still fearing some practical joke, I listened to the ticks until I felt sure of their tempo and then touched the wire and let go quickly.

Nothing.

I laughed. This was fun.

We carried on with the game, refining our ability to touch the wire for longer and longer periods as we became more and more familiar with the rhythm of the ticker and together, Donaldson and I bonded in one of those complete moments of childhood friendship that last only as long as the particular period of play, each of us knowing that the next time we met we would be no closer than we had been before.

We were soon joined by other boys, returning from their cricket, rounders and athletics, and Donaldson and I, masters-of-ceremony, initiated them into the Ways of the Ticker.

Then I had an idea.

'What about this?' I said. 'Suppose we all link hands and stretch out in a line. Then one of us grabs the wire and actually *gets* a shock. The current should go all along the line getting weaker and weaker until it reaches the last person.'

'What's the point of that?'

'Well, the winner is the person with the most points. How many of us are there? Fifteen. So the person who actually touches the wire gets fifteen points, the person next to him fourteen and so on, down to the last person who gets one. If you break the link you're out.'

It took a certain amount of organisation, but eventually some rules were roughed out that allowed everyone to get the chance to be the Fifteen Man, the one who touched the wire and bore the brunt of the current.

Never physically brave I decided for who knows what reason, that I should be the Fifteen Man first. Donaldson was next to me and grasped my free hand. When we were all firmly linked I leaned towards the wire.

'Remember,' I said sternly, 'anyone who lets go is O-U-T out. For ever.'

Fifteen heads nodded solemnly. I reached forwards, held my breath and grasped the wire.

The first tick sent a surge through me that almost knocked me off my feet, but I held on for a second tick, almost unaware of the screams and giggles that were spreading out along the line.

After the third or fourth shock, I let go and looked back.

Fifteen boys were jumping up and down, yelling and giggling. The line had held.

The boy at the end, who had received the least shock was none other than Bunce and he was pink and grinny with the pleasure of having kept his nerve and held on.

We played this game for another half hour and I'm not sure I had ever been so completely happy. There was a combination of delights here that had never come together for me before: the knowledge of sweets and sweets and sweets in my pocket, the pride of a new-found physical courage, the pleasure of being not just part of a game, but master of it, the delicious awareness that I had somehow persuaded fifteen boys to break a school rule. We were in it together. I hadn't joined in with them, they had joined in with me.

Bunce had never overlooked the casual kindness of our first meeting in the Paddington train. He didn't ever tag, having too much dignity to be one of nature's hangers on, but he always liked me, no matter what I did, and he always grinned when he caught my eye and looked sad when I was teased or shouted at or in trouble.

Everyone had enjoyed a turn as the Fifteen Man, we had worked out the right number of pulses to hold on for to ensure the maximum pleasure and now Donaldson and I were conferring on refinements. He suggested that the chain should actually be a semi-circle and that the last man in the line should touch the wire at the same time as the first. Someone warned with awe and dread in their voice that this would cause a Short Circuit and that the person in the middle, when the two pulses of current met, would be burnt to a cinder. Perhaps we should collect a pony and use that as a guinea-pig. A pony in the middle of the semi-circle seemed a very funny idea, and a pony being fried to a crisp struck Donaldson as the most fantastically amusing proposition he had ever heard.

'Oh, we've just *got* to,' he said. 'Look! There's Cloud. We'll use Cloud.'

Cloud was an elderly grey pony with a great Thelwell-style underhang of a belly. Cloud was the first pony I had ever ridden and I hated the idea of her being electrocuted. I had inherited from my parents a love of animals that I frankly confess to be anthropomorphic, sentimental and extreme. The very sight of bears, seals and the more obviously endearing mammals will cause us all to weep copiously. I shall never forget the red mist that descended over me, years later, when I once saw youths throwing stones at some ducks in a park in King's Lynn. I picked up some huge pieces of builder's rubble nearby and started to hurl them at the boys, roaring the kind of meaningless obscenities that only pure fury can put into the mind. 'You shit spike wank turdy bastardheads ... how do you fucking like it, you tossing tossers ...' that kind of thing.

Were Donaldson and I going to fall out over the use of Cloud in the game? I really did not want that, but nor did I want to be the wet-blanket that doused the spreading warm glow of the moment, the kill-joy that dislocated that perfect rhythm of these unfolding new ideas. Improvised childhood games, like children themselves, are imponderably unpredictable in their robustness *and* their fragility.

I don't want to paint Donaldson as some cruel monster. I am certain he would no more have countenanced the zapping of an innocent old pony than any of us.

But this was never put to the test.

A voice came clear down the hill to interrupt us. It was the deep and almost broken voice of Evans, a prefect and the school's best bowler. One of his faster deliveries had once cracked a middle stump in two. He took the Cricket Ball Throwing Cup every year, on one occasion throwing the ball so far that it went clean over a lane and was never found.

'Fry! Is Fry Minor down there?'

'Uh oh!' said Donaldson, nudging me.

I brushed silently past Donaldson and the others, all pleasure drained from me, and started to climb the hill towards the silhouette of Evans outlined on the ridge.

What had I done wrong?

That's absurd, I *knew* what I had done wrong, but I could not understand how I could have been found out. It was impossible.

Maybe Mr Dealey *had* seen me coming out of Cromie's study. Maybe someone had missed a few pennies from their pocket and had guessed that I had stolen them. Maybe there had even been a witness.

'Get a move on, will you?' Evans stood under the great horsechestnut at the top of the hill and glowered down at me as I laboured up towards him. 'Haven't got all day.'

He was in his cricket whites, streaked with the long green grass stains of a man who isn't afraid to dive.

'Sorry, Evans,' I said. 'Only, it's my asthma. I can't run too much in this weather . . .'

'Oh yes, your asthma. Well, never mind that, I'm to take you to the headmaster's study.'

'Sorry?'

'Asthma and deafness too?'

'But why? What have I done?'

Evans turned away as I reached the ridge of the hill, not even looking to see whether I would follow. 'You'd know that better than me. Cromie just puts his head out of his study door, sees me and says, "Evans, track down Fry the Younger and bring him to me *at once*."'

For Evans the event was merely a distraction from nets or from whatever else he had on his mind and I could see that he led me without either relish or sympathy, only with careless disinterest. I trailed behind him like a wet spaniel wondering furiously what it was that Cromie could know.

We reached the outside of his study too early for any excuse to have come to my head, nor had I had time to rehearse fully in my mind the stout and stolid style of blank innocence that would come to me when Cromie confronted me with my crime, the hot indignation of my denial, the hooting outrage that would possess me the moment he accused me of . . . of *what*?

'Enter!'

Evans had rapped on the door. I stood there, legs braced.

'That means "come in",' said Evans, swinging the door open for me.

Cromie was not at his desk. He was sitting in one of his two leather armchairs, reading. The first thing I looked for, with the quickest darting glance, was any sign that the secret drawer to the desk was open. It was not.

'Thank you, Evans. Very prompt.'

'Sir.'

Evans vanished with another turn on his heel. He went on in later life to Harrow, playing cricket for the school and shining in the cadet force, where his ability to turn smartly on his heel won him, I have no doubt, the Sword of Honour and the admiration of all.

I lingered in the threshold. There was a jaunty gleam in Cromie's exceptionally blue eyes, and a crisp upturn to his russet moustache that puzzled and frightened me.

For all I know Cromie's eyes are brown and his moustache was green: I hope he will forgive any inaccuracy. I believe he is a wise enough man to know that false memory can be more accurate than recorded fact.

'Come in, Fry, come in!' he cried with the affable assertive-
ness of an archdeacon inviting a curate in for a friendly talk on
Pelagianism.

'How kind, sir,' I said, ever pert.

'Sit,' said Cromie, indicating the other armchair, the
armchair whose seat and cushions, up until this moment, I had
only ever seen from upside-down, while bent over one shining
leather arm preparing to receive the cane.

I sat in some bewilderment.

I was too far away from leaving the school to be ready to
receive the famous Leaver's Talk about which the school
whispered fiercely at the end of each term, the Leaver's Talk
which told everyone what they already knew about Vaginas
and Babies and Testicles and Urges and Some Other Boys.

I stared at the carpet hopelessly confused.

After what seemed an age, Cromie put down whatever it was
that he was reading and twinkled across at me.

'Fry,' he said, slapping a cavalry-twilled knee. 'I am going to
make a prediction.'

'Sir?'

'You are going to go far.'

'Am I, sir?'

'Believe me, yes. You are going to go very, very far. Whether
to the Palace of Westminster or to Wormwood Scrubs I can't
quite tell. Probably both, if I know my Fry.' He rubbed the
knee he had already slapped in the manner of an older man, a
man whose arthritis or war wound might be playing merry
hell, but was none the less a companionable reminder of better
days. 'Do you know why you will go far, Fry?'

'No, sir.'

'You'll go far because you have *the* most colossal *nerve*.'

'Have I, sir?'

'For colossal nerve, for sheer, ruddy cheek, I have never met
anyone to match you.'

All this said so easily, so chummily so – there was no
escaping the word, mad as it seemed – so *admiringly*.

'Fry has a problem,' Cromie went on, seeming now to be
addressing the bookcase. 'He has a parcel he wishes to send,

but, drat and curse it, he has no stamp. So what does he do? He goes into Sir's study, cool as you please, sees a heap of letters and packages waiting to be stamped, puts his own on top of the pile and leaves. "Old Dealey will take the whole lot out to the post office and mine will be stamped along with the rest of them," he thinks to himself. How was he to know that Sir might come along before Dealey had taken them away and recognise the highly individual handwriting of the most impudent scoundrel this school has ever had the honour to house?'

God, God, God . . . the joke shop order . . . the pennies stuck together. I had clean forgotten.

In all the excitement of discovering those sweets I must have laid the package down on the desk when fiddling with the secret drawer.

Great heavens almighty.

'Such cavalier insolence deserves a reward, Fry,' said Cromie. 'Your reward is that Dealey has duly taken your parcel to Uley along with the others and it will be sent to its destination at the school's expense and with my compliments.'

He rubbed his chin and chuckled.

Maybe Jesus Christ and Granddaddy did not judge and punish. Maybe they loved me.

I knew what was expected of me in return and gave Cromie the full repertoire: the ruefully apologetic stretching of the lips, the bashfully sheepish grin, the awkwardly embarrassed shifting in my seat.

'Well, you know, sir. I just thought . . .'

'I know very well, sir, what you just thought,' said Cromie, smiling back as he stood. He looked about him. 'This must be the first time you've been inside this room without leaving it with a sore backside. Well, count yourself lucky. Use some of that colossal nerve to better account in future.'

It was true that the only times I had been in that study in Cromie's company had been to receive two or three of the best. The last time had been for a visit to the village shop. Three strokes, with a promise of double that amount next time.

I stood up now, and squeezed my eyes tight in horror as I heard the rustle of paper bags in my trouser pockets. This would be no time for illegal sweets to tumble from me like coins from a one-armed bandit.

'It's all right, there's no need to look so frightened. Off you go.'

'Thank you very much and I'm sorry, sir.'

'Go and sin no more, that's all I ask. Go and sin no bloody more.'

Sitting under a cedar of Lebanon half an hour later, stuffing foam shrimp after foam shrimp into my mouth, I mused on fate. Maybe I was brave, in a certain sort of way. It took courage to be deceitful and dishonest and conniving and wicked. More courage than it took to toe the line.

The late summer light was lovely on the lawns and lake, there were more fruit salads and a bag of flying saucers left in my blazer pocket.

'*F-r-r-r-ry!*'

When the name was called with such rolling menace, it could only mean Pollock, Pollock the head boy with raven black hair and a sadistic hatred of all things Fry the Younger.

He came round from behind the tree and had snatched the bag from out of my hand before I knew what was happening.

'So we've been to the village shop again, have we?'

'No!' I said, indignantly, 'we have *not*.'

'Don't bother lying. Shrimps, milk bottles, flying saucers and blackjacks. Do you think I'm an idiot?'

'Yes I do Pollock. I do think you're an idiot. I *haven't* been to the village shop.'

He struck me across the face. 'Don't be cheeky, you little creep. Empty your pockets.'

Because of that fall at Chesham Prep my nose has always been immensely sensitive to the slightest percussion. The least strike will cause tears to spring up. In those days the tears were added to by the humiliating realisation that they looked like real tears.

'Oh for God's sake, stop blubbing and empty your pockets.'

There is nothing like a false accusation to cause even more tears.

'How many times do I have to tell you,' I howled. 'I *haven't been to the village shop!*'

'Yeah, yeah, yeah. Sure you haven't. And what have we got here then?'

If the memory weren't so absurdly anachronistic, I could almost swear that Pollock ripped open one of the flying saucers and put his tongue to the sherbet like a Hollywood cop tasting white powder.

'But it's not from the village shop! It's not, it's not!'

There was no getting through to this idiot.

'Christ, you're for the high jump this time,' said Pollock, turning away with all my spoils.

As he spoke we both heard the bell ring for tea. He looked up towards the main school buildings.

'By the ships straight after tea,' he grunted and stumped up the hill.

How strange that the phrase 'by the ships' has only just come back to me.

At one end of a corridor, the other end of which led to the headmaster's study, there were two model battleships mounted in glass cases. A prefect who sent you to see the headmaster always said 'By the ships, after lunch . . .' or 'One more squeak from you, and you'll be outside the ships'. Odd that I didn't remember those ships earlier on in the telling of the story. I think one of them may have been HMS *Hood*, but maybe I'm wrong. I am certain too that they had red paint on the funnel which seems unlikely in a royal naval vessel. Perhaps they were cruise liners. Whatever they were, they spelled disaster.

With rising panic I stumbled up after Pollock screaming at him that I hadn't, I hadn't, I *hadn't* been to the village shop. I heard only answering echoes of laughter as he disappeared into the school.

I heard a small voice at my elbow.

'What's the matter, Fry? Whatever is the matter?'

I looked down to see the anxious brown eyes of Bunce blinking up at me.

I wiped a sleeve across my snot-running nose and

tear-stained cheeks. I could not bear it that one who so admired me should see me in such a state.

As I was wiping that sleeve the idea came into my head fully born and fully armed. The speed of its conception, birth and growth almost took my breath away. I had followed Evans earlier in the afternoon all the way from the electric fence to Cromie's study without being able to think of any defence to any accusation and now – in deeper trouble by far – a rescue plan had emerged in a second. It was complete in my mind before I had even removed the sleeve from my face.

As Biggles never tired of telling his comrades, there is *always* a way. Always. No matter how tight the squeak, and remember chums, we've been in tighter squeaks than this, there is *always* a way out. Algy, look lively and pass me that rope . . .

'Pollock's just caught me with a load of tuck from the village shop,' I said in a low voice, laden with doom.

Bunce's eyes rounded still further. I could tell that the glamour and exoticism of village shop tuck frightened and fascinated him. This was by now at least his second year, I suppose, but somehow, like little Arthur in *Tom Brown's Schooldays*, he was always functionally the youngest boy in the school. I remember that earlier on this summer term, a master had casually pointed out to him that he had turned up to a PE lesson in white plimsolls instead of black and he had gone redder than a geranium and wept and wobbled for days afterwards. His sixth term at the school, he hadn't even been *close* to punishment or the gentlest chastisement, but it was his first ever deviation from the letter of school law and it had upset him deeply.

'Golly,' he said. 'Didn't you get the whack last week for . . . ?'

'Exactly,' I said, interrupting. The thing was to keep the little chap off balance. 'And Cromie said if I was caught again I would be expelled.'

'*Expelled?*' Bunce breathed the word in a terrified whisper as though it were nitro-glycerine that might explode if handled too roughly.

I nodded tragically. 'I don't know what my mother and father would do if I were expelled,' I said, sniffing a little sniff.

'But *why*?'

'Why? Because it would upset them so much, of course!' I said, nettled by such denseness.

'No, I mean why did you go to the village shop again if you knew you would get expelled?'

Well, I mean *really*. Some people.

'It's . . . it's hard to explain,' I said. 'The thing is, never mind why, there's just no way out, that's the point. Pollock's confiscated the evidence and he's going to . . .' My voice trailed off in sudden wonderment as an idea seemed to catch hold. 'Unless, that is, unless . . .'

'Unless what?'

'No, no . . . it's asking too much,' I said, shaking my head.

'Unless what?' squeaked Bunce again.

'It's no good, I'd better face it. I'm done for.'

'Unless *what*?' Bunce almost stamped the ground in his desperation to be told.

'Well . . . I was thinking that if I could say that *I* hadn't been to the village shop but that I had got the tuck from *someone else* . . .'

I let the thought hang in the air.

'You mean,' said Bunce, 'that if a boy said that he was the one who had been to the village shop not you then you wouldn't be the one who had been and you wouldn't be expelled?'

I didn't bother to follow the literal meaning of that peculiar sentence but assumed he was along the right lines and nodded vigorously. 'Trouble is,' I said grimly, 'who on earth would do that for me?'

I watched, with the detached and curious interest of the truly evil, as Bunce blinked, bit his lip, swallowed, bit his lip and blinked again.

'*I* would,' he said at long last.

'Oh, no!' I protested. 'I couldn't possibly ask *you*. I mean you're far too . . .'

'Far too *what*?'

'Well . . . I mean, everyone knows, you're a bit of a . . . you know . . .'

I allowed myself to stumble, too tactful to finish the thought.

Bunce's face grew dark. 'A bit of a *what*?' he said, in something close to a growl.

'Well,' I said gently, 'a bit of a *goody-goody*.'

He flushed and looked at the ground. I may just as well have charged him with complicity in the holocaust.

'It's okay,' I said. '*I'm* the idiot. I don't know what it is with me. I just can't help being bad.'

He looked up at me, suddenly and for the first time annoyed with himself because he just couldn't help being *good*. Which is what I had wanted him to feel. Christ, I'm smart, I said to myself. Perhaps this is what is meant by 'approaching genius'. Do I know how to play a person like a fish, or do I not . . .

I could see that Bunce was coming to an independent decision, or rather that he believed he was coming to a independent decision.

'What's got to happen,' Bunce said, in a voice firm with resolution, 'is that you've got to tell Mr Cromie that it was me who went to the village shop. Me not you.'

'Oh but, Bunce . . .'

'No. That's what you've go to do. Now come on, or we'll be punished for being late for tea as well.'

'Good Christ, Fry!' Cromie yelled, pacing up and down the study like a caged Tasmanian devil. 'Not an hour after I congratulate you on your nerve than you're back here proving to me that it's not nerve, it's cheek, it's rudeness, it's *bloody insolence*!'

I stood on the carpet, biding my time.

'Did I, or did I not, boy, warn you last time that if you dared so much as to *smell* that blasted shop again I would have your guts for garters? Well?'

'But , sir . . .'

'*Answer* me, damn you! Did I, or did I not?'

'But sir, I haven't been to the village shop.'

'What?' Cromie stopped mid-stride. 'Are you trying to tell me . . .' he gestured towards the bags of confiscated sweets on his desk. It simply amazed me that the thought hadn't crossed his mind to check his own stash in the secret drawer. Maybe he had forgotten all about it.

'No, sir. I *was* eating those, but . . .'

'But what? You picked them off a tree? You fished them out of the lake? I wasn't born yesterday, you know.'

I wasn't born yesterday. Pull the other one. Have your guts for garters. Don't try to teach your grandmother to suck eggs. Pull your socks up. Buck up your ideas.

I wonder if schoolmasters still talk like that.

'No, sir, it's just that *I* didn't go to the village shop.'

'What do you mean?' Cromie almost clawed the air in his frustration. 'What *on earth* do you mean?'

'Well, sir, what I say, sir.'

'Are you trying to tell me that someone *else* gave you those sweets?'

I nodded. At last he understood.

'And who, may I ask, is this charitable person, this extraordinary philanthropist, who visits the village shop just so that he might bestow sweets on his friends like some benevolent lord of the manor distributing largess to his villeins? Hm? Who might this person be?'

'I . . . I don't like to sneak, sir . . .'

'Ho, no. Ho no you don't,' Cromie wasn't buying *that* one. 'If you don't want your promised six strokes, then you had better tell me and tell me *this minute.*'

My lower lip wobbled as the betrayal was wrung from me. 'Well, sir. It was Bunce, sir.'

I do not believe I have ever seen a man more surprised. Cromie's eyebrows shot up to the ceiling and his lips went instantly white.

'Did you just say Bunce?' he asked in a hoarse whisper of disbelief.

'Sir, yes, sir.'

'Bunce as in *Bunce*?'

I nodded.

Cromie stared at me, eyeball to eyeball for about five seconds as if trying to pierce through to the very back of my soul. He shook his head, strode past me, flung open the door and yelled in a voice that thundered like Krakatoa, '*Bunce! Bunce!* Somebody find me Bunce!'

'Oh dear,' one of the parrots remarked, kicking the husk of a nut out of its cage. 'Oh dear, oh dear, oh dear.'

I waited, standing my ground as I listened to the cries for Bunce echo around the school like calls for courtroom witnesses.

During tea I had looked across at Bunce's table from time to time. He had been listlessly pushing fried bread into his mouth like a condemned man who has chosen the wrong last breakfast. When he had looked up and happened to catch my eye, his cheeks had blazed scarlet but his head had nodded emphatically up and down and his mouth had formed the word 'Yes'. I had no doubts about my Bunce. Bunce was brave and Bunce was true.

Within three minutes Bunce was beside me on the carpet in Cromie's study, his hands behind his back, his mouth set in a firm line, but his legs wobbling hopelessly in their shorts.

'Bunce,' said Cromie, sweetly, 'Fry tells me that . . . '

This was as far as he managed to get.

The dam burst and the torrent filled the room.

'Sir, it's true, sir. I went to the village shop, sir. I went. I did. I did go there. Fry went. I didn't. I mean, I went, Fry didn't. *I* went to the village shop, not Fry. I got the sweets for him. He didn't buy any. It was me. I bought them all. I went to the village shop. I went to the village shop. I *did* . . .'

All this came at a pace that made Cromie blink with astonishment. It ended in a howling cyclone of weeping that embarrassed us all.

'Fry, get out,' said Cromie.

'Sir, does that mean . . . ?'

'Just go. Wait outside. I shall call for you later.'

As I closed the door I heard Bunce's voice squeaking out the words, 'It *is* true, sir. Every word. I went to the village shop and I'm so sorry, sir, I shan't ever again . . .'

There were too many people milling about to allow me to stay near and eavesdrop. The great cry for Bunce had fascinated the school.

'What's up, Fry?' everyone wanted to know.

I shrugged my shoulders as if I didn't care and walked to the end of the corridor down towards the ships.

Higher up the wall, above the *Hood* and the *Dreadnought*, or the *Invincible* and the *Repulse* or whatever they were, were wooden panels where the gilt names of scholars and other great achievers had been painted. I stood and looked at them. Le Poidevin, Winship, Mallett, de Vere, Hodge, Martineau and Hazell. I wondered for a brief second if my name would ever be up there, but dismissed the idea at once. I knew that it would never be. This was a list of the names of those who had joined in. They had gone on from being captains of rugger and captains of cricket to being captains of school and captains of industry. I wondered if, in a phrase that Major Dobson loved, they had also become Masters of their Fate and Captains of their Soul.

'Are you a *Major* of your Soul then, sir, and is that better than being a Captain of your Soul?' I remember I had asked him this once when he had read that Whitman poem to us and he had smiled cheerily at the question. I had loved Major Dobson because he had been a good teacher and because, in that strange and inappropriate way that children have, I had felt sorry for him. I think my mother had taken me to see a production of Rattigan's *Separate Tables* at the Maddermarket Theatre in Norwich when I was quite young, and since then I had always associated Majors with disappointment, regret and, that awful phrase, 'passed over'.

'Not bad for a passed-over Major . . .' Colonel Ross says to Major Dolby in *The Ipcress File*.

In fact, I now know, Major Dobson had been captured by the Germans with the British Expeditionary Force at Dunkirk. He then escaped and fought throughout the war right up through Sicily and Italy. True to the old cliché, he never talked about it. No more than did Mr Bruce who had spent the war years in a Japanese internment camp and taught History and Divinity with the panache and brio of an ancient fabulist. Being fiercely Scottish, the history he taught with such passion was of William Wallace, the Montrose Rebellion and the Jacobite

Wars of 1715 and 1745. I have special reason to bless Jim Bruce as you will discover later.

I discovered these and other biographical details only two weeks ago when Ant Cromie kindly sent me a list of answers to a cartload of questions about Stouts Hill. Charles Knight, who taught me Latin and Greek and looked like Crippen the murderer but was the kindest and gentlest man who ever taught me, a man who loved to teach, had no interest in discipline or punishment whatsoever, and took immense pride in my taking the school's Senior Greek Prize when I was twelve (I have it still, the collected works of John Keats) – he fought in the desert and in Italy too. I remember so clearly history lessons that involved the war, I remember its universal fascination to all of us, for all that it had ended twelve or thirteen years before we were born. Almost every boy in the school could identify the silhouette of a Dornier and a Heinkel and draw Hurricanes, Spitfires and Panzer tanks. Yet not once do I remember a single master refer to war as a personal experience. I would have bombarded, strafed and sniped them with questions, had I known. It puzzles me still, this silence of old soldiers.

Looking up at the names of the old boys always made me think of the war. Although the school had only been founded in 1935, those names above the ships looked like the names of the war dead, they shared that same melancholy permanence. A contemporary school roll, however *outré* or grand the names, always sounds perky and chipper; the school roll of a generation ago has the sombre muffled note of a funeral bell.

I had not been staring up at le Poidevin and Winship and Mallett for long before I saw, reflected in the glass case of the ships, the study door open at the end of the corridor. I turned.

Cromie stood in the doorway and beckoned with a single curling finger. I walked down the corridor jauntily.

Somehow, I knew the game was up. I think too that I knew that it was right that it was up. Like a scared mutt darting out from between his master's legs, Bunce shot from the study and rocketed down the corridor towards me. I caught the rolling whites of his eyes as he passed and thought I heard a panted word, which may have been 'Sorry'.

As I approached Cromie and the open study door he turned to the six or seven boys who were hanging around, pretending to talk to the parrots and examine the pictures on the walls.

'What are you lot doing here?' he yelled. 'Nothing better to do? Want some extra work?'

They fled in instant silent panic.

Now there was only me in the corridor, walking towards Cromie who was framed against the doorway, his outline dark against the window at the back of his study. The corridor seemed to be getting longer and longer, as in some truth-drug induced hallucination scene in *The Avengers* or *Man in a Suitcase*. Still his finger seemed to beckon, still every step that I took seemed to take me further from him.

When the door did close behind us the room was deadly quiet and the sounds of the school could not be heard. Even the parrots and the mynah bird had fallen into silence.

Cromie turned towards the window where the shutters were. The shutters that housed the canes.

'Of course you know,' said Cromie with a sigh, 'that I am going to beat you, don't you, Fry?'

I nodded and licked my lips.

'I would just like to believe,' he went on, 'that you know *why*.'

I nodded again.

'To go to the village shop is one thing. To send a boy like Bunce to go in your place is quite another. Let us not fool ourselves. Bunce would never have gone unless at your bidding. If you can see how cowardly that is, how vile and low and cowardly, then perhaps there is a scintilla of hope for you.'

That was the first time, I remember, that I ever heard the word 'scintilla'. It is funny how the exact meaning of a new word can be so precisely understood in all its connotations, just from its first hearing.

'Eight strokes, I think,' said Cromie. 'The most I have ever given. I hope never to have to give so many again.'

Bunce never forgave himself, in all the time I knew him, for letting me down. He remained convinced that somehow he could have played it better. He should have swaggered, acted the part of the real, wicked, dyed-in-the-wool village-shopper. I wanted to hug him for his sweetness. Just a great hug to reward such goodness of nature.

I wanted to hug myself too.

I wanted to hug myself for fooling Cromie.

He still didn't get it. Still didn't know the real truth. I had stolen his sweets, stolen money from his pupils and verbally tortured a fine child into lying for me. And all I had been beaten for was the schoolmasterly crime of being a 'bad influence'.

The boys of Cundall Manor School loved me to tell them that story when I was a schoolmaster in the late 1970s. I didn't paint myself in *quite* the terrible colours I should have done, I left out the parts involving *real* theft, but otherwise I told it as it was and they *loved* it.

'Tell it again, sir. The story of you and Bunce . . . go on, sir!'

And I would light my pipe and tell them.

I look back now at Stouts Hill, closed during my first term at Cambridge, and I shake my head at the person I was. The child was more malevolent, I think, than the adolescent, because at least the adolescent had love as an excuse. All the child wanted was to tear at sweets with his teeth.

It never quite managed to move with the times, Stouts Hill. Ant Cromie was ambitious and built a fine theatre. But he never liked the idea of too many day boys. The fees were high, the uniform remained fabulously classy and meanwhile the parents became less interested in ponies and Greek and more interested in Common Entrance results and money. They had voted Mrs Thatcher in and they voted out Cloud the pony and the boathouse and the lake and the old Majors and Commanders. On my bookshelf I still have a copy of Fitzroy Maclean's *Eastern Approaches*, lent to me by Paddy Angus's husband, Ian. I really must send it back to him some time. Fitzroy Maclean is dead now and so is Stouts Hill.

I wonder what those who have used it as a Time Share Facility make of the place. I wonder if I left any guilt and shame

in the air? I wonder if Bunce's grief at his own goodness is
soaked into the walls?

I was happy there. Which is to say I was not unhappy *there*.
Unhappiness and happiness I have always been able to carry
about with me, irrespective of place and people, because I have
never joined in.

Falling In

I

UPPINGHAM SCHOOL was founded in the reign of Queen Elizabeth the First, but like most public schools did nothing but doze lazily where it was, in the cute little county of Rutland, deep in prime hunting country, until the nineteenth century when a great pioneering headmaster, as great pioneering headmasters will, kicked it up the backside and into a brief blaze of glory.

Uppingham's great pioneering headmaster was Edward Thring and one must suppose he had some connection with Gabbitas and Thring, the scholastic agency. Certainly Edward Thring founded the Headmasters' Conference, the public schools' defining body. Even today, if you are not a member of the HMC you are not a public school, merely an Independent.

Thring believed, like all Victorian pioneering headmasters, in simply enormous side-whiskers and in the Whole Boy. Uppingham School, under his command, was the first public school in Britain to build a swimming pool. Thring encouraged the development of carpentry, woodwork, pottery, printing and crafts. He believed that every child had a talent and that it was the duty of the school to find it. If a boy was a duffer at Latin, Greek or the Mathematics, Thring argued, then something else must be found at which he could excel, for Every Boy Is Good At Something. Edward Thring had wider and more substantial sideburns by far than Thomas Arnold of Rugby School, but Uppingham had no Webb Ellis to invent a new field game and no Thomas Hughes to invent a new literary genre, and thus, despite the staggering impressiveness of Thring's whiskers, that flew from his cheeks like banners of flame, Uppingham never quite attained Rugby's heights of fame and glory and throughout the passage of the twentieth century it slowly floated down to its current middle level of middle-class, middle-brow, middle-England middledom.

The English have a positive mania for attaching the word 'philosophy' to the most rudimentary and banal platitudes: 'Our philosophy is to please the customer', 'do as you would be done by, that's my philosophy,' 'a blend of traditional comfort and modern convenience is very much the Thistle Hotel's philosophy,' that kind of nonsense. The word gets its most savage mistreatment in the mouths of that peculiarly pompous animal, the public school headmaster, that creature so ruthlessly and brilliantly slaughtered, stuffed, mounted and put on permanent display by Peter Jeffrey in Lindsay Anderson's film masterpiece *If*...

The public school headmaster and the public school prospectus use the word 'philosophy' much as Californian Valley Girls use the word 'like', ceaselessly and senselessly.

It was Very Much Uppingham's Philosophy, for example, to apply the precepts and principles of Edward Thring to the modern world.

In other words, they had added a metalwork division and a screen-printing room to the carpentry shop.

It was Very Much Uppingham's Philosophy to develop the potential of every pupil.

In other words, the school's A-level results and Oxbridge success rate were well below the average.

It was Very Much Uppingham's Philosophy (even in my day unironically expressed) to turn out polite, cheerful, all-round chaps.

In other words the average Uppinghamian is a well-mannered, decent fellow with a stout heart but not too much between the ears.

If all this sounds like mocking criticism, it is not meant to.

Well-mannered, decent fellows with stout hearts and not too

much between the ears were the gravy and potatoes of two world wars. The well-maintained memorials in Uppingham catalogue a greater roll of the dead than the size of the school warrants. If other, smarter schools provided the brilliant generals and tacticians who moved counters on maps at Staff HQ, then Uppingham served up the gallant young fellows who sprang so cheerfully and so unquestioningly up the trench ladders, leading their men into the certainty of muddy, bloody slaughter. What is more, Uppinghamians who survived would never be so unsporting or so tasteless as to write clever sceptical poetry about the experience afterwards.

There is a word which still means much to the English and which was for many years a rod for my back, a spur to prick the sides of my intent, a Fury from which to flee, a nemesis, an enemy, an anathema, a totem, a bugaboo and an accusation. I still recoil at its usage and its range of connotation. The word stands for everything I have always wanted not to be and everything and everyone I have felt apart from. It is the shibboleth of the club I would never join, could never join, the club outside whose doors I might stand jeering, while all the time a secret part of me watched with wretched self-loathing as the elected members pushed through the revolving doors, whistling, happy and self-assured. The word is

HEALTHY

– a word that needs some unpicking. Its meaning derives from whole and hale and is cognitively related to such words as holy and healing. Heal is to weal (as the Eleven Plus might say) as health is to wealth. To be healthy is to be whole and holy. To be unhealthy is to be unclean and unholy, insanitary and insane.

For the English the words healthy and hale, at their best, used to carry the full-bellied weight of florid good cheer, cakes and ale, halidom and festive Falstaffian winter wassail. By the end of the seventeenth century, the hale health of pagan holiday was expelled from the feasting-hall along with Falstaff and Sir Toby Belch by the sombre holy day piety and po-faced puritanism of Malvolio, Milton and Prynne. 'Health!' became no longer a bumping boozer's toast but a quality of the immortal soul. Health no longer went with heartiness, but with purity.

'For your soul's health's sake . . .' said the priest.

Thomas Arnold, and behind him Edward Thring and a squadron of other great Victorian pioneering headmasters, whiskers flowing in the breeze, found a new meaning for health. They twisted a poor Roman satirist's cynical hope into the maxim of the Muscular Christian: *Mens sana in corpore sano.*

'A healthy body makes a healthy mind,' became the wilfully syllogistic mistranslation upon which a 'philosophy' was founded. Cleanliness, generation upon generation of Britons were led to believe, was next to godliness. Health of body was to be looked upon as an outward and visible sign, to misappropriate the glorious poetry of the Eucharist, of an inward and spiritual health.

Thring had some reason to believe in Health, where health meant hygiene. During his headmastership of Uppingham School he had become infuriated by Uppingham Town's refusal to do something about its sewers, whose antiquity and medieval inefficiency were causing regular outbreaks of typhus and typhoid amongst pupils and staff. With the furious energy and implacable will of all great Victorians, he moved the entire school hundreds of miles away to the seaside village of Borth in Wales until such time as Uppingham's local economy suffered enough to force its burghers to do something about their sanitation and, literally, to clean up their act. Thring and the school returned in triumph to a hygienic Uppingham and the school's Borthday is annually celebrated still.

It is one thing to build sanitation systems that inhibit the breeding of unhealthy bacteria and bacilli, but it is another to build educational systems that inhibit the breeding of unhealthy ideas and beliefs. Besides, while we can universally agree that cholera, typhus and typhoid are unhealthy we are unable to come anywhere close to consensus as to the healthiness or otherwise of *ideas*. I suppose today, the

fashionable word to apply is 'meme', the evolutionary
scientist's new buzz-word, a concept that applies the model of
the selfish gene and the greedily self-replicating virus to
movements in thought, to philosophies, religions, political
tendencies, trends in individualism and sexual license, to
growth, development, change and ideo-diversity in everything
from the rights of animals to the rights of man. One model is
as good as another, but today's memologists kid themselves if
they think they were the first to look on ideas as diseases. Their
twist is to call religion the virus, where their predecessors
looked on atheism, humanism and free-thinking as the
contagions. Scientists bring the pure neutrality of φυσις and
the beautiful self-working holiness of nature to bear upon the
problem. Their grandfathers, Charles Darwin's furious contemporaries, invoked the Bible, the edicts of Empire and that
curious Victorian morality that believed worthiness to be the
same as worth and healthiness the same as health.

The religiosity of the public schools had sown into it, praise
the Lord, the seeds of its own destruction, for the cornerstone
of public school education was a study of the languages of
classical antiquity, Latin and Greek, and a study of the classics
leads the alert reader away from the revealed claims of
ecclesiasticism and towards the beauty and holiness of
Socrates, Plato and Lucretius.

Uppingham School has very few alumni of whom it can
boast in terms of that fell whore, Fame. The odd politician
(Stephen Dorrell being the current foremost example), the even
odder explorer and eccentric (the Campbells, Donald and
Malcolm, for example) an odd actor or two (William Henry
Pratt was in my House and achieved eternal glory under the
wisely altered name of Boris Karloff), the great director John
Schlesinger was there too, but very few writers and artists.
Indeed the best known writers to have attended Uppingham
include a most exotic trio of early twentieth-century minors.
James Elroy Flecker for example, a poet and dramatist whose
best known work *Hassan* was set to incidental music by Delius
and contains splendid mock Arabian felicities like, 'Shall I then
put down the needle of insinuation and pick up the club of

statement?' and the couplet that should be the motto of every unhealthy schoolboy:

> For lust of knowing what should not be known,
> We take the Golden Road to Samarkand.

Flecker's contemporary at Uppingham was the exotic Arthur Annesley, better known as Ronald Firbank, whose books included *Vainglory*, *Valmouth* and *Sorrow in the Sunlight*, unfortunately retitled as *Prancing Nigger*. Firbank remains even today near the top of the essential reading list of every well-read literary queen. He was a great favourite of 'better' writers like Evelyn Waugh, Aldous Huxley and Ivy Compton-Burnett, and his writing exemplifies *par excellence* that style of poisonous, luxuriant prose that Cyril Connolly defined as the Mandarin. As E. M. Forster wrote of him and his *louche* created world of birettas, lace-stays and pomanders, 'Is he affected? Yes always ... Is he himself healthy? Perish the thought!'

A little older, but longer-lived than either, was Norman Douglas, the third of the Uppingham triumvirate, and at one time a kind of literary and social hero to me and a writer whose first editions I still collect to this day. Here is something that Douglas wrote about Uppingham in his 1933 memoir *Looking Back*.

> A mildewy scriptural odour pervaded the institution – it reeked of Jereboam and Jesus; the masters struck me as supercilious humbugs; the food was so vile that for the first day or two after returning from holidays I could not get it down. The only good which ever came out of the place was cheese from the neighbouring Stilton, and that, of course, they never gave us. And the charges ... On my mother's death I found, among her papers, those Uppingham accounts: God, how they swindled her! I daresay all that is changed now.

The mildewy scriptural odour and that reek of Jereboam and Jesus still sometimes hung in the air around the more solid

Victorian buildings of Uppingham during my time there and we were certainly never fed on Stilton, but otherwise the place had certainly, as Douglas dared say, changed. The fees were, and still are, steeper than those of many schools with better reputations, but I don't think it could be accused of swindling. Most of the masters struck me as supercilious humbugs too, but then schoolmasters always strike cocky adolescents as supercilious humbugs. If anyone was a supercilious humbug it was most certainly me.

What I adored about Douglas and about Firbank is that they were, as Forster said

UNHEALTHY

The black bombazine bombast of their Victorian childhoods and educations gave those two writers a deep yearning for light, colour, exoticism and the pagan, in Firbank's case the Marian paganism of the Romish church, in Douglas's the real paganism of dryads, fauns and the Great God Pan. They strove instinctively for a style that is the antithesis of blackness and bombast and the best word for that style is not Connolly's Mandarin, but Camp.

What is camp? A much misunderstood word. Everyone has their own feel for it, here is mine.

Camp is not in rugby football.
Camp is not in the Old Testament.
Camp is not in St Paul.
Camp is not in Latin lessons, though it might be in Greek.
Camp loves colour.
Camp loves light.
Camp takes pleasure in the surface of things.
Camp loves paint as much as it loves paintings.
Camp prefers style to the stylish.
Camp is pale.
Camp is unhealthy.
Camp is not *English*, damn it.

But . . .

> Camp is not kitsch.
> Camp is not drag.
> Camp is not nearly so superficial as it would have you
>   believe.
> Camp casts out all fear.
> Camp is strong.
> Camp is healthy.

And, let's face it . . .

> Camp is queer.

(Mostly)

How much a sensitive *heterosexual* boy is drawn to the silks, the light, the paganism, the poison and the luxury of camp, is a question. How much a straight boy *needs* an alternative world, that too is a question. If he does need one, it is more easily found ready-made in the contemporary outside of rock and roll, sport, cars and girls. So easily found that it is not really an alternative world at all, merely one that is just different enough in emphasis from that of the older generation to enable the youth to feel rebellious and rorty.

A boy who knows that he is *other*, who knows that the world is not made for him, who reads the code implicit in words like 'healthy' and 'decent', he may well be drawn to the glaring light and savage dark of the ancient world and the poisonous colours and heavy, dangerous musks that lie the other side of the door into the secret garden, the door held open by Pater, Wilde, Douglas, Firbank . . . even Forster himself, missish and prim as he could be.

Without the 'benefits' of a classical education, a boy growing up knowing his difference, might in my day, have been drawn to *The Wizard of Oz*, *Cabaret*, musicals, glam rock and fashion. Today the gayboy in every section of society has a world of gay music, dance and television to endorse his identity. Manchester has its gay village, London has Old Compton Street, the gay world meets daily to chat, cruise and invigorate itself on the internet. They don't need a parcel of old poofs historically sequestered in Capri and Tangier to tell them who they are and where they come from and whether or not they have the right to hold their heads up high.

I did need them, however. I needed them desperately and without them I am not sure what I would have done to myself.

Queers are not the only unhealthy people to contaminate English society of course. There are Jews too.

I never much cared about my jewishness as a boy. The arbitrary oddity of difference between the western patronymic custom and the primacy of maternal bloodlines in Judaism meant that, by virtue of surname, I passed as gentile. My father's family name of Fry was as old English as could be, steeped in Quakerism as far back as the founding of the movement. John Fry, a parliamentarian ancestor, signed King Charles the First's death warrant. My Great Uncle George wrote a book called *The Saxon Origins of the Fry Family* as a counterblast to those heretical relations (the chocolate making swine from Bristol) who believed that they originated from the town of Fry in Normandy. The opening words of Uncle George's disappointingly little read work are:

> Unlike many so-called English families, the Frys did *not* come over with William the Conqueror in 1066 – they were there to meet him when he arrived.

My mother might be entirely Jewish, but my surname is entirely English, and that made all the difference to me in terms of my perceived identity. To the English it meant I was English, with faintly exotic overtones, to the Jews it meant I was Jewish, with only a venial blemish. I had, that is to say, the best of both worlds. There are plenty of children in Britain with Jewish fathers and gentile mothers who therefore count as non-Jews to the Jewish, but whose surnames being Goldberg, Cohen or Feinstein, find themselves being treated by the British, in Jonathan Miller's phrase, as the Whole Hog.

Besides, I don't really, so far as I can tell, *look* especially Jewish and these things too, make a difference.

I only remember three other Jewish boys at Uppingham: their names were Adley, Heilbronn and Green. Their jewishness was probably of greater importance to them than mine was to me. I used my mixed blood as a vague extra element of exoticism about which I could boast, for there was no palpable anti-Semitism at Uppingham – just the usual careless use of the words 'jew' or 'jewy' applied to anybody to indicate meanness with money, no more than that.

I have feelings about English anti-Semitism that are as mixed as my own blood. Those members of my mother's family who survived the holocaust went to live, with the single exception of my grandfather, in America or Israel. In conversation with them I would get very hot under the collar when they shook their heads wonderingly at my grandfather's decision to live in what they regarded as such an anti-Semitic country as England.

'What about Benjamin Disraeli?' I would retort. 'He was Prime Minister over a hundred years ago. He gave Queen Victoria the Suez Canal and the title of Empress. He died an Earl. When's the first Jewish President of the United States going to be sworn in?' I would conveniently forget to add, of course, that Disraeli's father had converted to Christianity. 'Or look at Rufus Isaacs,' I would say. 'Presidents and potentates would have to bow and call him Your Highness when he was Viceroy of India. He died a Marquess. Half of Margaret Thatcher's cabinet is Jewish. The New York Athletic Club didn't allow Jews in as members until a few years ago. Can you imagine such low, brash vulgarity in a London club?'

Very self-righteous and patriotic I would be. They might respond with talk about the British wartime reluctance to believe in the depths into which Nazi anti-Semitism had sunk and their handling of the Palestinian Mandate.

This is not an argument I feel qualified to pursue. There is no doubt in my mind, however, that there *is* a kind of anti-Semitism peculiar to Britain. I have mentioned before the use of the word *clever* and with what particularity it is applied to men like Jonathan Miller and Freddie Raphael. Jews, like homosexuals, are not quite *healthy*. They are part of that parade of pale, clever men who, at the turn of the century, confused the healthy world with all that talk of relativism and doubt and those weird ideas about determinant history and the divided self. Einstein, Marx and Freud took the old healthy guilt that sprang from Eden and the Cross and which Western Culture had somehow successfully purged of jewishness and gave us a whole new suite of guilts that a good cold shower and a game of rugger couldn't quite cleanse. Indeed, the perverted swine would probably look at that cold shower and that game of rugger and read all kinds of nasty things into them, the kind of nasty things that only a pale, unhealthy kind of outsider could possibly see. They'll read *anything* into the most innocent of pastimes, these Jews and these pansies. *Reading things into things*, if that isn't the favourite hobby of the intellectual I don't know what is. Come to think, dim stirrings of old Latin lessons here, doesn't intellectual actually *mean* 'reading into'? There you are then. People nowadays can't look a plain thing in the face and call it plainly what it is. Intellectuals to the left of us, intellectuals to the right, *reading*. Beastly, unhealthy swine.

Well, no one talks in quite that John Buchaneering way any more, but the modes of thought are still there, or rather modes of anti-thought: still there, still present and incorrect. The Jews still manage, in some people's eyes, that supremely clever trick of being to blame both for capitalism and its excesses through their control of banks and financial institutions *and* for socialism and the liberal consensus that threatens the very stability of capitalism and the free market. It's their bloody *torah* and their damnable *talmud*, simply encourages too much of reading things into things and too much smug rabbinical clever-clever cleverness.

The Uppingham mind certainly was not trained to read too much into things. Those schoolmasters with imaginations and intellects had enough to do to get the boys through O level examinations without worrying their heads with real ideas: they did their best, but it is easy to forget how much more powerful is the corporate mentality of schoolboys than the individual intellect of a schoolmaster. It was easier for the boys to brand a schoolmaster pretentious than it was for a master to call a boy unimaginative. Indeed, I can remember endless arguments (see, there's another thing you Jews are always doing ... *arguing*) with other boys about that great sin of 'reading too much into things'. It is a cliché amongst *healthy* schoolboys to say, 'You can read anything into anything. Bloody hell, all this Shakespeare stuff. I mean they read too much into it. In Braddy's English set today, you won't believe it, but he was going on about bloody Hamlet and his mother and he used the word "Freudian" about them ... I mean, Jesus, how stupid can you get? Doesn't he realise Freud wasn't born until hundreds of years later? Shakespeare couldn't have known anything *about* Oedipus complexes and all that rubbish. I can't believe our parents pay men like that to talk such pseudy wank.'

It's mean to attack so hopeless a brand of feeble stupidity or mock so terrible a lack of imagination, in the end it is its own tragic handicap, and those who go to the grave unilluminated by the light of ideas are the sufferers, but of course I didn't know that then, I thought such Philistines were already the victors and that the life of the mind and the imagination was under threat from all sides. Besides I was a terrible show off and I used to react angrily, with great moral fervour and all the jewy, pansy strength of my wicked tongue. Not that argument could ever swerve the stolid Uppinghamian mind away from his settled conviction that art, literature and the play of ideas were anything more than 'wank'. Indeed, the better one argued, the more it proved it was all words, words, words.

'Oh, you can argue *anything* with words, Fry. Doesn't make it right.'

It is one of the great ironies of British (anti-)intellectual life that a nebulous sense of twentieth-century relativism has taken hold, somewhere deep down, and is used to damn and distrust the logical and the rational. Thus a point of view about art can be dismissed as 'pretentious' and 'wank' – in other words, as not solid, not real, 'airy-fairy' and 'arty-farty' – while at the same time any logical, rational defence of it is dismissed as 'just opinion' or 'semantics' in a world in which, 'let's face it, everything is relative, anyway . . .'

I wished that Forster's 1934 obituary of the art critic Roger Fry (no relation so far as I know) could be mine . . . I can't think of a better encomium.

> What characterized him and made him so precious in twentieth-century England was that, although he was a modern, he believed in reason . . .
>
> [He] rejected authority, mistrusted intuition. That is why his loss is so irreparable . . . If you said to him 'This must be right, all the experts say so . . . Hitler says so, Marx says so, Christ says so, *The Times* says so,' he would reply in effect, 'Well. I wonder. Let's see.' He would see and he would make you see. You would come away realizing that an influential opinion may be influentially backed and yet be tripe . . .
>
> Intuition he did not reject. He knew that it is part of our equipment, and the sensitiveness he valued in himself and in others is connected with it. But he also knew that it can make dancing dervishes of us all, and that the man who believes a thing is true because he feels it in his bones, is not really very far removed from the man who believes it on the authority of a policeman's truncheon.

Forster, in other words, is talking about a classical mind, a Greek mind. It is so ironic that classical education, English style, produced nothing but anti-classical attitudes. The English public schoolboy product can easily live out his whole life believing that imagination is the same thing as fantasy, that ideas are deceptive ornament and that ornament itself is supernumerary to life's requirements, he reflects absolutely our age of unreason: the plodding and carefully plotted lines of Nuffield empiricism are fine, but inference is to be distrusted. He lives between the extremes of the revealed truths of convention and current morality on the one side, and the vague, ignorant madness of a misunderstood sense of relativism, opinion and New Age finger-wagging-more-things-in-heaven-and-earth-Horatio-ism on the other, confusing mysteriousness with mysticism, and relativism with the idea that any view is up for grabs without the need for the winnowing processes of logic, reason and personal experience. Catastrophe, breakdown, marital disaster, personal tragedy, injustice or abuse are often the only crises that drop the scales from their eyes. I speak as such a product myself, you must understand, not as one looking down from a Heliconian height.

For, in spite of all my differences, such as they are, I was never fully the sensitive outsider, the rejected Jew, the outrageous queen or the distanced intellectual that I liked to picture myself to be. I was never *quite* as intelligent as I thought I was, never *quite* as bold in my refusal to be conventional, never *quite* as alienated by my sexuality, never *quite* as sure of my belonging to the inner life of art and the mind. I absorbed the lessons of E. M. Forster readily and greedily. I collected him in first edition as avidly as I collected Norman Douglas. It is worth quoting almost in full that famous passage that hovers above all this. It is taken from 'Notes on the English Character', the first essay in his 1936 collection *Abinger Harvest*, whence also came the lines on Roger Fry and Firbank.

Note One is that the character of the English is essentially middle-class; after a little historical explanation as to why that might be safely stated, Forster continues:

> Solidity, caution, integrity, efficiency. Lack of imagination, hypocrisy. These qualities characterize the middle classes in every country, but in England they are national characteristics also, because only in England have the middle classes been in power for one hundred and fifty years. Napoleon, in his rude way, called us 'a nation of shopkeepers.' We prefer to call ourselves 'a great commercial nation' – it sounds more dignified – but the two phrases amount to the same.

The *Second Note* contains that famous phrase 'the undeveloped heart'.

Second Note. Just as the heart of England is the middle classes, so the heart of the middle classes is the public-school system ... How perfectly it expresses their character – far better, for instance, than does the university, into which social and spiritual complexities have already entered. With its boarding-houses, its compulsory games, its system of prefects and fagging, its insistence on good form and *esprit de corps*, it produces a type whose weight is out of all proportion to its numbers ...

And they go forth [the public-school boys] into a world that is not entirely composed of public-school men or even of Anglo-Saxons, but of men who are as various as the sands of the sea; into a world of whose richness and subtlety they have no conception. They go forth into it with well developed bodies, fairly developed minds and undeveloped hearts ... An undeveloped heart, not a cold one. The difference is important ...

Once upon a time (this is an anecdote) I went for a holiday on the Continent with an Indian friend. We both enjoyed ourselves and were sorry when the week was over, but on parting our behaviour was absolutely different. He was plunged in despair ... I could not see what there was to make a fuss about ... 'Buck up,' I said, 'do buck up.' He refused to buck up, and I left him plunged in gloom.

The conclusion of the anecdote is even more instructive. For when we met the next month our conversation threw a good deal of light on the English character. I began by scolding my friend. I told him that he had been wrong to feel and display so much emotion upon so slight an occasion; that it was inappropriate. The word 'inappropriate' roused him to fury. 'What?' he cried. 'Do you measure out your emotions as if they were potatoes?' I did not like the simile of the potatoes, but after a moment's reflection I said, 'Yes, I do; and what's more I think I ought to. A small occasion demands a little emotion, just as a large emotion demands a great one. I would like my emotions to be appropriate. This may be measuring them like potatoes, but it is better than slopping them about like water from a pail, which is what you did.' He did not like the simile of the pail. 'If those are your opinions, they part us forever,' he cried, and left the room. Returning immediately, he added: 'No – but your whole attitude toward emotion is wrong. Emotion has nothing to do with appropriateness. It matters only that it shall be sincere. I happened to feel deeply. I showed it. It doesn't matter whether I ought to have felt deeply or not.'

This remark impressed me very much. Yet I could not agree with it, and said that I valued emotion as much as he did, but used it differently; if I poured it out on small occasions I was afraid of having none left for the great ones, and of being bankrupt at the crises of life. Note the word 'bankrupt.' I spoke as a member of a prudent middle-class nation, always anxious to meet my liabilities. But my friend spoke as an Oriental . . . he feels his resources are endless, just as John Bull feels his are finite.

This is how Forster finishes.

. . . the English character is incomplete in a way that is particularly annoying to the foreign observer. It has a bad surface – self-complacent, unsympathetic, and reserved. There is plenty of emotion further down, but it never gets used. There is plenty of brain power, but it is more often used to confirm prejudices than to dispel them. With such an equipment the Englishman cannot be popular. Only I would repeat: there is little vice in him and no real coldness. It is the machinery that is wrong.

I hope and believe myself that in the next twenty years [this was written in 1920] we shall see a great change, and the national character will alter into something which is less unique but more loveable. The supremacy of the middle-classes is probably ending. What new element the working classes will introduce one cannot say, but at all events they will not have been educated at public schools . . .

The nations *must* understand one another, and quickly; and without the interposition of their governments, for the shrinkage of the globe is throwing us into one another's arms. To that understanding these notes are a feeble contribution – notes on the English character as it has struck a novelist.

Well, have we seen 'a great change'? Has the supremacy of the middle-classes ended? In a pig's arse has it ended. Even today, *mutatis mutandis*, the character of the English is defined by the character of its (still rising) middle-classes and even today, the character of those middle classes is defined by the character of the (still disproportionately) powerful public-school product. The schools of course have changed, to the extent that public schoolboys wear baseball caps and expensive Nike footwear, listen to rap music, raise the pitch of their voices at the end of sentences in that bizarre Australian Question Intonation picked up from the TV soaps, and say 'Cool' and 'Slamming' a lot. That is nauseating certainly, embarrassing obviously, but fundamentally it alters nothing. No one can seriously suggest that the average English public schoolboy emerges from his school with a South Central Los Angeles sensibility, or the outlook, soul and character of an unemployed working-class spot-welder. The body is probably even better developed, the brain as fairly developed but the heart just as undeveloped. The British have always absorbed cultural influences without losing their character. After all Humphrey Lyttelton and his generation listened to black jazz at Eton in the 1930s and probably called their friends 'cats' and 'daddy-o'. In our day we said that things were 'far out' and 'like, wow . . . ' but it altered our Englishness not a whit. *Plus ça change . . .*

It is worth remarking, I suppose, that the Indian 'friend' Forster referred to in his *Notes* was, of course, a lover; also worth remarking that Forster never points out that his impression of the English character was not only middle-class and public-school, but also *male*.

On that subject it so happens that the first edition of *Abinger Harvest* that I possess once belonged to the historian R. W. Ketton-Cremer who retained in its pages a pristine clipping from the *Sunday Times* of March 22nd, 1936 containing a review of the book by the eminent critic Desmond MacCarthy – in those days there really were such things as eminent reviewers.

MacCarthy makes the following delicate point with great perspicacity and elegance.

His [Forster's] peculiar balance of qualities is more often found in woman than in man; and if I could be confident of not being misunderstood by those who consider intellect a masculine speciality, I would add that his view-point ... both as a critic and a creator, is feminine rather than masculine ... Absurdities and tragedies, he seems to be saying are due to the failure to link experiences together – to *connect*. That is Mr Forster's "message." Now, the essentially masculine way of taking life is to handle it departmentally. A man says to himself: there is my home and my private life of personal relations; there is my business, my work; there is my life as a citizen. In each department he has principles according to which situations can be handled as they arise. But in each department these are different. His art of life is to *disconnect*; it simplifies problems ... The feminine impulse, on the other hand, whether on account of women's education or her fundamental nature, is to see life as more of a continuum. That is part of what I meant by saying that Mr Forster, as a creative writer and as a critic, takes the feminine view-point.

Intuiting, and finally knowing for sure that Forster was somehow, like me – Not As Other Boys – allowed me to form a more natural bond with him as a writer than I might otherwise have done. Certainly 'Notes on the English Character' and later *Howard's End* became sacred texts for me at Uppingham, together with Cyril Connolly's perfect *Enemies of Promise* and its *Theory of Permanent Adolescence*:

It is the theory that the experiences undergone by boys at the great public schools, their glories and disappointments, are so intense as to dominate their lives and to arrest their development. From these it results that the greater part of the ruling class remains adolescent, school-minded, self-conscious, cowardly, sentimental, and in the last analysis homosexual.

It was difficult for me to know quite how to handle that. On the one hand I believed that I was made homosexual the day I was born, on the other I loved the idea that it was School's Fault and that I was the victim of a wicked and corrupt system. Connolly, one sees now, meant socially as much as erotically homosexual, hence 'the last analysis' – but there were days when, unhappy with my sexual lot, I liked to blame my education for my nature. Ihab Hassan, as so often, is right on the money when he says in *The Anti-Hero*:

> The ambivalences of a bourgeois hero in an over-whelmingly middle-class society raise for him problems of estrangement and communion, sincerity and simulation, ambition and acquiescence . . . The sad history of the anti-hero is nothing more than the history of man's changing awareness of himself. It is the record of his recoil . . . Man, meanwhile, goes clowning his sentimental way into eternity.

It can come a bit hard sometimes to see one's own unique, heroic life pinned so pitilessly to a wall. At other times it can endorse, affirm and save, but as I go clowning my sentimental way into eternity, wrestling with all my problems of estrangement and communion, sincerity and simulation, ambition and acquiescence, I shuttle between worrying whether I matter at all and whether anything else matters at all but me.

I am sorry to borrow from others so much, but to do it one last time, I bring Montaigne to my defence:

> I quote others only the better to express myself.

Just in case you get the impression that from the age of thirteen onwards I spent all my time sitting in libraries reading Cyril Connolly, Michel de Montaigne (the fabulous edition translated by the fabulously named M. A. Screech was not available then), E. M. Forster, Ronald Firbank and Ihab Hassan, I should say that I have conflated and compressed time here.

None of this reading, none of this connecting or identifying with literature or the lives of others took place until the great event happened – the great event of my falling in love. Until that time I read a huge amount of Sherlock Holmes and P. G. Wodehouse, Talbot Baines Reed and G. Henty, Alastair Maclean and Agatha Christie, Biggles and Buchan, Hammond Innes and Len Deighton, Dornford Yates and Dorothy Sayers. What is more, I still do.

2

I believe Stouts Hill wanted me to leave them as early as possible. I had sat for the Uppingham scholarship examination aged twelve and failed to receive an award. I came close enough to an exhibition for Uppingham to recommend me to try for the exam again at a later date. I suspect, however, that Stouts Hill had Had Enough: the idea of me hanging around for another year did not please Cromie at all and it was agreed that I should leave as soon as possible, retaking the scholarship examination internally once installed in Uppingham. I bade goodbye to Stouts Hill then, aged twelve, without ever having been made a prefect, selected for a single athletic team, or achieving any distinction whatsoever save a record number of canings and a handful of academic prizes.

What am I *saying*? I won Third Prize (a grand certificate and a two pound book token) in the Independent Association of Preparatory Schools' *National* Art Competition for my portrait entitled *An Unforgettable Character*. I had misread a pot in the art room which I had thought announced itself to be 'Vanishing Fluid' and, in attempting to correct a defect around the eyes of my Unforgettable Character, varnished his features so thoroughly that the work more than lived up to its title. Indeed it is probable that the judges even to this day are unable to forget the lustrous, glittering eyes and glossily menacing brows, beard and spectacles of my subject and that he gleams still in their nightmares like a lacquered Rolf Harris.

Now I come to think of it, there was such a thing as a 'sub-prefect' at Stouts Hill whose duties were unclear and privileges non-existent. It sounds splendidly *Casablanca* – 'An exit visa may be obtained from the office of the sub-prefect for the usual fee' – but the position I believe came into being merely to offer an opportunity for hopeless cases like myself to put something down on their entrance forms for later life. I think I was also entitled to claim myself to have been 3rd XI Scorer, a role I filled once or twice, but only for Home Matches – Stouts Hill wasn't going to let me loose on other schools for a minute.

Not *quite* expelled then, I lived out the summer holidays, turned thirteen halfway through them, and arrived at Uppingham in the September of 1970. Roger had already had a year at Uppingham and was bracing himself with his usual good humour for the arrival, yet again, of his troublesome younger bro.

In those summer holidays he and I were inseparable, at school we did not expect to be. We had arguments, of course, as brothers will (I remember throwing a dart at him on one occasion: the image-memory of it sticking out of his knee sickens me still) but it is extraordinary, looking back, how creatively we managed to fill the holidays in a place so far distant from urban excitements. We were in the same predicament as the Reverend Sydney Smith who, finding himself stuck in the country, wrote to a friend that he could best describe his situation as being 'simply miles from the nearest lemon'. Sydney Smith, in case you don't know him, is well worth discovering, he had a unique brand of at once sophisticated, surreal and good-natured wit: he said, for example, of meeting Daniel Webster that he struck him as 'much like a steam engine in trousers' and was overheard telling a woman at a dinner party 'Madam, I have been looking for a person who disliked gravy all my life; let us swear eternal friendship'. Well, Roger and I were not only simply miles from the nearest lemon, we were simply miles too from the nearest café, the nearest cinema, the nearest toyshop, the nearest bowling-alley and the nearest friend. So we had each other. By this time too, we had our sister Jo, who was six that summer of 1970 and who adored and trusted me implicitly. I told her gravely that I knew how to fly and that when she was seven I would teach her the trick of it. Shortly after her seventh birthday, returned from my first term at Uppingham, she reminded me of this promise. I took her upstairs, sat her high on a window-ledge and told her that all she had to do was jump and that my magic would do the rest. After a little thought, she decided not to take me up on the offer. I am glad to say that she never gave the slightest outward show of disappointment or disillusionment in her brother.

To thirteen- and fifteen-year-old boys however, six-year-old girls are not very much more than toys and Jo spent most of her time in the company of the great Nanny Riseborough who had served in our house, for the previous owners, since she was a small girl.

Lest the reader run away with too Bridesheady a picture of my childhood, I had better describe life in Norfolk just a little. The house where I grew up, and where my parents live to this day is big certainly, but then it had to be big for my father had needed somewhere with space ever since he had settled against an academic career, discovered that life in mainstream industry did not suit him and decided to set up on his own. While we had lived in Chesham we had spent many days meandering around England looking for suitable properties with plenty of outhousery. I recall endless drives to huge, unsaleable houses with overgrown gardens. My mother would gulp at the kitchens and public rooms, my father frown and shake his head at the inadequacy of the outhouses. Roger and I would romp about in the unweeded kitchen gardens, bored to distraction.

One of my grandfather's employees, a sugar worker, happened one day upon a house for sale in the tiny Norfolk village of Booton. It was an imposing Victorian mansion, with an enormous stable-block and an absurd quantity of other outhouses, as well as an attached cottage the size of a substantial townhouse. It boasted, inexplicably, five outside lavatories as well as a splendid kitchen garden that offered asparagus beds, an apple orchard, a tennis court, a badminton lawn, a pigsty, a paddock, hen-coops, sinister rhubarb patches and a summer house. It was the size and condition of the stable-block that clinched the deal. This could be Father's laboratory. There was room for as many lathes, oscilloscopes and things that go beep, tweet, whoop and boing as the maddest boffin could hope for.

In those days it was well serviced too. Mrs Riseborough cooked and nannied Jo. She had sisters-in-law and friends from the village of Cawston who scrubbed and cleaned and lit the fires in winter. The Tubby brothers gardened, but they eventually left to be replaced by Mr Godfrey who ran the garden for many years and who delighted my brother and me by talking to himself a great deal in an endless stream of complaint about how the soil was 'a bitch' whenever it was cold. Given that he was an old man who consumed a large quantity of roll-ups every day, no doubt the frosty earth was indeed a bitch and I hate the picture of us giggling at him. It was quite a garden to run, fully Victorian and designed to provide a large household with fruit and vegetables the year round. The outhouses could store apples, pears and potatoes throughout the winter and Mrs Riseborough made jams, pickles and jellies from the plums, cherries, strawberries, raspberries, damsons, gooseberries, blackberries, redcurrants and blackcurrants that the garden bore. Always providing my mother didn't get to them first, that is. My mother has an absolute passion for sour fruit and can strip a gooseberry bush quicker than a priest can strip a choirboy.

I am not so very old you know, but this does seem another life: a life that moved with the rhythm of the seasons, a life that had essentially remained unaltered for decades. Everything was delivered: fish came on Wednesdays (not being Catholics we had no interest in reserving it for Fridays), delivered by horse and cart. It is ridiculous but true, I am really *not* that old, but to the house the fishman came, every week, his horse clopping along like Steptoe's Hercules. Bread was delivered too, three times a week I think. On Wednesday mornings my mother would call up Riches of Reepham and order the groceries which were delivered in a van by Mr Neale, who greeted me, as all Norfolk people greet young boys, with a 'Hello there, young man!' and a squeeze to the cheeks. Milk came from a local dairy in waxed cartons which, after use, made good fire kindling that hissed, spat and crackled. The yellowest sweatingest butter we had too, neatly patterned on all sides with the marks left by the patting paddles. Meat came by van from Tuddenhams's of Cawston, it being understood somehow in the community that the Cawston butcher was superior to the Reepham. The coal merchant came every month or so and a mobile library stopped by the house once a week.

Fruit and vegetables (oranges, lemons and bananas excepted) came from the garden.

'Never eat asparagus after Ascot,' was one of my mother's rules.

An asparagus bed needs to go to seed in late June, so this seems a sensible idea. Somewhat inconsistently however, my mother was forever raiding the beds for their exquisite ferns which look very well in flower arrangements. I remember that asparagus also needed huge quantities of salt in the autumn. Mr Godfrey (helped by me sometimes) would empty sack after sack of ICI salt on each raised bed until they twinkled and glittered as if struck by an early rime frost.

The kitchen garden itself had been divided up by its Victorian makers using row upon row of little gravel pathways, lined with box hedging, 'a bitch to keep tidy' as poor Mr Godfrey liked to remind me, my brother or any rabbits or jackdaws that might be listening.

Mr Godfrey lodged with a certain Mrs Blake and from time to time he would ask permission to take excess vegetables from our garden for their supper table. One day he startled Cawston by making an honest woman of her, but even after their marriage he continued to refer to her as Mrs Blake. Norfolk people are slow to change. I remember an old couple who used to live in a small cottage with an outside lavatory. They moved, many years ago, to a smart new council house in which all modern conveniences were installed. Even today however, if you visit them and one of them wants to go to the loo they will startle onlookers by saying, as they climb the stairs, 'I'm just going down the garden . . .'

At the back of our garden was a red wooden pigsty, sadly unused in our day, and behind that a paddock where for a time we kept a huge flock of geese, which were insupportably bad-tempered, loud and greedy, eating everything but stinging nettles, which gave the paddock a rather scrappy and tattered look.

Mrs Riseborough cooked lunch every day and cooked in a way that few people are capable of now. I don't suppose she had ever seen or looked at a cookery book, a food-mixer or a freezer cabinet in her life. She made egg custards, apple pies, rhubarb crumbles, steak and kidney puddings, marrow stuffed with mincemeat, cauliflower and macaroni cheeses and all manner of good English pies, tarts and flans. Roger liked treacle tart with cornflakes on top, I liked them without, so each Thursday we would alternate. Mrs Riseborough taught me how to make a rose for the centre of a pie by taking a layer of pastry and laying it on my thumb and then adding another layer at forty-five degrees to the first and so on, and then cutting them over the thumb gently with a knife. In August or September she made her mincemeat and the Christmas puddings, five or six of them in huge bowls. The pudding mixture included carrots and Mackeson Cream Stout. The mincemeat would then be steeped in brandy and stored for the mince-pies which were made later.

Mrs Riseborough's idea of a salad would be laughed at now, with its English kitchen garden produce of beetroot, radishes, Tom Thumb and butterheart lettuce, tomatoes and cucumber, topped with hard-boiled egg and a sprig of parsley, not a rocket, radiccio, frisée lettuce or coriander leaf in sight: I could never get enough of it, so long as there was enough Heinz Salad to go around.

She did have some strange ideas, however. She was firmly convinced that the addition of a lump of coal to a bowlful of lettuce in water would keep the lettuce crisp, and from time to time she believed that she had too much blood and needed a nosebleed. Again, who knows? I understand leeches have made a comeback in some hospitals, maybe cupping will return too.

She worked in the kitchen, which had no sink and one very

low tap, hardly a foot from floor level. We were not on the water mains in Booton, each day the procedure of 'pumping up' had to be gone through. There were two wells, one with hard drinking water from the water table, the other a rainwater collection cistern providing water for washing and bathing. The low tap in the kitchen was the only drinking water tap in the house. Guests, especially Londoners, always commented on the beautiful softness of the water when they bathed – it lathered beautifully and never left the scumline that lime-loaded London water does – but most of them wondered how we could go through the nonsense of daily pumping every day and why, in winter it was always colder inside the house than outside.

The pump house had been fitted with an electrically driven motor, I wouldn't want you to picture Roger and me labouring away like medieval parishioners on the village green. The motor drove enormous wheels which were connected by great belts that slapped away as the pump worked. When we had first arrived at Booton a health inspector had taken a sample of water for analysis (the bottom of the holding tank had been alive with bright red nematodes). Some months later a report came back saying that the water *could* be consumed, but not by infants under a year old. Since Jo had been drinking nothing else for months, it was decided to ignore such nonsense.

As the house had been untouched since it was built, its offices and amenities were (and still are) Victorian, a series of larders, game larders, sculleries, outer sculleries and something called a china pantry surrounded the kitchen. The lavatories were gigantic wooden affairs with chains that said 'pull' on them and wash-basins that you tipped on a swivel to empty. The ironing was done by a gigantic electric linen press, all levers topped with bakelite knobs. A great box made by Mann Egerton's of Norwich, before they decided there was more money in selling Rolls Royce's I suppose, high on a wall in the back passage shook a tin star to indicate in which room a bell had been rung, and next to it hung the thickened blue and red sally of a bell-rope, to be pulled to summon us children from the garden for lunch or tea, or for a ticking off.

In the afternoons, after the silent lunch (Father frowning at my inability to hold a fork properly or at the inanity of some Guinness Record I had solemnly announced), Nanny Riseborough would take Jo for a walk, first in her pram, then by pushchair, until finally they went on foot together. Sometimes Jemina the Siamese cat and I would accompany; according to season we would return with punnet upon punnet of blackberries or trug upon trug of daffodils, to which it transpired, after one afternoon's heavy picking, I was allergic. I had to be rushed to the nearby town of Aylsham (nearby being seven miles away) to receive an adrenalin shot from the doctor. Only champagne and a beer brewed by Trappist monks in Belgium have ever given me worse attacks.

The stable-block, where my father worked, was called Over The Way. 'Is Daddy over the way?' became the most urgent question of the day. If he was, then it meant we could muck about inside, slide down banisters, play games, relax and even, if we were daring, *watch television*.

If Daddy was *not* over the way, it meant he was in his study, in which case we trod gingerly about the house as though on eggshells. The most terrible thing was to *believe* he was over the way and then discover that you had not heard him returning. In the middle of some game we would hear the tell-tale sound of his pipe being banged down into an ashtray to dislodge the plug and dottle and realise that, horror of horrors, Daddy was In. Instantly, fun, freedom and relaxation turned into terrified silence. The best answer was to steal from the house and find something to do in the garden.

Sometimes there were magical days when he had to leave Booton entirely and drive to Norwich or even as far away as Yorkshire. If it was a weekday, this meant we could visit the Men over the way, the men who worked for Father in the stable-block. They would look up from their soldering irons, wink and give a cheerful, 'Hello there, young man' when we came in and we would twiddle with the knobs on the oscilloscopes and press the inviting green buttons on the machines.

At various times my father manufactured a whole range of

different items. He had invented an object called an Arc Rule which was actually demonstrated to my enormous excitement on *Tom-Tom*, the BBC's predecessor to *Tomorrow's World*. At one stage most of the stable-block was given over to the manufacture of electric Sellotape dispensers, cheerfully assembled by women from the surrounding villages who listened to Radio 2 when the Boss wasn't about. On another occasion Father helped the Ford motor company with electronic governing systems for their automatic transmissions and the place was littered with bits of Capri. There were objects made throughout the 1970s called 'thyristor controls' and I have no idea what they did, but they were cleverly sealed in Araldite so that no one who bought them could find out how they worked without smashing them to pieces.

Later, Father designed and built the most entertaining contraption the world has ever seen, a machine for chugging out Tack-Strip, something the furniture industry liked to have about the place. The machinery resembled the mongrel love-child of a cinema projector, a steam-hammer and a Toblerone production line, all put together on a day when Heath Robinson had thought it might be fun to try hallucinogenic mushrooms for breakfast. I could watch Tacky going for hours and hours; I would follow, in a trance, the thousands and thousands of little metallic blue tacks as they shuffled around in a great vibrating bowl and then scuttled like soldier ants down a chute that blasted them with an air-compressed hammer at a rate of six or seven a second into a moving strip of thick cardboard that then folded itself over and continued its journey towards the packing box. The boxes were stacked on to pallets and a small electric fork-lift truck hummed about tidying up. The fights between my brother and me, when Father was away, to be the one to drive the fork-lift truck were harrowing to behold.

My father was inevitably thought of in terms of awe by some local people who referred to him as the Mad Inventor. When strange noises came from the stable-block at three in the morning, I half expected to see a stolid posse of villagers surround the house, flaming torches in hand, demanding to know with what strange forces he be meddling. Years would pass without the villagers ever seeing him, which only added to his mystique. If my mother was not around to order the last detail of his life, as a result of a bout of flu for example, my father might be forced to drive two miles into the village of Reepham to stock up on tins of pipe tobacco. The sight of him helplessly proffering a palmful of coins to the tobacconist like a frightened foreigner was most extraordinary. I don't suppose to this day he could describe a twenty-pence piece or tell you which British heroes were on the back of which currency notes. I mustn't exaggerate: he managed to attend British Legion and Conservative Party meetings (in the 1960s and 1970s before the Conservative Party went mad), sail every now and then across the North Sea to Holland with a nautical friend and more recently he served as an exceptionally committed and hard-working governor of Reepham High School. He was never entirely Professor Caractacus Potts, but then he was never the beaming fellow from the Daddy's Sauce label either.

The most pleasing objects by far to emerge from his stable-block laboratories were a line of objects known as Things. Thing was a vast steel cabinet covered with more knobs and switches than you can imagine. It took weeks and weeks for Father and the men to make a single Thing, which was usually destined for a subsidiary of ICI in Mexico, Israel or Turkey where it sat there, Thing-like and Controlled. What it controlled and how it controlled, I have no idea, but Project Thing had taken Father months in the study with slide rules and paper to dream up and then even more months in the drawing office, designing the scores of circuit boards which slotted into Thing like honeycomb frames into a hive.

While Thing was being made it was all guts: wrapped in miles and miles of cabling and bulging with power supply objects tightly coiled in copper wire that looked like solenoids, Thing had a very vulnerable and naked look to it. When all the wiring was done and the circuit boards had been soldered and inserted down to the last one, Thing's metal cowling was stove-enamelled a wonderful 1930s green and the switches, dials and knobs were added. The last thing to go on was the plate which had Alan Fry Controls Ltd., Booton, Norfolk, England printed upon it and the company logo, which took the form of the letters f-r-y, designed by my father to resemble the trace of some pulse of power as shown up on an oscilloscope.

Meanwhile my mother would have been typing and telephoning away to arrange all the bills-of-lading, export documents and God knows what other administrative and bureaucratic nightmares that the despatch of a Thing entailed. Sheets and sheets of documentation seemed to be entailed and the sweetest-tempered woman in the world would become, for a week or so, a tiny bit of an old snap-dragon. Only the packing of the trunk for school occasioned more drama and crossness from a woman otherwise more cheerful than Pickwick, Pollyanna and Mrs Tiggywinkle on a sunny day in Happyville.

Finally, Thing, which was far too heavy to carry and which had been assembled in the largest room in the stable-block, which was upstairs, had to be lowered down into the stable yard through a giant trap-door by a system of chains and pulleys, what I suppose is called block and tackle, a principle I have never understood. The family would gather in pride as Thing descended, green, gleaming, perfect and entirely like something out of *Doctor Who*. We all wanted to pay our respects and to enjoy the atmosphere of a Clydeside ship launch, but most of all I wanted to watch the most amusing part of the whole operation, the part that preceded the loading on to the lorry and the final farewell. Thing, being nearly always destined for hot countries, had to be protected against the changes in temperature that it would inevitably undergo in transit. In other words, to inhibit condensation, Thing was wrapped in a huge sheet of transparent plastic, which was then heat-sealed until only a tiny hole remained. My father would then solemnly insert into this tiny hole the nozzle of a vacuum cleaner and proceed to suck out all the air.

The sight of the plastic sheet sucking in its cheeks as it were and snugly pressing itself against Thing's every declivity and protuberance was greatly impressive, comic and delicious, exactly the reverse of the pleasure you get from watching the stirring, twitching and swelling as a hot-air balloon or an airship is inflated. That naturally abhorrent phenomenon, the perfect vacuum, could naturally never be achieved by this method, but when the Hoover nozzle was removed and the tiny hole instantly sealed up, Thing looked like the most impressive object in the world and my pride in my father knew no bounds.

He was and is a simply remarkable man. Many sons are proud of their fathers, and no doubt have reason to be – for there are many remarkable men in the world. For sheer brainpower, will, capability and analytical power however, I have to say, all family loyalty aside, that I have never met anyone who came close to him. I have met men and women who had known more and achieved more, but none with so adaptive and completely powerful a brain. His ability to solve problems – mechanical, mathematical, engineering problems – is boundless, which is to say bounded only by the limits of the universal laws he holds so dear, the laws of Newton and the laws of thermodynamics. The clarity of his mind, the perfectionism and elegance of his abstract mathematical and intellectual modelling and practical design and his capacity for sustained concentration, thought and work stagger me, simply stagger me.

To grow up under the brooding, saturnine shadow (for in his thirties and forties he brooded greatly) of a man so fiercely endowed with mind power was immensely difficult for all of us. He worked every day, Christmas Day and bank holidays included, for years and years and years. No holidays, no breaks for television, nothing but work. Just occasionally one might hear the sounds of Beethoven, Brahms, Bach or occasionally Scarlatti or Chopin coming from the Broadwood grand piano he had taken apart and rebuilt in the drawing room, but that did not mean relaxation. Music too was something for analysis, deeply emotional analysis often, but analysis founded on a deep knowledge of theory and form.

A schoolfriend on first catching sight of him exclaimed, ' My God – it's Sherlock Holmes!'

My heart sank on hearing this, for Sherlock Holmes had long

been a passion. I was a member of the Sherlock Holmes Society of London (a membership that was directly to connect with my expulsion from Uppingham) and knew most of the stories almost by heart. I had never realised, or admitted to myself before, that whenever I thought of Holmes, or heard his voice, it was really my father whose voice and image came into my head. The descriptions Watson gives of that infuriatingly, cold, precise ratiocinating engine of a brain fuelled by a wholly egocentric passion and fire exactly tallied with my view of my father. Like Holmes, my father would never think of food, creature comforts or society when the working fit was upon him. Like Holmes he had a great musical gift; like Holmes he could be abominably rude to those close to him and charm itself to total strangers; like Holmes he delighted in piquancy and problem-solving for their own sakes, never for gain or fame; like Holmes he combined dreamy abstraction with ruthless logic and an infinite capacity for taking pains; like Holmes he was exceptionally tall, strong and gaunt. Damn it, my father even smoked pipes – for years he virtually lived inside a cloud of thick smoke.

Unlike Holmes my father never went out; unlike Holmes my father never solved life problems for others; unlike Holmes my father never achieved household fame and the respect of Popes, Princes and Prime Ministers. Unlike Holmes my father was real. He was my father.

I have rarely met a man so pig-headedly uninterested in the world of affairs. I was ever a greedy soul and have always loved the creature comforts and symbols of success. It frustrated me to see someone who could have made a massive fortune many times over, whether by designing top-end hi-fi, computer software, commercial gadgetry or industrial plant, stubbornly refuse to sell himself. I admire such a reluctance of course, and am proud of it: huckstering, boastfulness and noisy advertisement are not appealing, but there is an egotism in excess modesty too, and I thought I detected a misanthropy and arrogance in him that drove me to distraction, partly, of course, because it contrasted with my own worship of success, fame, money and status.

Maternal grandfather, Austro-Hungarian
cavalry, 1914

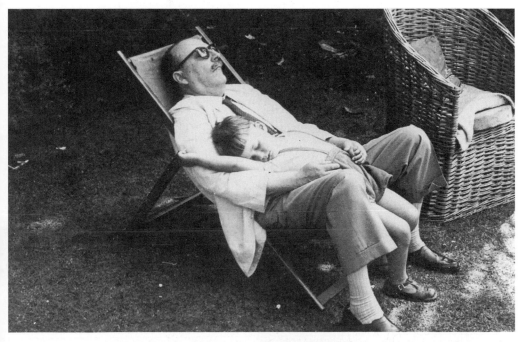

Same grandfather, Austro-Hungarian-English grandson, pudding-basin hair,
sandals by StartRite of England

Harnessed, strapped, restrained: Aged One

Above: Second birthday party surrounded by friends and admirers

Left: With mother, garden of Sherwood House, summer 1958

Admiring my brother's lederhosen, Sherwood House, 1959

Above: Aged Four: before the onset of
the crippling modesty described *passim*

Right: Pride in my brother's first day at
Chesham Prep

Above: With brother
(in Stouts Hill uniform)
alarming a primate

Right: Sitting on trunk
with brother and new
sister, awaiting despatch
to prep school, 1965

Much travelled photograph of the house at Booton

Booton Church: same architect, more extravagant style thoughts

Healthiness: a picture of everything I was not

Cat. No. M.F. 154 M.C. Rules 1981, r. 68. **Extract from regi**

Above: Catalogue of specimen charges from Swindon Magistrates' Court, 1975

Left: With brother and sister, outside the Tack House

ional Division of Swindon

ion] [an Order] entered in the Register of the Magistrates' Court sitting at Swindon

the 22nd **day of** October , 19 75

Nature of offence or matter of complaint.	Date of offence or matter of complaint.	Plea or consent to order.	Minute of Adjudication.	Time allowed for payment and instalments.
...tealing a wrist watch value ...).70 the property of the ...xford and Swindon ...–opprative Society. ...eft Act 1968 ...7	9th Sept	Guilty 1.10.75	Two years Probation with condition to reside where directed by the Probation Office	
...r Deception dishonestly o ...btaining a pecunairy ...dvantage forhimself. ...eft Act.1968 ...15	9th Sept	Guilty 1.10.75	Two years Probation with condition to reside where directed by the Probation Office	
...r Deception dishonestly ...btaining a pecunairy ...dvantage for himself. ...eft Act.1968 ...15	9th Sept	Guilty 1.10.75	Two years Probation with condition to reside where directed by the Probation Office	
...r Deception dishonestly ...btaining a pecunairy ...dvantage for himself. ...eft Act.1968 ...15	Btwn. 19&24 August 1975	Guilty 1.10.75	Two years Probation with conditions to reside where directed by the Probation Office	

...rtify the above Extract to be a true Copy. ....

Clerk of the said Magistrates' Court.

Dated the ....1st... day of ......November.................................,19.95.......

...eeding of a magistrates' court.   SHAW & SONS LTD., Shaway House, Lower Sydenham, London, S.E.26. MLX 00412-0

The prep-school master, summer term Cundall Manor School – second year of probation

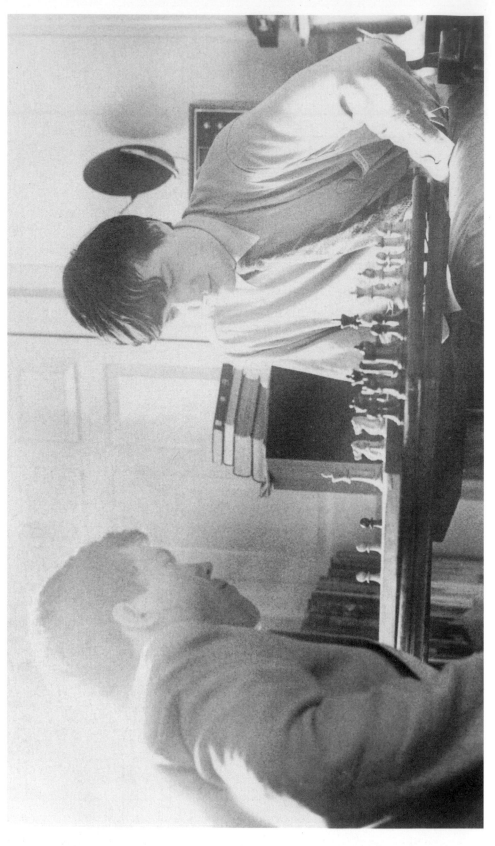

Playing chess with Hugh Laurie: my rooms at Cambridge, 1980

I used my mother as an excuse for resenting my father. I felt she deserved better than to have her life revolve entirely around the demands and dictates of a wilfully unworldly husband. I thought she deserved holidays in the sun, warmth in the winter, the right to accept a few more invitations and the chance to go on shopping trips to London. I have no doubt I was jealous too, jealous of the adoration she had for him and the energy she put into making his life as easy as possible.

I cannot remember my parents arguing ever. I only recall one occasion when I heard my parents' voices raised against each other and it terrified the life out of me.

It was night and I had been in bed for about an hour, when, through three floors of the house, there came to my ears the sound of my father shouting and my mother wailing. I padded fearfully into my brother's room and shook him awake.

'Listen!' I hissed.

We stared at each other in fear and astonishment. This was entirely unprecedented. Simply unheard of. Our parents *never* argued, *never* shouted at each other. At *us*, yes. Occasionally. But never at each other. Never, never, never.

We crept down the back stairs, my brother and I, and listened quakingly for perhaps ten minutes to the sounds that were emerging from my father's study. He was raging, simply raging while my mother howled and screeched unbearably. There was nothing we could do but tremble and wonder. We edged back up the stairs and talked to each other for a while about what it might mean and then went to our separate rooms to try and sleep.

The next morning I came fearfully into the kitchen, half-expecting to see my mother hunched over the table in tears.

'Morning, darling!' she said cheerfully, grinning as usual like a tree-frog who is having its toes tickled.

I waited until Mrs Riseborough was out of the room before tentatively asking whether everything was all right.

'All right? What do you mean?'

'Well, last night. Roger and I ... we couldn't help overhearing.'

'Overhearing?' She looked genuinely puzzled.

'You were crying and Daddy was shouting . . . '

'Crying . . . ?'A look of complete bewilderment crossed her face and then suddenly she brightened and began to giggle. '*Crying?* I was *laughing!*'

'What do you mean?'

'Well, it was the *funniest* thing . . . '

It turned out that the previous night in the study my father had started to hunt about on his desk for a file that he needed.

'Bloody hell, you put something down for a second and it completely disappears . . . I mean what is going *on*?'

My mother could see from her position on the sofa that he was actually sitting on this file, and for ten minutes my father continued to sit on it, all unaware, throwing papers around, pulling open drawers and getting more and more Basil Fawlty in his ungovernable fury at the thing's disappearance while my mother became more and more overcome by greater and greater transports of laughter.

That was what we had heard.

Not the greatest story in the world I know, but its point lies in the extreme oddity (as I now know it to be) of a married couple who never shouted at each other or had any kind of row – at least never within the hearing of their children. They *adore* one another, worship and value one another entirely. I'm sure they have been frustrated by each other sometimes, it would only be natural, and I know it upset my mother that for years my relationship with my father was a mess. She would have to bear my sulking adolescent grunts of 'I hate Father. I *hate* him,' just as she would have to hear him telling me how arrogant, shiftless and incapable of thought or application I was.

When I first heard other children's parents shouting at each other I wanted to die with embarrassment. I just did not believe such things could be, or that if they were, that they could be tolerated. I still find any sort of confrontation, shouting or facing off unbearable.

It is possible that the closeness, interdependence and uncon-ditional love each bears for the other may have contributed to whatever fear it was that kept me from partnering anyone for so many years. It always seemed impossible to me that I would ever find anyone with whom I could have a relationship that would live up to that of my parents.

They fell in love at first sight and knew instantly when they met that they would marry. They had both been students at London University, my mother a history scholar at Westfield College, my father reading physics and running the music society at Imperial. My father was pleased with my mother's jewishness, her father adored this brilliant young man and was, I think, especially delighted that my father could speak German, which he had learned in order to read papers on physics, so many of which were published in that language. My grandfather himself was ridiculously multilingual, speaking Hungarian, German, Yiddish, Czech, Slovak, Rumanian and English. I have a picture of him as a young man, splendid in his Austro-Hungarian cavalry officer's uniform, taken just before he went off to face the Serbian guns at the very start of the First World War. He came to England in the 1930s to teach British farmers how to grow sugarbeet, so my mother, the youngest of three girls, was born in London and grew up in Bury St Edmunds and Salisbury, attending Malvern Girl's College from a very young age, to all intents and purposes a very English little girl – for the Nazis were about to arrive in Britain at any moment, and my grandfather knew something of what Nazis did to Jews. His name was Neumann, which he changed in England to Newman. *His* father, my great-grandfather, a Hungarian Jew also of course, had lived for a time in Vienna, and it was always said of him that he was the kind of man to give you the coat off his back. You can imagine how my blood ran cold when I read this in Alan Bullock's *Hitler: A Study in Tyranny*, while reading about the early life of Hitler for my last novel, *Making History*:

> After their quarrel Hanisch lost sight of Hitler, but he gives a description of Hitler as he knew him in 1910 at the age of twenty-one. He wore an ancient black overcoat, which had been given him by an old-clothes dealer in the hostel, a Hungarian Jew named Neumann, and which reached down to his knees ... Neumann ... who had befriended him, was offended by the violence of his anti-Semitism.

I suppose there were many Hungarian Jews in Vienna in 1910, and I suppose many of them were called Neumann, but one can't help wondering if it really might be true that one's great-grandfather might have befriended and kept warm a man who would later decimate a large part of his family and some six millions of his people.

My parents wed secretly: my mother's scholarship would, for some odd reason, have been forfeit had it been known that she was married while still an undergraduate. Now, after forty-two years together, it still warms my heart when I hear them in another room, this remarkable couple, chattering away as if they've just met.

The house has hardly changed at all. The pumping up process for water is now simpler than it was, but the kitchen still has only one low tap – all the washing up goes out to a scullery. The Aga has to be riddled every night to shake the ash down and there is still no central heating. People who visit it show wonder at its time-capsule dignity and might even express envy at my good fortune in growing up in such a place.

I used to think I hated living there, but throughout all my years of rebellion, ostracism and madness I always carried a photograph of the house with me: I have it still, tattered and torn, but the only copy left in the world of an aerial picture taken, I think, around the very time of my life between prep and public school. Maybe I had just started my first term at Uppingham, maybe it was taken just before I left Stouts Hill for the last time, for my brother and I are nowhere to be seen in the picture, unless we were cantering about on the badminton lawn which is hidden from view. I wouldn't have kept this picture all those years if the house didn't mean something to me, and I wouldn't be gulping down tears now, looking at it, if the memories it invoked were impotent and sterile and incapable of touching me deeply.

It was the house where I grew up.

It contains my brother's bedroom, with its peeling William Morris wallpaper; it contains the bedroom I spent most of my life in, lying awake for hours and hours and hours with the self-induced insomnia of adolescence, peeing out of the window into the night air and killing the honeysuckle below because I was too lazy, slobby and sluttish to go downstairs to the lavatory; it contains the bedroom of my sister, with posters of the cricketer Derek Randall still hanging on the wall. It contains the study on whose carpet I stood so many times, facing my father over some new school report, some new disaster, some new affront to authority, some new outrage that might send my mother from the room clutching a handkerchief to her mouth in grief and upset. It contains the same objects and the same memories, and it contains the same two parents who made me from their flesh and whom I adore so much. It is home.

In the book of Uppingham school rules the first rule is this:-

A boy's study is his castle

The only other fortress of privacy afforded a boy at Uppingham came in the shape of the tish, a dormitory cubicle that housed his bed, a small table and such private items as might be fitted into the table or under the bed and *vice versa*. A curtain could be pulled across and then a tish too, became a boy's castle. One assumes that the word tish descends, not from the German for table, but from a contraction of the word 'partition', but applying logic to English slang is never a sound idea. I think we can be fairly sure however, that 'ekker' the word used at Uppingham for games, derived from 'exercise'. 'Wagger', or 'wagger-pagger-bagger', which was used to denote 'waste-paper basket', is an example of that strange argot prevalent in the 1920s and 1930s that caused the Prince of Wales to be known as the Pragger-Wagger. Even today, in the giddy world of High Anglicanism in such temples of bells, smells and cotters as St Mary's, Bourne Street, SW3, I have heard with my own two ears Holy Communion referred to by pert, campy priests as 'haggers-commaggers' and my mother still describes the agony and torture of anything from toothache to an annoying traffic jam as 'aggers and torters'.

The only other jargon to offload at this stage is the name for the prefects, who at Uppingham, as at some other public schools, were called 'praepostors', which happily preposterous name is, according to the Oxford English Dictionary, a 'Syncopated form of præpositor'. The OED then cites the following as an example of the word's usage:

> **1887** *Athenæum* 29 Oct. 569/3 He [Rev. E. Thring] strongly encouraged self-government among the boys, and threw great responsibilities upon the præpostors.

It is good to know that Thring of the enormous side-whiskers, or Dundreary Weepers (buggers' grips my mother calls them) was a master of the modern art of delegation.

Eighty-three years after that Athenæum article, a great deal of responsibility was still being thrown upon the praepostors, who were known universally as pollies. There were the House Pollies, who had authority only within their Houses, and the School Pollies, who had authority everywhere. A School Polly could carry an umbrella and wear a boater. With that embarrassingly *faux* anger that middle-class rebels have made a speciality, pollies were called, out of their hearing, 'pigs', as in: 'He's only a House pig, he can't tell you what to do,' or 'Did you hear that Barrington has been made a School Pig? Tchuh!' This sort of remark was usually made with the kind of muttered Worker's Revolutionary Party snarl that public-school boys are very good at reproducing, but which ill-suits their minor grievances.

But there again, whose grievances are ever minor? I am fully aware that *my* grievances, such as they are, are minor. The story of a sensitive young weed struggling to grow up in the robust thicket of an English public school is not likely to arouse sympathy in the breasts of every reader. It was a subject done to death in the earlier part of this century in novels, memoirs and autobiographies. I am a cliché and I know it. I was not kidnapped by slave traders, forced to shine shoes at the age of three in Rio or sent up chimneys by a sadistic sweep. I grew up neither in circumstances of abject poverty, nor in surroundings of fantastic wealth. I was not abused, neglected or exploited. Middle class at a middle-class school in middle England, well nourished, well taught and well-cared for, I have nothing of which to complain and my story, such as it is, is as much one of good fortune as of anything else. But it *is* my story and worth no more and no less than yours or anyone else's. It is, in my reading at least, a kind of pathetic love story. I would prefer to call it *pathétique* or even *appassionata*, but pathetic will do, in all its senses.

The first problem to dominate me at Uppingham was that of the fag test. Every new boy had to pass this blend of initiation rite and familiarisation exam in his first fortnight. He was instructed in this by a Fag Teacher, a second year boy, in my case an athletic fellow called Peter Pattrick.

The fagging system was in the process of winding down when I arrived. Personal fags, of the kind found in public school fiction, had become more or less extinct. Fags still had to run errands for pollies, but there was none of the toast-making, shoe-shining, study-tidying, bog-seat-warming, head-patting, thigh-stroking, buttock-fondling drudgery, slavery or abuse that I had dreaded. Fagging consisted essentially of communal chores, the most notable roles in which were to be Morning Fag, who had to wake the House (more on this later) and the unpleasantly named Lav Fag who only had to sweep the corridors, and so far as I can remember, had nothing to do with lavatories at all. The Paper Fag was obliged to go into town early in the morning, before breakfast, pick up the House's order of newspapers and deliver them to the studies. Another job was to go down twice a day and clear the school pigeonholes for senior boys, bringing up their messages to the House, that sort of thing. I can't remember what this duty was called – Pigeonhole Fag, I suppose, but again it is madness to expect logic, he might well have been called Kitten Fag, Balloon Fag or Ethics Fag for all I know.

When I use the word 'House', it must be understood that I am referring to the boarding-houses into which the school was divided, miniature versions of an Oxbridge college I suppose, in as much as one lived, ate and slept in the House, and went into the school itself for lessons, much as an Oxbridge undergraduate lives, eats and sleeps in college and goes to university faculty buildings for lectures. There again, the collegiate system is not very easy to explain either, so it is seems rather pointless my attempting to explain one mysterious system by reference to another equally baffling.

Essentially, Uppingham was six hundred boys strong, and had twelve Houses of fifty boys each, give or take. Each House had a housemaster, who was most directly responsible for one's discipline, direction and well-being, he was the man ultimately *in loco parentis*. Each House had a matron too, and a small number of staff. When I began at my House, Fircroft, there was a female kitchen staff, referred to by the boys, I am sorry to say, as skivvies. All I can offer in our defence is that we did not mean the word in any derogatory sense, it was simply the word used, we knew no other. The skivvies waited on the boys: if one wanted more water in one's jug or more tea in one's cup, one would, talking to one's neighbour all the while, simply hold up the hand containing the empty jug or mug and wave it about a bit. If service did not come quickly, one would shout 'Water!' or 'Tea here!' and eventually the jug or cup would be taken away, filled and returned. Now of course, everything is organised along cafeteria lines and involves serving-hatches and, probably, wide ranges of camomile tea, isotonic NRG drinks and vegetarian falafel. What I can't understand is why there wasn't bloody revolution in the town of Uppingham in my day. I suppose waiting hand and foot on loud public-school boys is marginally better than being unemployed, but I shouldn't wonder if some of the ruder, less considerate boys didn't get a fair amount of spittle in their tea-cups and bogeys in their baked beans.

Fircroft had a garden, a croquet lawn, a copse with a hammock, disused outside lavatories (the 'House rears' in local argot, later to prove the unromantic scene of my deflowering) and, being one of the Houses furthest from the school, two fives courts. Fives is a game much like squash, except that the ball is struck with a gloved hand instead of a racket. It comes in two flavours, Eton and Rugby. We played Eton Fives, a better game, all snobbery aside, because it involved a buttress projecting from one side of the court, presumably deriving from the buttresses of Eton College's great Perpendicular Gothic chapel, against which boys once sacrilegiously bounced balls. Fives was still played enthusiastically by some, but Eton's rival Harrow had its own old game which was rapidly becoming fashionable, not just in schools, but in the world of sweaty businessmen and newly emerging health clubs. Squash was already more popular than Fives at Uppingham by the time I arrived and the Fives Courts were really just places where bikes were parked and behind which one smoked, masturbated or sipped cider with, or without, companions.

My housemaster was a man called Geoffrey Frowde, an old friend of my parents. He had been up at Merton, Oxford, as an undergraduate, but his wife Elizabeth had been at Westfield with my mother. The Frowdes and my parents had camped out in the Mall together that rainy, rainy night before Queen Elizabeth's Coronation and waved together at Queen Salote of Tonga as she rode by with her famous lunch sitting beside her. These experiences no doubt form a bond and it was on account of Geoffrey Frowde being at Uppingham that Roger and I had been marked down for it from an early age. All this made my subsequent impossibility as a pupil all the more embarrassing of course. To be endlessly frustrated by the uncontrollable wickedness of the son of friends must put a man in a very difficult position.

Back to the fag test. This took the form of a written exam and required of its candidates a full knowledge of all the school Houses (in alphabetical order), their housemasters, their House-captains and their locations. One had to know too all the form masters by their names and initials and where in the school their form-rooms lay. Being an ancient establishment that had prospered in Victorian England, Uppingham, like a good English town, like the English language itself indeed, had rambled and swollen and bulged itself out in a higgledy-piggledy manner that demonstrated no logic, plan or rationale. The new boy had to know where each games field was, the

layout of the music school and the art school and the carpentry
and metalwork shops and all manner of other places. These
were the compulsory and predictable elements of the fag test
and held no terrors for me. I have always been able to rely on
that excellent memory of mine; the unknown factor in the test
lay in the right of the House-captain, whose job it was to mark
the results, to top off all of this factual quizzing with school
slang tests and unpredictable questions about nicknames,
customs and traditions. A cobbled pathway that led past the
library through to the central colonnade, for example, was
known as the Magic Carpet and an alley whose flooring was
made of small square raised tiles sometimes went under the
name of the Chocolate Block. There were dozens and dozens
of similar nicknames for people, places and regions of the
school that one naturally absorbed over a period of months and
years, but to find them all out in a week and a half was difficult.

The price of failure in the fag test was high: a flogging from
the House-captain. I had a dread conviction that boys beat
much more mercilessly than prep school headmasters. The
captain of the House, whose name was Peck, sported splendid
sideburns, nothing to Edward Thring's Dundreary Weepers of
course, but impressive none the less and an indicator, to my
mind, of huge reserves of strength. There was something
horrible too about the very word 'flogging' which conjured
images of naval punishment at the mast, the victim biting on
wads of leather as the lash was laid on.

Peter Pattrick my fag teacher set about his task with vigour,
for if I failed, he too would be punished. If I passed, and passed
well, there was a reward: Pattrick would have to stand me a tea
at the buttery. The school had three butteries, sort of cafés-
cum-tea-rooms-cum-tuck-shops-cum-ice-cream-parlours. There
was the Upper Buttery, the Lower and the Middle. The one I
came to love and cherish was, as befits my nature, the Lower
Buttery, a cash only, high cholesterol joint run by a couple
called Mr and Mrs Lanchberry, or possibly Launchberry. Mrs
Lanchberry (we will settle on that, I have only a limited
number of 'u's at my disposal) had a way of dropping two eggs
into a lake of boiling lard that I have yet to see rivalled. To this

day, double-eggs on toast with baked beans, a glass of sparkling dandelion and burdock and I'm simply *anybody's*. The Upper Buttery was run by a Mrs Alibone and was really more of a shop, selling sweets, coffee, biscuits, bread, cheeses, ices and other consumables on tick. There was some system of order-forms involved and she always knew exactly when one was bust, which I found irritating and in rather poor taste. The Middle Buttery was hidden somewhere in the Middle, one of the largest playing fields in England, on which dozens (literally) of cricket matches could be played simultaneously, as well as games of tennis, hockey, rugger and Christ knows what else besides.

For the fag test then, they dangled a carrot and they brandished a stick. Like most small boys at new schools I was far more driven by the stick than I was drawn by the carrot. To tell the truth, the prospect of being bought a huge tea by Peter Pattrick frightened me almost as much as being flogged by Peck.

Pattrick – I think I mentioned that he was athletic? Especially good at tennis – decided that the way to teach me was to take me to the House library, find the largest book he could, Liddell and Scott's *Greek Lexicon* probably, and hold it over my head while he tested me. A mistake or hesitation from me and – *bang!* – down would crash the book on to my skull. This was of no help and only served to confuse me. I remembered everything perfectly well almost the first time I was told it, the sight of that huge *eau de nil* jacketed dictionary looming above me simply mesmerised me into stupidity. At one point, while the book was hovering and I was havering, the door to the library opened and my brother came in. He took in the situation at a glance, I rolled a pleading eye towards him and then he spoke:

'That's it, Peter,' he said. 'If he gives any trouble, knock some sense into him.'

I *hate* myself for telling that story, for it gives quite the wrong impression of Roger who is just about the kindest man I know, with less malice in him than you would find in a bushbaby's favourite aunt. He will squirm with embarrassment and shame at reading this, which is undeserved. Facts must out, however, and I must record that I *was* a little hurt by his failing to come to my aid or defence. No grudge of course, for I thought it must be my fault and that this was how things were done at big schools. Prep school is, it goes without saying, no kind of preparation at all for public school, any more than school is a preparation for life. The alteration in scale, the sudden descent from seniority to absolute insignificance, these make any social lessons learnt worse than useless. Those whose early days at public school were least happy were those who had won most prizes, rank and power at their preps. Worth noting here the oddity too of my brother calling Pattrick by his Christian name. It was considered rather cool and adult amongst second, third and fourth years to be on first name terms.

'Hi, Mark,'

'Guy! How's it going?'

When Mark and Guy subsequently leave school and find each other again in their twenties, after university, working in the same merchant bank it becomes cool, of course, to revert back to surnames.

'Bloody hell! It's Taylor!'

'Hallett, you old bastard!'

All very puzzling and absurd.

In the event, whether Liddell and Scott had anything to do with it or not, I scored 97 per cent in the fag test, a House record. I remember the thrill of seeing the word 'Excellent!' scrawled next to my result in Peck's hand. Peck wore the striped trousers and black waistcoat of the sixth-former as well as the boater of the School Polly, but I seem to remember that he also (unless I have gone stark mad) affected a sort of cream-coloured silk stock of the kind huntsmen wear. I thought him little short of a god – even more so when I watched him playing Volpone in the school play and saw that he was a magnificent actor. I think he was the only boy older than me that I ever had a thing for, if you'll forgive the prissy phrase. I can't call it a crush exactly, or a 'pash' as they were sometimes odiously called, a 'thing for' about sums it up.

I can still remember the twelve Houses in alphabetical order, I suppose every Old Uppinghamian can – I'll recite them for you.

> Brooklands
> Constables
> Farleigh
> Fircroft
> The Hall
> Highfield
> The Lodge
> Lorne House
> Meadhurst
> School House
> West Bank
> West Dean

I do that to show the pleasingly bourgeois nature of the names of the most of the Houses. 'Meadhurst', 'Farleigh' and my own House, 'Fircroft' – they sound as if they belong in Carshalton or Roehampton, peeping through laurel bushes and shaded by monkey-puzzle trees. These Houses were necessarily larger than the average suburban villa however, despite their names, because they had to fit in dormitory and washing facilities for fifty boys, study accommodation, shower rooms, a dining hall and kitchens, as well as boot rooms, storage space and what estate agents once called 'the usual offices'. There had to be too the housemaster's area, the 'private side' as it was called, where he could live some sort of life with his wife and family. The Frowdes had two children and a golden labrador called Jester. I don't suppose an active dog could have a better life than in the boarding-house of a school. No matter how pissed off a boy might be with existence, authority or himself, there was always room to share food and affection with a dog. A dog allowed an adolescent, struggling to be manly, cynical and cool, to romp and giggle and tickle and tumble like a child.

Each House had its own character, its own nature, its own

flavour and atmosphere. Some were known for having more than the average number of the academically able, others provided a disproportionate number of athletes. One House might have a reputation for being messy and ill-disciplined, another for being a hotbed of queering and tarting. Fircroft lay somewhere in the middle. Frowde was not a martinet and did not beat or terrify the boys. The housemaster of West Bank (you don't need much imagination to guess the nickname of *that* House) was as fearsome a man as I have ever met and was rumoured to thrash like an engine ... he taught me Latin and his contribution to my school report one term read:

> Feckless, fickle, flamboyant and evasive. A disappointment.

Which about summed me up. I rather admired and liked him, he was at least more or less consistent. Masters who inspired complete, abject terror were rather a relief to me. Had this man, Abbot, been my housemaster however, I think I should have run away by the end of my first week. He once, in the middle of a Latin lesson, fell silent in the middle of some talk about Horace. We all looked up from our slumbers and saw that he was staring at a pigeon that had landed on an open window-sill. For three minutes he stared at the pigeon, saying nothing. We began to look at each other and wonder what was up. At last the pigeon flapped its wings and flew away. Abbott turned to the form.

'I am not paid,' he said, 'to teach pigeons.'

School House was the province of the headmaster, a most extraordinary man called John Royds, one time Indian Army colonel and ADC to Orde Wingate in Burma. He was physically short but had powerful presence and possessed all the techniques for inspiring awe that one looks for in a headmaster, the ability to swish a gown in an especially menacing way, for example, and a telegraphic, donnishly tart and lapidary way with words. His noticeboard in the colonnade fluttered with memos, smartly typed by an IBM golfball:

Re: The wearing of lapel badges
I think not.

JCR

or

Re: The birthday of Her Majesty the Queen
The occasion falls today. Hurrah etc. Let joy be unconfined.

JCR

or

Re: Litter in the Old School Room
We begin to weary of this nuisance. Be aware: our vigilance is ceaseless.

JCR

That sort of thing. Every morning he would step out of his House, walk with a firm tread and upright gait that concealed the most painful arthritis and snip a red rosebud from a bush in the garden which he would attach to the buttonhole of his charcoal grey suit. At one stage he developed shingles, causing him to wear the blackest and most impenetrable dark glasses at all times and in all situations, including the pulpit which, coupled with the sub fusc of his clothing, gave him the sinister look of Alan Badel in *Arabesque* or the menacing cool of a Tarantino hitman *avant la lettre*.

The application form to Uppingham required a recent photograph of the candidate to be affixed to it. By the first day of term Royds would have studied these and knew every single new boy in the school by sight.

All these things I would get to know later of course. For the time being I had passed my fag test and could find my way around. That was what mattered.

Peter Pattrick was pleased as punch, and punched me pleasedly and proudly on the arm to prove it. Being very well off (he was one of those boys I envied, who seemed endlessly to be in receipt of jaw-droppingly large cheques through the post connected with mysterious trust funds and shares, as if life for him were a continually successful game of Monopoly and the Community Chest eternally benign – I have a dim memory of getting myself, years later, hopelessly into debt with him) Pattrick could afford to stand me just about the biggest blow-out the Lower Buttery had ever seen. Unfortunately he ordered for me, amongst the eggs, bacon and sausages, a huge quantity of chips. Unlike almost everyone else I have ever known, I am not drawn by the appeal of chips and my heart sank as I saw that he was going to watch me eat my way through this heaping plateful down to the last greasy atom.

It is on occasions like this where years of dorkily studying books on magic come in really useful. From the earliest days of Booton's visiting mobile library I had fallen hungrily on any magic book I could find on its shelves. My 'chops' as magicians call technique, are not of the first order, it takes the kind of practice a concert musician is prepared to put into his music to perform just the standard pass with a pack of cards, but I can misdirect very well. Every now and then, without his knowing it, I would get Pattrick to look in a particular direction, gesturing with my fork towards a boy who had come in and asking his name for example, while with my other hand I would secretly grab a handful of chips and drop them on to a napkin in my lap.

Magic, in the form of close up sleight of hand in particular, is an art-form I venerate, but it must be confessed that almost every technique in it was invented primarily for some venal purpose. Almost all of the palms, passes, jogs, steals, glides, culls, crimps, undercuts and fakes that form the repertory basis of playing-card magic, for example, were devised by riverboat gamblers in the nineteenth century in order, to put it baldly, to cheat, swindle and steal. These techniques can be found in the masterwork on the subject, *Expert Card Technique*, by Jean Hugard and Frederick Braue, published still, I hope, by Faber and Faber. I suppose those who do not like or approve of magic sense firstly that magicians are the kind of disreputable or vengefully nebbish outsiders who relish putting one over on others and secondly that they themselves, as the victims of a trick, are not quite confident enough in themselves to take it laughingly. They are the kind who tug violently at the magician's sleeves halfway through a performance or say, with snorting contempt, that it is, after all, only a bloody trick.

I suppose, and it grieves me to say it, that there was a connection between my love of magic and my stealing. I wouldn't want you to argue backwards from that and say that any amateur of magic, from Orson Welles to David Mamet, is necessarily a potential thief, but in my case I fear it was true. The techniques of magic made me an excellent thief, I could *sell* a theft, I could *patter* a theft. Fortunately – in the last resort fortunately – the showman in me, as far as theft was concerned, always worked against the sly in me and I was usually found out, aces of spades raining from my grasped sleeve . . .

Pattrick, anyway, hadn't the least clue what I was up to. I got through every forkful of my gigantic feast, having transferred the napkinfuls of chips to another table at an opportune moment.

I was in. I had passed the test and was now an entity.

3

The first year at Uppingham passed more or less uneventfully for me. I found the work easy. The maths and the science I simply didn't attempt, which made it easier still. I had decided years ago that I had a 'maths block' and it infuriated me that this condition was not as properly recognised as dyslexia, for example, which was just beginning to be acknowledged as a syndrome or accepted condition. In fact I don't have the numeral equivalent of dyslexia, if there really is such a thing, it was all, I fear, to do with my father. Anything at which he excelled I seemed to go out of my way to be not just bad at, but quite staggeringly and impressively awful at. Not just maths and science therefore, but music too. The combination of my singing hang-ups and my father's talent made sure that music and I were never going to be public friends. Hemuss at Stouts

Hill had written to my parents and begged to be excused the
nerve-fraying task of teaching me the piano. At Uppingham I
elected, Christ knows why, to learn the cello, which was taught
by a rather sexy and stylish woman called Hillary Unna, whom
I always think of whenever I see that impeccable screen
goddess Patricia Neale. Hillary Unna liked me (I think) and I
shall never forget that she said to me in a husky, vampy voice
at our first meeting, 'Well, here's a lissom one . . .' At that time,
and at that age, such a compliment to a boy so physically
unsure made me glow for weeks. 'Lissom', what a kind word
to give to a gangling youth. I was thin in those days of course,
more than thin I was skinny and growing upwards at a
frightening speed, but I believed myself to be awkward and
physically uncoordinated, in fact the unpleasant word 'unco'
was always hooted at me whenever I dropped a ball or tripped
over. There's no point beating about the bush, I had Lord
Nelson's hand–eye co-ordination and the grace of a Meccano
giraffe.

Privately, the music school was my favourite place. There
were double-doored practice rooms where one could sit at the
piano and hammer furiously away like Beethoven in his last
years of deafness. For hours I used to stamp out the descending
chords and rising arpeggios that opened Grieg's piano
concerto fancying myself on the stage of the Wigmore Hall.
There was a record library there too, where I locked myself in,
screaming and roaring with pleasure as I wildly and doubtless
unrhythmically conducted Beethoven's *Egmont* and the
overtures of Rossini – which to this day I still secretly place
above the deeper artistic claims of Bach and Bruckner. I am still
unable to smell the peculiar smell of vinyl records, dusty
amplifiers and anti-static cleaning cloths without being
transported back to that room, with its blackboard of ruled
staves and its stacked jumble of music stands and chairs; back
to that overwhelming surge of rapturous, tumultuous joy and
the inexpressibly passionate deluge of excitement that flooded
through me when the music bellowed from that one single
Leak speaker. I could spend thousands now on the highest end
hi-fi in the world and know that, for all the wattage and purity

of signal, the music would never *quite* touch me again as it did then from that primitive monaural system. But nor could anything quite touch me now as it did then.

Amongst the boys of Fircroft there were the cool and the uncool. This was not, after all Edwardian England, not a world of 'May God forgive you, Blandford-Cresswell, for I'm sure I shan't,' or 'I say, that's beastly talk, Devenish,' or '*Cave*, you fellows, here comes old Chiggers.' This was 1970 and hippiedom and folk rock were making their sluggish, druggy moves.

In my first week Rick Carmichael (way cool) stopped me in the corridor and said, 'You're Roger Fry's brother aren't you?'

I nodded.

'Well, could you take a message for me?'

I nodded again.

'See that bloke over there?' Carmichael pointed down the corridor towards a boy with dangerously long hair, hair that nearly reached his collar, hair at which this boy pulled, stroked and twiddled, thoughtfully, lovingly and dreamily as he leaned against a wall.

'Yes,' I said. 'I see him.'

'Well, his name is Guy Caswell and I want you to say this to him. "Captain Beefheart is better than Edgar Broughton." Got that?'

'Sorry?' I had heard Captain Beefheart as Captain 'Bee-fart' and thought this might be some terrible trick to get me into trouble.

'It's not difficult. "Captain Beefheart is better than Edgar Broughton." Okay?'

'All right, Carmichael.' I gulped slightly and moved down the corridor, repeating the strange mantra to myself over and over again under my breath. 'Captain Beefheart is better than Edgar Broughton, Captain Beefheart is better than Edgar Broughton, Captain Beefheart is better than Edgar Broughton.' It was utterly meaningless to me. May as well have been Polish.

I reached the boy with the long hair and coughed tentatively.

'Excuse me . . .'

'Yeah?'

'Are you Caswell?'

'Yeah.'

'Er, Captain Beefheart is better than Edgar Broughton.'

'*What?*' Caswell let his left hand fall from its ministrations to the glossy locks.

Oh Christ, surely I hadn't got it wrong? Maybe he had misheard.

'Captain Beefheart,' I said with slow and deliberate emphasis, 'is better than Edgar Broughton.'

'Oh yeah? And what the *fuck* do you know about it?' snarled Caswell, straightening himself up and starting towards me.

I hared off down the corridor as fast as I could go, past Carmichael, who was doubled up with laughter, and out into the quad, not stopping until I reached the back of the fives courts, panting and terrified.

After tea, as I was making my way towards the study I shared with Whitwell, a new boy in my intake, there came a tap on my shoulder.

'Hey, Fry . . .' It was Caswell. 'No, no. It's okay,' he said as he saw the fear leap into my eyes. 'It was Rick, right? It was Carmichael. He told you to say that.'

I nodded.

'Okay, here's the deal. Go to Carmichael's study and tell him that The Incredible String Band is better than Jethro Tull.'

Oh Lord, what had I got myself into here?

'The Amazing String Band is . . .'

'Incredible, yeah? The *Incredible* String Band is better than Jethro Tull.'

'Jethro Tull?'

'That's it. Jethro Tull.'

'As in the drill?' My factoid-rich, Guinness Book of Records mind knew that Jethro Tull was the name of the man who had invented the seed-planting drill in 1701, though why this rendered him inferior to an incredible string band, I couldn't begin to guess.

'The Drill?' said Caswell. 'Never heard of them. Just say what I said, 'kay?'

There was enough friendliness of manner for me to know that there was no danger for me in this, and the idea of running messages appealed to the frustrated cub scout in me. I liked being thought of as useful.

Carmichael had a study to himself in another corridor. I knocked on the door, only slightly nervously. Loud music was playing inside, so I knocked again. A voice rose from within.

'C'min . . .'

I opened the door.

Every boy decorated his study differently, but most went to some lengths to make them as groovy as their incomes would allow. Fabrics were hung on walls and depended from ceilings, which gave the impression of Bedouin tents or hippy dens. These fabrics were known as tapestries, or tapos. Joss-sticks were sometimes burned, to hide the smell of tobacco or just because they were far-out and right-on. Carmichael's study was highly impressive, a psychedelic tapo here, a low wattage amber light bulb there. It was nowhere near as impressive as his older brother Andy's study, however. Andy Carmichael was something of an engineer and had constructed out of wood elaborate levels and ladders within the study, turning it into a cross between an adventure playground and Victor Frankenstein's laboratory. At the moment, the House was abuzz with the rumour that Andy Carmichael had nearly completed a hovercraft he had been building and that it was going to get its trial run on the Middle very soon. He did finish it eventually, I remember, and it worked too: every bit as noisy, useless and disgusting as the commercial hovercrafts that ply the channel today.

I believe there was a yet older Carmichael called Michael, but he had already left the school. I liked the idea of his being told to get into the family car and used to repeat endlessly to myself, 'Get into the Carmichael car, Michael Carmichael . . . get into the Carmichael car, Michael Carmichael.'

What stunned me about *Rick* Carmichael's study however, was the sight of the books on his bookshelf. Six Penguin copies of P. G. Wodehouse Jeeves stories. On the frontmost, *Jeeves in the Offing,* I could see a photograph from a BBC series of three or four years earlier which had starred Dennis Price as Jeeves and, as Bertie Wooster . . . Ian Carmichael.

Rick looked up and followed the direction of my eyes.

'Are you . . . is he? I mean . . .' I stammered. 'You know, on the telly . . . ?'

'He's my uncle,' said Rick, turning down the volume on his record-player, which had been pushing out a rather appealing song about tigers and India, of which more later.

'I *love* P. G. Wodehouse,' I said solemnly. 'I *adore* him.'

'Yeah? Do you want to borrow one?'

I had read them all, all the Jeeves stories, ever since Margaret Popplewell, a friend of my mother's from her schooldays, had given me a copy of *Very Good, Jeeves* for my birthday. I had been collecting him in all editions for some time and had a massive collection. The great man wrote nearly a hundred books, so there was still a long way to go.

'Could I?'

He passed *Jeeves in the Offing* over to me. I am looking at that very copy now, it is on the desk next to my keyboard. On the front we see a photograph of a beautifully dressed Ian Carmichael wearing a monocle (a source of much debate amongst Wodehousians – there is only one actual reference to Bertie wearing an eye-glass, and that was in a painting of him which became a poster, but you really don't want to know that) a red carnation is in his buttonhole and a wonderfully dim good-natured look of startlement beams through his exceptionally blue eyes. Above the tubby Penguin that stands next to the title is printed '3/6' (which was shortly to become known as seventeen and a half pence) and on the back we read:

> The cover shows Ian Carmichael as Bertie Wooster in the B.B.C. series 'The World of Wooster' (Producer: Michael Mills, by arrangement with Peter Cotes. Photographer Nicholas Acraman)

Many years later I worked for Michael Mills, who was a formidably shrewish and frightening man. There was very little he had not done in the world of Light Entertainment and he did not take kindly to unpunctual actors. I was booked for a part, very early on in my 'career' on a half-hour comedy called *Chance in a Million* which starred Simon Callow, whom I was desperate to meet, since his book *Being an Actor* had been a huge inspiration at university. I had not known that Teddington Lock, where Thames TV studios had their being, took well over an hour to get to from Islington, where I was living at the time, and had arrived at least half an hour late. Michael Mills, who was the kind of man who wore spacious cardigans and half-moon spectacles that dangled on black string, gave me a withering look and told me that he would be writing to my agent about the unprofessional hour at which I had arrived. He has died since I believe and I never got a chance to talk to him about the making of that 1960s 'World of Wooster' series.

It is strange to touch this book now and know that it was handed to me, lazily and charmingly, by Rick Carmichael more than a quarter of a century ago. Stranger still, I suppose, in the light of the fact that I was to spend four years myself playing Jeeves in another television adaptation of those same stories.

'Anything else?' Rick said.

'Oh!' I jerked up from my reverent gaze at the book. 'Oh, yes. The Unbelievable String Band is better than Jethro Tull.'

Carmichael smiled, 'Er, I think you mean "The Incredible String Band", don't you?'

'Oh,' I said. 'Damn. Yes.'

'Right,' said Carmichael. 'You tell Guy that Carol King is better than Fairport Convention.'

I can't remember how many times I shuttled between Carmichael and Caswell delivering insulting messages on the subject of their favourite music, but it meant that somehow I became more or less accepted early on by these two and by Rick's best friend, Martin Swindells, who was known as Mart and sometimes as Dog. They were also friendly with a boy called Roger Eaton, who was red-haired and called Roo. They were cool, this group, Guy, Rick, Mart and Roo. They knew more about rock music than I thought I could ever, ever learn. They were cool and they were amiable. They were not interested in status, ambition, gossip about the staff or schooly, status-bound things. They didn't take joy in teasing the weak or sucking up to the strong. They liked music and they liked fun. One of them, I won't say which in case their parents are reading this, showed me the first ever joint I had ever seen. He didn't let me smoke it, but he showed it to me. For all I know it wasn't a joint at all, just a cigarette rolled up to look like one.

Rock music, of course, was not the same as rock and roll. Nor was it the same as pop. Since the demise of The Beatles, pop and the single-play record had become singularly unhip, at public schools at any rate. Albums were where it was at. Albums meant Pink Floyd, Van de Graaf Generator, King Crimson, Deep Purple, Led Zeppelin, Genesis (nice Charterhouse boys with a cockney drummer) and – at the folksy end – Jethro Tull, Procul Harum, Steeleye Span and, bless them, The Incredible String Band.

A lot of that rock would now be called Heavy Metal: Uriah Heep, Iron Maiden and Black Sabbath were, unless I've leapt ahead of myself, already going, and cool people already knew about David Bowie whose 'Major Tom' had flopped the year before but was a coming man. There was a rumour too that Long John Baldry's old keyboard player, Elton John, had produced an album that was so far out it was far in. These were things I did not know.

There was one band, however, that I soon came to know everything about. About halfway through my first term, Rick Carmichael ran out of cash and decided to hold a Study Sale, an auction in which all the stuff, gear and rig he could do without became available to the highest bidder. I came away from this sale with the complete set of BBC tie-in Jeeves Penguins and an LP, the very album whose first track 'Hunting Tigers Out in India' had been playing when I had first knocked on Rick's door. It was called *Tadpoles* and was the work of The Bonzo Dog Doo-Dah Band.

I had heard of them because they had enjoyed their one and only Number One hit with 'The Urban Spaceman' while I was still at Stouts Hill. This album was most strange and wonderful to look upon. It had holes pierced in the eyes of the band members on the front and, inside, a card which you could slide backwards and forwards, which made all kinds of shapes pass in and out of the blank eye sockets. Below the title *Tadpoles* was the phrase . . .

Tackle the toons you tapped your tootsies to in Thames TV's *Do Not Adjust Your Set*

. . . which, it grieves me to say, meant nothing whatever to me, our house not being an ITV house. I am not even sure if my parents' television could *get* ITV at this stage. I remember, to divert for a moment, that when we had moved up to Norfolk, aged nine and seven, Roger and I had been *desperate* to watch television that first evening because the week before, in Chesham, we had seen the first ever episode of *Doctor Who* and were already hopelessly hooked. Something had happened in transit to the mahogany Pye television with its tiny grey screen and it wouldn't work. We missed that second episode and I grieve still at the loss.

Do Not Adjust Your Set, I now know was an early evening comedy show which had featured Michael Palin, Terry Jones and Eric Idle, who had by this time already gone on to join John Cleese, Graham Chapman and Terry Gilliam in *Monty Python's Flying Circus*, which was just beginning to seep into our consciousnesses. The music for *Do Not Adjust Your Set* was provided by a very strange collection of art-students and musicians who called themselves The Bonzo Dog Doo-Dah Band. By the time I began seriously to get into them, they had dropped their Doo-Dah and were just The Bonzo Dog Band. The two leading lights of the band were the immensely skilled musical *pasticheur* Neil Innes (who continued his association with the *Python* people by writing the songs for and appearing in *The Rutles* and *The Holy Grail* and so on), and the late, majestic and remarkable Vivian Stanshall, one of the most talented, profligate, bizarre, absurd, infuriating, unfathomable and magnificent Englishmen ever to have drawn breath.

Stanshall (Sir Viv to his worshippers) died in a fire a few
years ago and I felt terrible because I hadn't been in touch with
him for years – ever since I had helped him out a little by
investing in a musical he had written called *Stinkfoot* which
played, to generally uncomprehending silence, in the Shaw
Theatre, London some ten or so years ago.

Over the next year at Uppingham I bought their other
albums, *Gorilla*, *A Doughnut In Granny's Greenhouse*,
Keynsham and finally *Let's Make Up and Be Friendly*, their
last, which contained Stanshall's short story, 'Rawlinson End'
which I can still recite by heart and which he went on to
develop into that *outré* film masterpiece, *Sir Henry At
Rawlinson End* starring Trevor Howard as Sir Henry and J. G.
Devlin as his butler, Old Scrotum, the wrinkled retainer. When
I first heard the joke, 'Scrotum, the wrinkled retainer,' I
laughed so much I honestly thought I might die of suffocation.

Oh, very well, it isn't Alexander Pope or Oscar Wilde, but
for me it was as delicious as anything could be delicious. With
Stanshall, it was as if a new world had exploded in my head, a
world where delight in language for the sake of its own
textures, beauties and sounds, and where the absurd, the
shocking and the deeply English jostled about in mad
jamboree.

It was Stanshall's voice, I think, that delighted me more than
anything. It had two registers, one light and dotty, with the
timbre almost of a 1920s crooner, and capable of very high
pitch indeed, as when he sang songs like the Broadway
standard 'By A Waterfall'; the other was a Dundee cake of a
voice, astoundingly deep, rich and fruity, capable of Elvis
impersonations (the song 'Death Cab for Cutie' for example)
as well as great gutsy trombone blasts of larynx-lazy British
sottery, to use a Stanshally sort of phrase.

Most people will know his voice from the instruments he
vocally introduces on Mike Oldfield's otherwise entirely
instrumental album *Tubular Bells*, which sold in its millions
and millions in the early 1970s and founded the fortune of
Richard Branson.

The Bonzos were my bridge between rock music and

comedy, but comedy was more important to me by far than rock music. I did eventually buy an Incredible String Band album called, it grieves me to relate, *Liquid Acrobat As Regards The Air* as well as *Meddle*, *Obscured By Clouds* and other early Pink Floyd, but my heart wasn't really in them. It was comedy for me. Not just the modern comedy of the Bonzos and Monty Python, nor the slightly older comedy of Peter Cook and Dudley Moore, much as I adored those geniuses. I also collected records with titles like *The Golden Days of Radio Comedy* and *Legends of the Halls* and learned by heart the routines of comics like Max Miller, Sandy Powell, Sid Field, Billy 'Almost a Gentleman' Bennett, Mabel Constandouros, Gert and Daisy, Tommy Handley, Jack Warner and most especially, Robb Wilton.

Perhaps we're getting back to that 'can't sing, can't dance: won't sing, won't dance' subject. If I learned all the comedy, I could repeat it, *perform* it, which was as close as I could come to singing or dancing. I'm not a bad mimic, no Rory Bremner or Mike Yarwood, but not bad, and I could repeat back the comedy I had learned, word for word, intonation for intonation, pause for pause. Then I might be able to try out some of my own.

I was not alone in this. Richard Fawcett, a boy of my term, shared this love of comedy. He was a fine mimic too, and an astoundingly brave and brilliant actor. He and I would listen to comedy records together, pointing out to each other why this was funny, what made that even funnier, trying hard to get to the bottom of it all, *penetrating* our passion, wanting to hug it all to us in heaping armfuls, as teenagers will.

Fawcett had a collection which included routines by Benny Hill and Frankie Howerd, as well as an extraordinary song called 'The Ballad of Bethnal Green' by someone whose name I fear I have forgotten, (I think his first name was Paddy, I expect someone will write to me and let me know) and which included delightfully weird lyrics like:

> Rum-tiddle-tiddle, rum tiddle-tiddle
> Scum on the water

> Lint in your navel and sand in your tea

And somewhere in this ballad came the splendid phrase,

> With a rum-tiddly-i-doh-doh
> I hate my old mum

Fawcett also shared with me a passion for words and we would trawl the dictionary together and simply howl and wriggle with delight at the existence of such splendours as 'strobile' and 'magniloquent', daring and double-daring each other to use them to masters in lessons without giggling. 'Strobile' was a tricky one to insert naturally into conversation, since it means a kind of fir-cone, but magniloquent I did manage.

I, being I, went always that little bit too far of course. There was one master who had berated me in a lesson for some tautology or other. He, as what human being wouldn't when confronted with a lippy verbal show-off like me, delighted in seizing on opportunities to put me down. He was not, however an English teacher, nor was he necessarily the brightest man in the world.

'So, Fry. "A lemon yellow colour" is precipitated in your test tube is it? I think you will find, Fry, that we all know that lemons are yellow and that yellow is a colour. Try not to use three words where one will do. Hm?'

I smarted under this, but got my revenge a week or so later.

'Well, Fry? It's a simple enough question. What is titration?'

'Well, sir . . . it's a process whereby . . .'

'Come on, come on. Either you know or you don't.'

'Sorry sir, I am anxious to avoid pleonasm, but I think . . .'

'Anxious to avoid *what*?'

'Pleonasm, sir.'

'And what do you mean by that?'

'I'm sorry, sir. I meant that I had no wish to be sesquipedalian.'

'*What*?'

'Sesquipedalian, sir.'

'What are you talking about?'

I allowed a note of confusion and bewilderment to enter my voice. 'I didn't want to be sesquipedalian, sir! You know, pleonastic.'

'Look, if you've got something to say to me, say it. What is this pleonastic nonsense?'

'It means sir, using more words in a sentence than are necessary. I was anxious to avoid being tautologous, repetitive or superfluous.'

'Well why on earth didn't you say so?'

'I'm sorry, sir. I'll remember in future, sir.' I stood up and turned round to face the whole form, my hand on my heart. 'I solemnly promise in future to help sir out by using seven words where one will do. I solemnly promise to be as pleonastic, prolix and sesquipedalian as he could possibly wish.'

It is a mark of the man's fundamental good nature that he didn't whip out a knife there and then, slit my throat from ear to ear and trample on my body in hob-nailed boots. The look he gave me showed that he came damned close to considering the idea.

Christ, I could be a cheeky, cocky little runt. I gave the character of Adrian in my novel *The Liar* some of the lines I liked to use to infuriate schoolmasters.

'Late, Fry?'

'Really, sir? So am I.'

'Don't try to be clever, boy.'

'Very good, sir. How stupid would you like me to be? Very stupid or only slightly stupid?'

I regret that I cut such an odious, punchable figure sometimes, but I don't ever regret those hours spent alone or with Richard Fawcett trawling the dictionary or playing over and over again comedy record after comedy record.

Whether we are the sum of influences or the sum of influences added to the sum of genes, I know that the way I express myself, the words I choose, my tone, my style, my *language* is a compound which would be utterly different, utterly, utterly different if I had never been exposed to any one of Vivian Stanshall, P. G. Wodehouse or Conan Doyle. Later on the cadences, tropes, excellences and defects of other writers and their rhetorical tricks, Dickens, Wilde, Firbank, Waugh and Benson, may have entered in and joined the mix, but those primal three had much to do with the way I spoke and therefore, how I thought. Not how I *felt* but how I thought, if indeed I ever thought outside of language.

I have diverted into this world of The Bonzos and comedy because I am coming soon, all too soon, to my second year at Uppingham, and I don't want to create the impression of a lone mooncalf Fry, absorbed only in love and the pungent pain of his lonely pubescence. There was a context: there were fifty boys in the House, they had their own lives too and we were all touched by the outside world and its current fads and fantasies.

In my first year I had Fawcett as a friend, and later, a boy called Jo Wood, with whom I was to share a study in my second year. Jo Wood was sound, sound as a bell. Solid, cynical, amused and occasionally amusing, he did not appear to be very intelligent, and unlike Richard Fawcett and me, seemed uninterested in words, ideas and the world.

But one day he said to me:

'I've got it now. It's reading isn't it?'

'I'm sorry?'

'You read a lot, don't you? That's where it all comes from. Reading. Yeah, reading.'

The next time I saw him he had a Herman Hesse novel in his hands. I never saw him again without a book somewhere on his person. When I heard, some years later, that he had got into Cambridge I thought to myself, I know how that happened. He decided one day to read. He taught me a lot about the human will, Jo Wood. But more than that, he was a kind patient friend who had much to put up with in our second year when he had to share a study with a boy whose life had suddenly exploded into a million pieces.

The only real fly in the ointment that first year, senseless brushes with authority aside, came in the form of Games. Ekker. Sports.

There is a fine Bonzo number called 'Sport' which follows a sensitive boy at school (called Stephen pleasingly enough) who prefers to lie in the long grass with his pocket edition of Mallarmé (another Stephen) while the big rough boys are at their football. The chorus calls out gruffly:

> Sport, sport, masculine sport
> Equips a young man for society!
> Yes, sport turns out a jolly good sort
> It's an odd boy who doesn't like sport!

I laughed at that song, but I inwardly I wept at it too. I *hated* sport, ekker, games, whatever they wanted to call it. And it was a fuck sight harder to get off ekker at Uppingham than it had been at prep school. 'A fuck sight' was the kind of language one used at Uppingham all the time, out of the hearing of staff. It was one of the first things I had noticed about the difference between Stouts Hill and Uppingham, the *language*, just as for Robert Graves in *Goodbye To All That* it had been the transition from Charterhouse to the Royal Welch Fusiliers that had marked a startling move up in the swearing stakes. From a world of 'bloody heck' and the occasional 'balls' I had been hurled into a society where it was 'fuck', 'wank', 'bollocks', 'cunt' and 'shit' every other word. To say that I was shocked would be ridiculous, but I was slightly scared. The swearing was part of the move up towards manliness, part of the healthiness. Study sales, butteries and shops, that kind of independence I could appreciate, but things that were manly frightened me. And nothing was more manly than Games.

Games *mattered* at Uppingham. If you had your First Fifteen colours, you were one hell of a blood. If you represented just your House, let alone the school in some sport, it gave you something, an air, a reason to feel good about yourself, a sense of easy superiority that no amount of mental suffering with irregular verbs could threaten. Work was ultimately poofy and to be bad at work was no cause for shame.

Games went on all the time. House ekker was a daily thing,

except on Fridays. It was no good cheering when Fridays came around however, for Fridays were compulsory Corps days, when we had to march up and down in Second World War battle-dress as part of the school's Combined Cadet Force. I was Army, poor bloody infantry; my brother wisely chose the Air Force. I must have looked as much like a military unit as Mike Tyson looks like a daffodil, shuffling about the parade ground in my badly blancoed webbing, clodding corps-boots, an overtight black beret that would never fold down and made me look more like a French onion seller than a soldier, writhing in an itchy khaki shirt, trying to march in step with a clunking Lee Enfield rifle over my shoulder and the school sergeant-major, RSM 'Nobby' Clarke yelling in my ear.

But you could fuck me with a pineapple and call me your suckpig, beat me with chains and march me up and down in uniform every day and I would thank you with tears in my eyes if it got me off games. Nothing approached the vileness of games, nothing.

Grotesque 'Unders versus Overs' matches would arise from time to time, in which under sixteens played over sixteens, and school matches that you had to watch and cheer at. PE lessons cropped up in the syllabus, in *academic* time: absurd Loughborough-educated imbeciles calling everyone 'lads' and using Christian names as if they found the snobbery of public school inimical to their healthy, matey world of beer, *bonhomie*, split-times and quadriceps.

'Good lad, Jamie!'

Oh, there was always a Jamie, a good-lad-Jamie, a neat, nippy, darty, agile scrum-halfy little Jamie. Jamie could swarm up ropes like an Arthur Ransom hero, he could fly up window frames, leap vaulting horses, flip elegant underwater turns at the end of each lap of the pool, somersault backwards and forwards off the trapeze and spring back up with his neat little buttocks twinkling and winking with fitness and firmness and cute little Jamieness. *Cunt.*

Then they had the nerve, these barely literate pithecanthropoids in their triple-A tee-shirts and navy blue tracksuit bottoms, with their pathetically function-rich stop-watches around their thick, thick necks, to write school reports citing 'motor development percentiles' and other such bee's-wank as if their futile, piffling physical jerks were part of some recognised scientific discipline that mattered, that actually *mattered* in the world. Even a tragic management consultant bristling with statistics and psychological advice on the 'art of people handling' – art of the so-fucking-obvious-it-makes-your-nose-bleed more like – has *some* right to look himself in the mirror every morning, but *these* baboons with their clip-boards and whistles and lactic acid burn statistics, running backwards with a medicine ball under each arm, shouting 'Come on, Fry, shift yourself, let's see some *burn* . . .'

Yeugh! The squeak of rubber soles on sports hall floors, the rank stench of newly leaking testosterone, the crunch of cinder racing tracks, the ugly, dead thump of a rugger ball taking a second later than the ugly, dead sight of it hitting the hard mud as you sullenly watched the match, the clatter of hockey sticks, the scrape of studded boots on pavilion floors, the puke-sweet smell of linseed oil, 'Litesome' jock-straps, shin-guards, disgusting leather caps worn in scrums, boots, shorts, socks, laces, the hiss and steam of the showers.

Fu-u-u-u-u-uck! I want to vomit it all out now, the whole healthy spew of it. It ate into my soul like acid and ate its way out again like cancer. I despised it so much . . . so much . . . so much. A depth and height and weight and scale of all consuming hatred that nearly sent me mad.

Games! How *dared* they use that grand and noble word to describe such low, mud-caked barbarian filth as rugby football and hockey? How *dared* they think that what they were doing was a *game*? It wasn't ludic, it was ludicrous. It wasn't gamesome, it was gamey, as a rotten partridge is gamey.

It was *shit*, it was a wallowing in shouting, roaring, brutal, tribal *shit*. And the shittiest shit of it all was the showers.

Yes, I might have been tall, yes, I might have been growing almost visibly, yes, my voice might have broken, but *what was happening down there*? Fuck all, that was what was happening.

If I heard the word 'immature' used, even in the most innocent context, I would blush scarlet. Immature meant me having no hair down there. Immature meant me having a salted snail for a cock. Immature meant shame, inadequacy, defeat and misery. *They* could peacock around without towels, *they* could jump up and down and giggle as bell-end slapped against belly-button, and heavy ball-sack bounced and swung, *they* could shampoo their shaggy pubes and sing their brainless rugby songs in the hiss of the shower-room, it was all right for them, the muddy, bloody, merciless, apemen *cunts*.

And you want to know the joke, the sick, repulsive joke?

I *love* sport.

I *love* 'games'.

I *a-fucking-dore* them. All of them. From rugby league to indoor bowls. From darts to baseball. Can't get enough. Cannot get e-fucking-nough.

Now I do, *now*.

Part of the reason for this book being a month and half late in delivery is that the England–Australia test matches and Wimbledon, and the British Lions Rugby Fifteen's tour of South Africa have all been tumbling out of the screen at once. I had to watch every match. Then there were the golf majors, the Formula One season building to its climax and Goodwood too. And now the soccer season is about to begin, and it'll be *Ford Monday Night Football* and more precious hours sat in front of the television lapping up sport, sport, sport, one of the great passions of my life. Those poor buggers in the gym trying to get my hopeless weedy body to do something *healthy* like climb a rope or spring over a vaulting horse, they did their best. They weren't stupid, they weren't mean. They would write witty reports on me: 'The only exercise he takes is the gentle walk to the sports centre to present his off-games chit,' that kind of thing. 'Physical exertion and Stephen Fry are strangers. I have tried to introduce them, but I feel they will never get on.' Good men, trying to do a good job.

Talk about betrayal.

How am I ever going to apologise to that miserable, furious, wretched thirteen-year-old, huddled in a scared bony heap on the changing room bench trying to work out how to shuffle to the showers without being *seen*? All he has is his anger, his fury, his verbal arrogance, his pride. Without that, he would shrivel into a social nothingness that would match his shrivelled physical nothingness. So forgive him the intemperance of his fury, forgive him his rage, his insolence and the laughing cockiness he is prey to: they are just a ragged towel. A towel to hide his shame, to cover up the laughable no-cockiness he is prey to.

Can so much be explained by (literally) so little?

Le nez de Cléopâtre: s'il eût plus court, toute la face de le terre aurait changé . . . didn't Pascal write that? If Cleopatra's nose had been shorter the whole face of the world would have been changed. I've never quite understood why he said 'shorter', not 'longer' – maybe in Pascal's day, or Mark Antony's for that matter, a short nose was considered uglier than a long one. Maybe I've misunderstood the whole thrust of the thought. Anyway, when I first came upon that *pensée*, (a favourite with French masters in dictation on account of its silent, subjunctive circumflex) I remember thinking about the face of *my* world. *Le nœud d'Étienne: s'il eût plus long* . . .

But then, as Pascal also said, the heart has its reasons, which Reason knows nothing about. Your guess is almost certainly better than mine. The spectator sees more of the game.

So back to that sad little creature.

It's an average weekday lunchtime halfway through his first term. As the meal has progressed, he has become quieter and quieter because he knows that after lunch he must face the House polly and the Ekker Book. He has to tick everyone off, this officious polly. He will want to see either a note from matron explaining why you are Off Ekker, or he will Put You Down for a game.

I wait in the queue, my stomach pumping out hot lead. The polly looks up briefly.

'Fry. Unders Rugger. House pitch.'

'Oh. No. I can't.'

'What?'

'I'm fencing.'

'*Fencing?*'

I had heard someone say this the other day and they seemed

to have got away with it. The polly flips through his book. 'You're not on the list as a fencer.'

Bollocks, there's a list. I hadn't thought of that.

'But Mr Tozer told me to turn up,' I whine. Mr Tozer, known inevitably as Spermy Tozer, was big in the world of sports like fencing and badminton and archery. Uppingham's Tony Gubba. 'I had expressed an interest.'

'Oh. Okay. Fencing, then. Make sure you bring back a chit from him so I can put you in the book.'

Hurray!

One afternoon taken care of. One afternoon where, so long as that polly doesn't see me, I can do what I like, roam where I like. He'll forget about that chit from Spermy Tozer.

But there will be other afternoons, and new excuses needed. Every day is a fresh hell of invention and sometimes, just sometimes, I actually have to turn up and sometimes, I am caught skulking unhealthily, and I am punished.

Peck I think, was the last House-captain to have the right to beat boys without the housemaster's permission. The most common form of punishment not corporal, was something called the Tish Call. Tishes, as I have already explained, were the cubicles that divided up the beds of the dormitory. Everyone, in every House in the school, slept in a tish.

A Single tish call was a small slip of paper given by a polly to an offender. On it was written the name of a polly from another House. A Double tish call contained two names of two different pollies, again from two different Houses. I was for ever getting Triple tish calls, three different pollies, three different Houses.

The recipient of a tish call had to get up early, change into games clothes, run to the House of the first polly on the list, enter the polly's tish, wake him up and get him to sign next to his name on the slip of paper. Then on to the next polly on the list, who was usually in a House right at the other end of the town. When all the signatures had been collected, it was back to your own House and into uniform in time for breakfast at eight o'clock. So that offenders couldn't cheat by going round in the most convenient geographical order, or by getting up before seven, the official start time, the pollies on the list had to write down, next to their signatures, the exact time at which they were woken up.

A stupid punishment really, as irritating for the pollies who were shaken awake as it was for the poor sod doing the running about. The system was open to massive abuse. Pollies could settle scores with colleagues they disliked by sending them tish callers every day for a week. Tit-for-tat tish call wars between pollies could go on like this for whole terms.

Of course pollies could do each other favours too.

'Oh Braddock, there's a not half scrummy scrum-half in your Colts Fifteen, what's his name?'

'What, Yelland you mean?'

'That's the one. Rather fabulous. You . . . er . . . couldn't find your way clear to sending him over one morning, could you? As a little tishie?'

'Oh, all right. If you'll send me Finlay.'

'Done.'

The only really enjoyable part of the tish call for me was the burglary. Officially all the Houses were locked until seven, which was supposed to make it pointless to set off early and take the thing at a leisurely pace. But there were larder, kitchen and changing room windows that could be prised open and latches that could yield to a flexible sheet of mica. Once inside all you had to do was creep up to the dorm, tiptoe into the target polly's tish, adjust his alarm clock and wake him. That way you could start the call at half-past five or six, bicycle about at a gentle pace and save yourself all the flap and faff of trying to complete the whole run in forty minutes.

That entire description of the tish call is lifted, almost whole, from *The Liar*, but then, when I wrote *The Liar* I lifted that description, almost whole, from my life, so it seems fair to take it back.

Because of the simplicity with which the rules of the tish call game could be circumvented, because of the *frisson* of sexual possibility that they hinted at and because I always enjoyed early mornings anyway, they held no particular terror for me as a punishment. Some boys came away from being given a tish call with their faces white as a sheet. They would dutifully get up at the right time, actually get into full games kit, actually run from House to House, puffing and sweating, and actually shower before coming into breakfast and presenting their filled-in slip of paper to the polly who had punished them. I *never* presented it, always waited for the polly to chase me up, allowing him a moment's triumphant thought that maybe I had actually dared not to do the tish call and that this time I was really for it.

'Where is it, Fry?'

'Second on the left, you can't miss it. Smells of urine and excrement.'

'Don't be clever. I gave you a triple tish call yesterday.'

'You *did*? Are you sure you're not thinking of my brother?'

'Don't be cheeky, you know bloody well.'

'I'm afraid it entirely slipped my mind.'

'*What?*'

'Yes. Awful, isn't it?'

'Well, in *that* case . . .'

'And then I remembered, just in time. Here it is . . . Copping's signature is especially elegant don't you think? Such a handsome swagger in the curve of the "c" . . . such careless grace in the down-swoop of that final "g" . . .'

Another duty to enjoy was that of Morning Fag. Most juniors hated it when their turn came round, but I counted off the days with mounting excitement. It involved some of the things I loved best: early mornings, the sound of my own voice, efficient service and a hint of eroticism. Maybe I should have been an airline steward . . .

At seven-fifteen at the latest I would spring out of bed, get dressed and tiptoe out of the dormitory. I would go downstairs to the Hall, where the skivvies would be laying the table for breakfast, bid them good morning, maybe blag a slice of bread and butter off them and check my watch against the clock on the wall. Then upstairs to a table on the landing where was laid out a huge brass bell with a leather loop for a handle. At precisely half past seven I would lift the bell and start to ring. It was heavy and took three or four shakes before the clapper really set itself in rhythm. I would go to each of the dormitories in turn and then, ringing the bell furiously all the time, shout as loudly as I could in an incantatory chant that was identical to that of all morning fags, and is impossible to set down here without musical entablature:

'*Time half past seven!*'

As soon as that had been done in the threshold of each of the four dormitories I would then have to dash from tish to tish waking each boy individually, counting – and this was the tricky part – backwards in five second increments. That is to say, I would have to tell them how long they had to go before ten to eight, which was the last time-call they received before eight o'clock and brekker.

Thus, entering each tish and shaking each shoulder I would yell in each ear, 'eighteen minutes and forty-five seconds tooo go . . . eighteen minutes and forty seconds tooo go . . . eighteen minutes and thirty-five seconds tooo go' and so on until the time for the next general cry and the next ring of the bell which came at twenty to eight.

'*Ten minutes toooooo go!*' was the chant, and then back to the tishes. 'Nine minutes and twenty-five seconds tooo go . . . nine minutes and twenty seconds tooo go . . .' before returning to the bell and the final, triumphant pealing and roaring of:

'*TI-I-I-ME TEN TO EIGHT!*'

By which time boys would be clattering and roaring and streaming past me, swearing, cursing, doing up their final buttons, foaming with toothpaste and bad temper.

Some boys were terribly hard to wake, and if you didn't succeed in rousing them fully and they were senior, they would blame you for not being up in time and make your life hell. Other boys were deliberately hard to wake and played secret unspoken games with you. They might sleep nude, under one sheet and present you as you entered the tish with all the signs of deep sleep and an innocent but perky morning erection. The unspoken game was that, as you tried to shake them awake by their shoulder, your elbow or a lower part of the arm might just accidentally rub against their twitching dick. Never a word spoken, this game sometimes went all the way, sometimes was just a little game. In my year as Morning Fag one got to know which boys played this game and which didn't, just as they presumably got to know which Morning Fags played it, and which didn't.

This was before I had ever masturbated myself, and although I knew all the theory and was titillated by the idea of sex, I didn't really get the whole fuss of it. At Stouts Hill I had already learned the hard way just how complex the attitude of the healthy boy was towards queering.

At my last year at prep school, it had become very much the thing amongst a handful of us in our senior dormitory to do a fair amount of fooling around when the others were asleep. A couple of the boys were equipped with a set of fully operational testicles and bushy pubic undergrowth, others like me were not. I greatly enjoyed creeping over to another boy's bed and having a good old rummage about. I never quite knew what it was that I enjoyed, and certainly the first time I saw semen erupt from a penis it gave me the fright of my life. I have to confess I found it frankly rather disgusting and wondered at nature's eccentricity: like Noël Coward's Alice I felt that things could have been organised better. One of the boys in that dorm, we'll call him Halford, like me not fully ripened but of a sportive disposition, took the same pleasure that I did in wandering around the school naked. Together we would, with roaring stiffies, or what passed for roaring stiffies in our cases, creep around the bathrooms simply glorying in the fact of our nakedness. We might point and prod and giggle and fondle each other a little, and experiment with that curious squashing of dicks in closing doors and desk-lids that seems to please the young, but it was the nakedness and the secrecy that provided all the excitement we needed.

One afternoon, this same Halford was climbing out of the swimming pool when he suddenly got the most terrible cramp in one leg. He yowled with pain, flopped forward on to the grass and started to thrash his legs up and down in agony. I was standing close by so I went and helped him up and then walked him around the pool until the cramp had gone. Fully recovered, he streaked away to change and I thought no more about it.

As the afternoon wore on it became apparent to me that I seemed suddenly to have become extremely unpopular. One is highly sensitive to these things at twelve, I was at least. Highly. My popularity rating was something I was more aware of than the most sophisticated political spin-doctor. But I simply couldn't understand it. It must have been one of those rare afternoons when I knew I had done absolutely nothing wrong. It was bewildering, but inescapable: boys were cutting me dead, sneering openly at me, sending me to Coventry and falling sullenly silent when I entered rooms.

At last I ran into someone who could explain. I found myself approaching a fat boy called McCallum in the corridor and he whispered something as I passed.

'What did you say?' I asked, stopping and spinning round.

'Nothing,' he said and tried to move on. McCallum was someone of little account and I knew that I could master him.

'You muttered something just now,' I said grasping him by both shoulders, 'you will tell me what it was or I will kill you. It is that simple. I will end your life by setting fire to you in bed while you are asleep.'

McCallum was the sort of gullible panicky fool who took that kind of threat very seriously indeed.

'You wouldn't dare!' he said, proving my point.

'I most certainly would,' I replied. 'Now. Tell me what it was that you said just now.'

'I just said . . . I said . . .' he spluttered to a halt and coloured up.

'Yes?' I said. 'I'm waiting. You just said . . . ?'

'I just said "Queer".'

'Queer?'

'Yes.'

'You said "Queer", did you? And why was that?'

'Everyone knows. Let me go.'

'Everyone knows,' I said, strengthening my grip on his shoulders, 'but me. What is it that everyone knows?'

'This afternoon . . . ow! You're hurting me!'

'Of course I'm bloody hurting you! Do you think I would be exerting this much pressure for any other reason? Go on.

"This afternoon . . ." you said.'
  'When Halford got out of the pool . . .'
  'Yes, what about it?'
  'You . . . you put your arm round him like a queer. Halford is hopping mad. He wants to beat you up.'
  In my shock, outrage, horror and indignation I let go of McCallum completely and he took his opportunity, scuttling away like a fat beetle, shouting 'Queer!' as he rounded the corner out of sight.
  I didn't even remember putting my arm round Halford's shoulder. I suppose I must have done as I had walked him round the pool.
  All the blood drained from my face and I came close to one of those early adolescent fainting fits which sometimes stay with you till late in life, a physical sensation that can overwhelm you if you stand up very suddenly – a feeling that you are close to blacking out and falling down.
  Halford thought I was queer because I had put my arm round him. Put my arm round him to support him! The very same Halford who was wandering naked with me around the bathroom not two nights previously. The Halford who taught me how to shut my cock in a door. The Halford who did a backward somersault naked on the floor at me and pushed his finger up his arse, giggling. *He* thought *I* was queer? Queer for putting an arm round him when he had cramp? Jesus.
  I stumbled to a back stairway to try and find a private place to go and weep. I had got no further than the first landing when I walked straight into the hairy tweed jacket of Mr Bruce, history master and quondam internee of the Japanese Army.
  'Hello, hello, hello! What's up here?'
  The tears were streaming down my face and it was no good pretending it was hayfever. Racked with sobs, I explained about Halford's cramp and the disgust I had apparently caused him when just trying to be helpful. I did not, of course, mention our night-time prowls in the nude, the sheer *hypocrisy* of Halford's reaction, the unfairness and injustice and cruelty of which was what had really knocked me for six. Mr Bruce nodded gravely, gave me a handkerchief and disappeared.

I crawled my way on up to a bed and lay there weeping until tea, when I decided that I might as well get used to my unpopularity and face the howling mob in the senior refectory.

As I tried to wedge myself into my place on the bench, an artificially huge gap appeared as the boys either side made a huge show of distancing themselves from the disgusting homo who was polluting their table. Pale but resolute I started to eat my tea.

Halfway through the meal a gong sounded. Everybody looked up in surprise.

Mr Bruce was standing at the end of the room, an arm upraised for silence.

'Boys,' he said. 'I have a special announcement to make. I have just heard of a heroic act of kindness that took place by the swimming-pool this afternoon. It seems that Halford got into difficulties with cramp and that Fry helped him to his feet and did exactly the right thing. He walked him about, supporting him carefully all the way. I am awarding Fry five merits for this sensible, cool action.'

I stared down at my plate, unable to move a single muscle.

'Oh, by the way,' continued Bruce, as if the thought had just struck him. 'It has also come to my ears that some of the younger, sillier boys, who are ignorant about such things, think that someone putting their arm around a friend in distress is a sign of some sort of perversion. I look to you senior boys, who have a rather more sophisticated understanding of sexual matters, to quash this sort of puerile nonsense. I hope, incidentally, that Halford has thanked Fry properly for his promptness and consideration. I should think a hearty handshake and good manly bear-hug would be appropriate. That's all.'

A squeak of brogues on floorboards and he was gone. After one and a half seconds of unbearable silence, palms began to rain down congratulatory thumps upon my back, Halford rose sheepishly from his bench to thank me and I was in favour once more.

Ant Cromie writes me that Jim Bruce died a couple of years ago, God rest, nourish and soothe his immortal soul. He walks

now with Montrose, William Wallace and Bonnie Prince
Charlie himself. He saved my last term at Stouts Hill and I will
honour his memory for ever.

But does that, or does that not tell you something of the
psychological minefield one trod through in those days, when
it came to questions of sexual nature, of *sexuality*, as we would
say now? The difference between sexual play and *queering*; the
blind terror that physical affection inspired, but the easy
acceptance of erotic games.

At Uppingham, much the same views obtained. Those
whose morning prongers one brushed as Morning Fag did not
think of themselves or of me as queer in any way at all. I am not
sure anyone really knew what queer really, *really* meant. The
very idea of it made everyone so afraid that each created their
own meaning, according to their own dread of their own
impulses.

You could openly admire a pretty boy, and all the middle
and senior boys did. It was a sign of manliness indeed to do so.

'Just ten minutes alone, me and that arse . . .' a sixth former
might say as a cute junior walked past. 'That's all I ask,' he
would add looking skywards in prayer.

'Oh no!' One senior would clutch another as they caught
sight of a comely new boy, 'I'm in love. Save me from myself.'

I *think* that the logic of it was that new boys, pretty boys,
were the closest approximation Uppingham offered to *girls*.
They were hairless in the right places and sweet and cute and
comely like girls, they had fluffy hair and kissable lips like girls,
they had cute little bottoms like . . . well, they had cute little
bottoms like *boys*, but hell, any port in a storm, and there's no
storm like pubescence and no port like a pretty boy's bum. All
that public swooning however, was no more than macho
posture. It proved their heterosexuality.

Some boys however had the most definite reputation for
being *queer*, in the fully snarled out, spat out sense of the word
as it was then used – before, that is to say, its triumphant
reclamation by the proud homosexuals of today. I never quite
understood how these reputations arose. Perhaps they came
about because the accused had been caught looking furtively at

someone of their own age in the showers – the furtiveness was more likely to earn you the label queer than open, frank inspection – perhaps they gave off some signal, nothing to do with campness or effeminacy, some signal that the *healthy* adolescent male responded to with hostility or guilt or desire. Perhaps it was all a dress-rehearsal for the tribal tom-tomming of irrational rumour, bigotry and dislike, dressed up and explained as instinct, that today in the wider world decides daily on the nature, character and disposition of the well-known: that asserts Bob Monkhouse to be unctuous, David Mellor to be a creep, Peter Mandelson Machiavellian, John Selwyn Gummer odious and John Birt sinister.

I certainly didn't know. My own view is that most homophobia, if one wants to use that rather crummy word, has almost nothing to do with sex.

'But have you any idea what these people actually *do*?'

Self-righteous members of the House of Commons loved standing to ask that question during our last parliamentary debate on the age of homosexual consent.

'Shit-stickers, that's what they are. Let's be clear about that. We're talking about sodomy here.'

Oh no you aren't. You *think* you are, but you aren't, you know.

Buggery is far less prevalent in the gay world than people suppose. Anal sex is probably not much more common in homosexual encounters than it is in heterosexual.

Buggery is not at the end of the yellow brick road somewhere over the homosexual rainbow, it is not the prize, the purpose, the goal or the fulfilment of homosexuality. Buggery is not the achievement which sees homosexuality move from becoming into being; buggery is not homosexuality's realisation or destiny. Buggery is as much a necessary condition of homosexuality as the ownership of a Volvo estate car is a necessary condition of middle-class family life, linked irretrievably only in the minds of the witless and the cheap. The performance of buggery is no more inevitable a part of homosexuality than an orange syllabub is an inevitable part of a dinner: some may clamour for it and instantly demand a second helping, some are not interested, some decide they will try it once and then instantly vomit.

There are plenty of other things to be got up to in the homosexual world outside the orbit of the anal ring, but the concept that really gets the goat of the gay-hater, the idea that really spins their melon and sickens their stomach is that most terrible and terrifying of all human notions, love.

That one can love another of the same gender, that is what the homophobe really cannot stand. Love in all eight tones and all five semitones of the word's full octave. Love as agape, Eros and philos; love as romance, friendship and adoration; love as infatuation, obsession and lust; love as torture, euphoria, ecstasy and oblivion (this is beginning to read like a Calvin Klein perfume catalogue); love as need, passion and desire.

All the rest of it, parking your dick up an arse, slurping at a helmet, whipping, frotting, peeing, pooing, squatting like a dog, dressing up in plastic and leather – all these go on in the world of boy and girl too: and let's be clear about this, they go on *more* – the numbers make it so. Go into a sex shop, skim through some pornography, browse the Internet for a time, talk to someone in the sex industry. You think homosexuality is disgusting? Then, it follows, it follows as the night the day, that you find *sex* disgusting, for there is nothing done between two men or two women that is, by any objective standard, different from that which is done between a man and a woman.

What is more, one begs to ask of these Tony Marlowes and Peregrine Worsthornes and Paul Johnsons, have the guts to Enquire Within. Ask yourselves what thoughts go through *your* head when you masturbate. If the physical act and its detail is so much more important to you than love, then see a doctor, but don't spew out your sickness in column-inches, it isn't nice, it isn't kind, it isn't Christian.

And if the best you can do is quote the Bible in defence of your prejudice, then have the humility to be consistent. The same book that exhorts against the abomination of one man lying with another also contains exhortations against the eating of pork and shell-fish and against menstruating women daring to come near holy places. It's no good functionalistically claiming that kosher diet had its local, meteorological purposes now defunct, or that the prejudice against ovulation can be dispensed with as superstition, the Bible that you bash us with tells you that much of what *you* do is unclean: don't pick and choose with a Revealed Text – or if you do, pick and choose the good bits, the bits that say things like 'Let he who is without sin cast the first stone', or 'Love thy neighbour as thyself'.

And please, whatever you do, don't tell us that what we do, either in love or lust, is *unnatural*. For one thing if what you mean by that is that *animals* don't do it, then you are quite simply in factual error.

There are plenty of activities or qualities we could list that are most certainly unnatural if you are so mad as to think that humans are not part of nature, or so dull-witted as to believe that 'natural' means 'all natures but human nature': mercy, for example, is unnatural, an altruistic, non-selfish care and love for other species is unnatural; charity is unnatural, justice is unnatural, virtue is unnatural, indeed – and this surely is the point – the *idea* of virtue is unnatural, within such a foolish, useless meaning of the word 'natural'. Animals, poor things, eat in order to survive: we, lucky things, do that too, but we also have Abbey Crunch biscuits, Armagnac, *selle d'agneau*, tortilla chips, *sauce béarnaise*, Vimto, hot buttered crumpets, Chateau Margaux, ginger-snaps, *risotto nero* and peanut-butter sandwiches – these things have nothing to do with survival and everything to do with pleasure, connoisseurship and plain old greed. Animals, poor things, copulate in order to reproduce: we, lucky things, do that too, but we also have kinky boots, wank-mags, leather thongs, peep-shows, statuettes by Degas, bedshows, Tom of Finland, escort agencies and the Journals of Anaïs Nin – these things have nothing to do with reproduction and everything to do with pleasure, connoisseurship and plain old lust. We humans have opened up a wide choice of literal and metaphorical *haute cuisine* and junk food in many areas of our lives, and as a punishment, for daring to eat the fruit of every tree in the garden, we were expelled from the Eden the animals still inhabit and we were sent away with the two great Jewish afflictions to bear as our penance: indigestion and guilt.

I will apologise for many things that I have done, but I will not apologise for the things that should never be apologised for. It is a little theory of mine that has much exercised my mind lately, that most of the problems of this silly and delightful world derive from our apologising for those things which we ought not to apologise for, and failing to apologise for those things for which apology is necessary.

For example none of the following is shameful or deserves apology, in spite of our suicidal attempts to convince ourselves otherwise:

- To possess a rectum, a urethra and a bladder and all that pertain thereto.
- To cry.
- To find anything or anyone of any gender, age or species sexually attractive.
- To find anything or anyone of any gender, age or species sexually unattractive.
- To insert things in one's mouth, anus or vagina for the purpose of pleasure.
- To masturbate as often as one wishes. Or not.
- To swear.
- To be filled with sexual desires that involve objects, articles or parts of the body irrelevant to procreation.
- To fart.
- To be sexually unattractive.
- To love.
- To ingest legal or illegal drugs.
- To smell of oneself and one's juices.
- To pick one's nose.

I spend a lot of time tying knots in my handkerchief reminding myself that those are things not be ashamed of, so long as they are not performed in sight or sound of those who would be pained – which also holds true of Morris dancing, talking about Terry Pratchett and wearing velour and many other harmless human activities. Politeness is all.

But, I fear I spend far too little time apologising for or feeling ashamed about things which really do merit sincere apology and outright contrition.

- Failing to imagine what it is like to be someone else.
- Pissing my life away.
- Dishonesty with self and others.
- Neglecting to pick up the phone or write letters.
- Not connecting made or processed objects with their provenance.
- Judging without facts.
- Using influence over others for my own ends.
- Causing pain.

I will apologise for faithlessness, neglect, deceit, cruelty, unkindness, vanity and meanness, but I will *not* apologise for the urgings of my genitals nor, most certainly, will I ever apologise for the urgings of my heart. I may *regret* those urgings, rue them deeply and occasionally damn, blast and wish them to hell, but apologise – no: not where they do no harm. A culture that demands people apologise for something that is not their fault: that is as good a definition of a tyranny as I can think of. We British are not, praise the Lord, in Stalinist Russia, Nazi Germany or Baptist Alabama, but that does not mean, and has never meant, that we must therefore reside in the fields of Elysium.

Bloody hell, I do rattle on, don't I? Doth the lady, once again, protest too much? I don't think so. And if I am protesting, it is not on my own behalf, but on the behalf of my fourteen-year-old self and its confusion.

I knew then, *knew* I was queer. I had no idea, no idea at all, what anybody else meant by the word: all that inconsistency, that subtle coding that allowed one both to leer at pretty boys' bottoms and to sneer at faggots, it confused me and it rattled me, but it never stopped me knowing. I knew I was queer for all kinds of reasons. I knew because I just plain knew, and I knew for that negative reason which is so easy to demonstrate to oneself: my loins never twitched at female bodies or the thought of them, there is simply no escaping such a primitive ineluctable fact and its implications. I knew that I could like and love women as friends, because since childhood I had always found the company of women and girls welcome and easy, but I knew just as strongly that I would never be aroused or excited at the thought of any physical intimacy with a girl, that I would never yearn to share my life with a female.

There was physical evidence of women at Uppingham only in the two-dimensional shape of the copies of *Forum* and *Penthouse* that were self-consciously passed around from boy to boy like joints at a teenage party, or in the three-dimensional shape of the kitchen-staff and the girls one saw in the town.

Lest anyone think such an atmosphere is enough to make any child homosexual, I should say that most of the boys in the same situation as me (my brother included, whose home life, let's face it, was identical to mine) lived, breathed, ate and drank girls. One boy whom I have already described to you, but whose blushes I shall spare, was in fact expelled for a sexual liaison with one of the kitchen girls. He could no more have been made homosexual by his time at Uppingham than I could have been made straight by a stint at Holland Park Comprehensive or Cheltenham Ladies' College. I think it is certainly true that our circumstances made it very difficult for some of the boys around me to *cope* with girls, but then you see I believe that all boys find it very difficult to cope with girls, and none of my straight friends who went to mixed state schools has ever told me anything different. I operate a sympathetic and comprehensive listening service for many friends in relationship difficulties (as they do for me when I'm brave enough to let them) and from all I have ever heard (or read in the autobiographies of others) sex is every bit as difficult, awkward, embarrassing and heart-rending for the straight as for the bent.

But knowing I was homosexual was one thing, disentangling its meaning (both its perceived cultural meaning and the real meaning it was to have to me) was very difficult. I was, as I have said, not yet masturbating, I had no definable physical or sexual appetites to assuage. All I had was a void, an ache, a hunger, a hiatus, a lacuna, a gap, a *need.* There's pleonasm for you . . .

I remember being at the bedside of a boy at prep school, playing with his (as it seemed to me at the time) colossal and strainingly hard penis. I stared at this phenomenon and – I can recall this scene so exactly in my mind in its every detail – I thought to myself: What now? I know this is fun, this has meaning, this is part of something big, but what now? Do I *eat* it? Do I kiss it? Do I try and merge with it, become one with it? Do I cut it off and take it back to my own bed? Do I try and stuff it into my ear? What is this supposed to lead to? I don't find this cock attractive or pretty, in fact it's frankly rather ugly, but I do know this it is *part of something* that matters.

For all my foregoing rant at those who believe homosexuality is simply about buggery, I should make it clear that I was not asserting that homosexuality has *nothing* to do with sex, I was merely trying to suggest that the sexual element is not what threatens and unhinges the homophobe.

Does homosexuality involve sex? Oh dear me yes, homosexuality involves sex. It involves sexual appeal, stimulation, excitement, arousal and ultimately, of course, orgasm. There can't be any doubt about that. There is love too and love is bigger than anything else in the world as you know, but that doesn't mean sex isn't in there too, doing its best to simplify things. If only it were *only* about sex . . . how simple and jolly homosexuality would be, how simple and jolly *heterosexuality* would be. Still, at least we get Shakespeare and Tolstoy and Beethoven and Cole Porter as a reward for all the pain and heartache.

I had been there then, at the bedside, worshipping at the throne of the cockhead as it were, knowing that this was something that was always going to have meaning for me. But it was *disconnected*, it was just a great gristly fat thing – all the poor lad wanted was for me to finish him off so that he could get to sleep of course, he had no interest at all in my psychic or romantic destiny – but for me this thing in my hands was at once a potent symbol of something that mattered *and* just a dick belonging to another boy, nothing more; the very disconnectedness of this dick, coupled with its swollen urgency and such a perplexed presentiment in me of the

momentous weight and meaning such scenes as this were to
have in my life, made the whole experience, and the dick itself,
highly absurd, highly comic and very slightly frightening.

So I giggled.

4

The beginning of my second year at Uppingham saw me no
more clued up about this whole business of sex than I ever had
been: I probably had a clearer idea of the terms and their
meanings: cunnilingus, urinobibe, Fallopian tubes, epi-
didymus, snatch, pussy, tit, jizz and clit, I knew the words all
right. But then I knew what a diminished seventh was, but it
didn't mean I could play or sing. I knew what a googly was and
I still couldn't bowl a cricket ball without causing twenty-one
boys to collapse in a heap of laughter. Knowledge is not always
power.

The erotic in life did not occupy me or engage my attention
much because I was still neither physically developed nor
sexually aware enough to have that need to 'get my bloody
rocks off' that seemed so to exercise the other boys, passing
their *Penthouses*, sniggers, phwors and Kleenex boxes from
study to study. Games and how to avoid them, that was still
what mattered most to me. Sweets and where to get them from,
that too. Sex, that could take a powder.

And then . . .

And then I saw *him* and nothing was ever the same again.

The sky was never the same colour, the moon never the same
shape: the air never smelt the same, food never tasted the same.
Every word I knew changed its meaning, everything that once
was stable and firm became as insubstantial as a puff of wind, and
every puff of wind became a solid thing I could feel and touch.

This is where language is so far behind music. The chord that
Max Steiner brings in when Bogart catches sight of Bergman in
his bar in *Casablanca*, how can I bring that into a book of black
ink marks on white paper? The swell and surge of the
Liebestod from Tristan, Liszt's Sonata in B minor – even
Alfred Brendel can't conjure that up from *this* keyboard, this
alphanumeric piano beneath my fingers. Maybe, because
sometimes pop music can hit the mark as well as anything, I
could write you out a playlist. We would start with the
Monkees:

And then I saw her face, and now I'm a believer

Naaah . . . it's no use.

There's nothing for it but old words and cold print. Besides,
you've been there yourself. You've been in love. Why am I
getting so hysterical? Just about every film, every book, every
poem, every song is a love story. This is not a genre with which
you are unfamiliar even if by some fluke (whether a cursed
fluke or a blessed one I would be the last to able to decide) you
have never been there yourself.

It was the first morning of the winter term, the beginning of
my second year at Uppingham. After breakfast, as was usual, I
went to my study, now newly shared with Jo Wood, and
collected the textbooks and blocks I would need for the
morning's teaching. A block was a pad of paper, special
Uppingham-sized paper, shorter and squarer than A4, which
could only be bought from the official school bookshop:
essays, notes and everything else had to be written on paper
from a block.

The routine at a school with boarding-houses goes like this,
you see. The Morning Fag awakens you. You breakfast in your
House, you walk into school for chapel and morning lessons
and you don't return to the House until lunchtime. All the
form-rooms, science labs and sports halls, the Chapel, Hall and
Library, they are grouped around the main school. Ekker
(eugh!), then back to the House for showers (don't get me

started . . .) followed by afternoon lessons in school and another (sometimes the last of the day) return to the House for supper. After supper there's a little free time before a bell will go, summoning you, if you are a junior, to hall where you do your prep (which means homework), supervised and kept silent by the praepostor on duty. If you're a senior, your prep is done in the privacy of your study. Then there's some more free time in which, unless through some infraction of the rules you've been gated (no doubt they now use the Americanism 'grounded', as in 'your ass is grounded, Mister'), you can go down to the Art School or the Thring Centre (named after the side-whiskers and containing electric typewriters, design studios, pottery shops and so forth: it has since been replaced by a splendid complex called, rather wetly in my opinion, The Leonardo Centre, designed by Old Uppinghamian architect Piers Gough and containing a TV studio, computers and all manner of larky toys) or you can see a play, listen to a concert, attend a lecture, go to play rehearsals, turn up for choir practice, or band practice or orchestra practice, or a meeting of the chess club, bridge club, judo club, poetry reading group, entomological society or whatever gathering of like minds suits your taste. Then it's back to the House in time for evening prayers, which are taken by the housemaster or the House Tutor, a master who hasn't got his own House yet and acts as a sort of locum to the housemaster proper from time to time. Then, essentially, it's cocoa, buns, biscuits and bed – the whole cycle to repeat itself the following day. On Saturdays, evening prayers take the form of a more informal compline. On Sundays, there are no games and no lessons, just two compulsory hours in your study that go under the strange name of Sunday Qs, short for Sunday Questions and designed, no doubt, to inculcate religiosity, healthiness and inward spiritual cleanliness. Dotted throughout the day in House there is a series of call-overs, what they called _appel_ in prisoner-of-war films. A list of all the boys in order of seniority downwards will be read out by the House-captain, and each boy has to call 'Here' at the sound of his name. One thinks of Rowan Atkinson's inspired Schoolmaster sketch, or that creepy play by Giles Cooper which was turned into a film with David Hemmings, the title of which came from the last three names of the roll . . . *Unman, Wittering and Zigo.*

There. If you require any more information and believe in Buddhism, I suggest you live your life wickedly and get reborn as a middle-class English boy in the mid-1950s: you'll get the experience firsthand.

So, back to Day Two, Term Four.

I had stuffed what I needed for morning lessons into my briefcase and Jo Wood and I walked together out of our study and down the corridor that led to the path that led to the road that led to School.

Four Houses were up at our end of town, Brooklands and Highfield were two. Brooklands was further away from the centre of Uppingham, so far away indeed, that it had its own swimming-pool. Opposite my House, Fircroft, was the Middle, that huge playing field I told you about, and perched next to it was Highfield, so named because it was on top of a hill and by a field. The fourth House was a little further down the hill, towards the town and school, and we will call this House Redwood's.

Redwood's doesn't exist.

There is no House between Highfields and the bottom of the hill.

I want nothing I write in this book to cause anyone needless pain, shame or embarrassment. Everything I write will be true according to the light of my own memory, but the truth will be told with tact and with due recognition of fiction's often greater capacity to convey reality than can any bald recitation of fact. Some names and the setting, styling and structure of some scenes must be fictionalised. I do not believe you will always be able to tell *which* scenes and *which* settings, nor would I want you to try. You have stayed with me thus far and must trust me when I say that although there is rearrangement, there is no exaggeration or sensationalisation. If anything the contrary might be the case, for certain scenes and events of my school life, however heavily disguised, would enable any school contemporary of mine instantly to ascribe names and identities, and that would be grossly unfair. Two people, if they read this book, will recognise themselves but see that they have been well enough disguised for no one else to know but themselves who they really are.

Enough already, Stephen – cut to the chase.

It is a clear mid-September day, the kind of day that contains in exactly equal proportion a mix of summer and of autumn, the leaves are not yet in their October reds, golds and yellows, but their greenness is becoming just a little shagged by now, not as brightly, squeakily sappily green as it was in midsummer. To make up for it the light has lost its August haze and has a great softness, the rotten marshy smells of late summer have been dispelled too and there is a nutty, barky freshness in the air.

Naturally, academic hours are the same throughout the whole school, so as we Fircroftians walk out on to the road, we join a stream of Brooklanders walking towards school, and a crowd of boys from Highfield cross the road towards us, for there is no pavement on their side; as we move down the hill, boys from Redwood's will cross over too, so that the observer looking down the dip of the London road from the centre of Uppingham at the right time will see a third of the school swarming towards him, two hundred boys dressed in identical black jackets, black trousers, black ties, black waistcoats, black shoes and white shirts, lugging their briefcases and if, poor sods they are slated for PE that morning, their duffle bags as well. Pollies will bicycle alongside whistling or twang-humming Claptonian guitar-licks, their boaters tipped at what they hope is an angle that says, 'Boaters are fucking square, man. I wear mine, like *ironically* . . . ' Yes, but you still wear it. You don't *have* to, you know.

I once got out my old Stouts Hill boater and wore it to school. This *enraged* a School Pig I encountered on the way.

'And just what the fuck do you think you're doing wearing a boater?'

'But this isn't a boater, Merrick, it's a sun-hat. I am highly susceptible to excess heat.'

'You'll be highly susceptible to a kick up the arse if you don't take it off.'

This morning though, I'm thinking of nothing in particular. Still settling back into the rhythm and enjoying the fact that there is a whole crop of new boys who are now the lowest of the low. Indeed, I have to train one of them for the fag test.

I will be taking my O levels this year. Fourteen seems a young age for them, but in those days, if they reckoned you could do them, you did them. I would take my A levels two years later and leave school at sixteen, then university at seventeen, that was my future, all charted out before me. That was how things were done then. If they felt you needed an extra year to cope with O levels, you were put into a form called the Remove. At prep school there had been a Remove and a Shell. I had been in Shell and I never understood quite what it meant.

I know, I'll look it up in the OED.

Well, bless my soul. Does one live and learn, or what?

15. The apsidal end of the school-room at Westminster School, so called from its conch-like shape. Hence, the name of the form (intermediate between the fifth and sixth) which originally tenanted the shell at Westminster School, and transf. **of forms (intermediate between forms designated by numbers) in other public schools; see quots.**
1736 *Gentl. Mag.* VI. 679/2 Near these [forms] ye shell's high concave walls appear.
1750 Chesterfield *Lett.* ccxxviii, Observe . . what the best scholars in the Form immediately above you do, and so on, till you get into the shell yourself.
1825 Southey *Life & Corr.* (1849) I. 151 He was floated up to the Shell, beyond which the tide carried no one.
1857 Hughes *Tom Brown* i. v, The lower fifth, shell, and all the junior forms in order [at Rugby].
1877 W. P. Lennox *Celebr. I have known* I. 43 The noise grew louder and louder, until the birch was safely deposited in a small room behind the shell,

as the upper end of the room was called from its
shape [Westminster].
1884 <u>Forshall</u> *Westm. Sch.* 3 The Headmaster faced
all the boys excepting the tenants of the Shell.
1903 *Blackw. Mag.* June 742/2 The third shell, a
form within measurable distance of the lowest in
the school [Harrow].

Well, there you go then.

There was no shell at Uppingham so far as I remember.

Actually, I am feeling rather pleased with myself as I walk
along with Jo Wood this morning because the new form I have
been put in this year is Upper IVA. This is more luck than a
reflection of any academic brilliance from me during my first
year: the school alternated annually between awarding the A
status to the top English set and the top Maths set – all part of
that good all-round chap 'philosophy'. This year it is the turn
of English, so I find myself in Upper IVA and all the brilliant
mathematicians have to put up with the indignity of being
grouped in Upper IVB.

You can be in the top form of your year, but be in lower sets
according to subject. So I was in the top sets for English,
History, French, Latin and so on, but in the bottom for
Physics, Maths and Chemistry. Geography I had given up in
favour of German.

My form-master and English teacher I find to be an excellently civilised man called J. B. Stokes, housemaster of
Meadhurst, given to a most peculiar use of what, if I have parsed
this correctly, is an imperative interrogative form of a future
conditional tense. In other words instead of saying 'Shut up' he
would say, 'You'll be shutting up?', 'You'll be sitting down?'

It is too early in the season to shuffle leaves along the
pavement as we walk down the hill, but Jo and I have our heads
bowed down towards the pavement none the less. As a child
one gets to know every crack in every paving stone on every
section of one's walk to school. Are we looking down because
we don't want to see or because we don't want to be seen?

I don't know what it is that makes me look up. A vague
awareness I suppose that the boys from Redwood's opposite

are crossing the road from their House to join the pavement, a little good-natured jostling might result, and the thick black line of boys will have swollen to its maximum size before the left turn, up the Chocolate Block, along the Magic Carpet and towards the Chapel, whose bell even now is ringing us to morning prayers.

His head isn't even turned towards me but I know.

How is that possible? How can it be that just the gait of him, the stand of him, the shape and turn away of him, can be enough for me to know and to know at once?

Looking at it coolly one can say that anyone might be drawn to such a fine head of fair hair, seen from behind. One might say that anyone could see that this was a classy, peachy and supreme pair of buttocks confronting us.

One might add too, in cynical tones, 'You say "you knew", but just suppose he had turned his head and revealed the face of a pig with a harelip, a twisted nose and a squint, would you now be writing this?'

Did I *really*, really *know*?

Yes, reader, I did. I swear I did.

The moment I lifted my head from the pavement and glanced across the road I saw, amongst the Redwood's boys crossing, one of their number looking the other way, as if to check that there was no traffic coming. And *at that moment*, before his face came into view, it happened. The world changed.

If he had turned out to be ugly, I think my heart would have sunk, but still the world would have been different, because that thing that stirred and roared in me would have been awakened anyway and nothing could ever have put it back to sleep.

As it is, he was not ugly.

He was the most beautiful thing I had ever seen in my life.

I stopped dead so suddenly that a boy behind walked straight into me.

'Watch where you're going, you dozy tosser . . .'

'Sorry.'

Jo turned patiently and gave me the sour, constipated look that was peculiarly his own and had caused his nickname to be 'Woodeeeeee' pronounced in the tones of one who groans on the lavatory, clutching the seat as he strains violently to disgorge a turd the size of Manchester.

'What have you forgotten?' he said.

He must have assumed that I had stopped because I had suddenly realised that I had left a vital textbook behind in the study. I knew from the heat in my cheeks that my face had turned the fieriest red imaginable. I somehow found the presence of mind to mumble, 'Laces,' and stoop to fiddle with my shoes. When I stood, the redness in my face, I hoped, might seem to be the result of my head having hung upside-down while I was lacing, a strategy that every human being uses to cover a blush and which fools no one.

I was up quickly though and immediately I started to walk forwards. I *had* to see that face again.

He had just reached the pavement and gave now the smallest, quickest of glances back up the hill, in our direction. Our eyes didn't meet, but I saw that he was even more beautiful than I had supposed. Even more beautiful than I had ever imagined it was possible to imagine imagining beauty. Beautiful in a way that made me realise that I had never even known before what beautiful really meant: not in people, nature, taste or sound.

There are many in Norfolk for whom 'big city' means Norwich.

'I been to Norwich once and I didn't like it,' they say. 'Swaffham's big enough for me.' They can only guess at what London, Los Angeles or Manhattan might be like.

I realised at this moment that I had only ever experienced the townships of 'charming', 'pretty', 'attractive', 'comely', 'sweet', 'delicious', 'handsome' and 'cute' and now I had finally penetrated the city limits of Beautiful. I was instantly aware of Beauty and the whole Greek and Keatsian fuss about it made sense.

Just as when an artist shows you a new view of something –

as Matisse for example might show you a quality in an apple that you had never noticed before and from then on you are able to see that same quality in every apple you encounter – so I would from this second onwards be able forever to see beauty, real beauty, in familiar things all around me. Before this moment I may have thought a particular sunrise or hillside was stunning or attractive but after this moment I would be able to see beauty there. Absolute beauty.

'What the fuck is going on?' said Jo, panting to keep up with me as I strode forwards.

This apparition was now perhaps three ranks forward of me. I could see that he was shorter than average. He wore the same uniform as everyone else, but it was transformed, as even the air around him was transformed.

'Don't want to be late, do we?' I said.

'You're off your fucking trolley,' grunted Jo.

If I could just hear the *voice*, maybe draw alongside and steal a look at the profile . . .

Then I saw Maudsley just ahead of me, a Fircroft sixth former and a rugger colour, nudge his neighbour and I heard him say in a voice too loud to be borne.

'D'you see that one, then? Fer-uck *me*! Herwow!' He shook his right hand backwards and forwards as if it had just been burned. 'I mean get the *buns* on it . . .'

My heart sank and the blood hammered in my ears.

'*Now* what?' Jo was as patient as a man can get, but even he had limits. I had almost stopped again.

'Nothing, sorry . . . nothing. Sorry, I just . . . nothing.'

It was unbearable, *unbearable* to think of a great ape like Maudsley even so much as *looking*. I knew at once, in an instant churn of misery that there would be others, others smitten by this thing, this vision, this impossibility. They would be cruder, they would be more obvious, their motives would be baser and, of course, of *double-course* they would be more attractive. They would be so much more attractive, so much more co-ordinated, so much more graceful, so much more seductive in their status and appeal. They would take my holy flame and extinguish it with thick thudding yellow wads of filthy spunk, snuff it to a hissing nothing in a hairy slimeball of lust. It was too terrible. They were looking at Sex. I knew they were, while I – I was looking at Beauty.

'Now calm down, Stephen,' you are saying. 'We know you're a poof. We know too, because let's face it you've rubbed our bloody noses in it enough times, that you don't deny sex, or the sex-drive in you. Don't kid us that this 'holy flame' of yours was some kind of pure abstracted love with no erotic overtones.'

I am telling you the feelings that ran through me and, painfully predictable and mimsy and effete and bloodless as they may seem, those *were* my feelings, arrived at in my head in less time than it takes for light to travel a yard. But I tell you another thing too with my hand on my heart and my fingers uncrossed. Although I was to develop, like every male, into an enthusiastic, ardent and committed masturbator, *he* was never once, nor ever has been, the subject of a masturbatory fantasy. Many times I *tried* to cast him in some scene I was directing for the erotic XXXX cinema in my head, but it always happened that some part of me banished him from the set, or else the very sight of him on screen in the coarse porn flick running in my mind had the effect of a gallon of cold water. Sex *was* to enter our lives, but he was never wank fodder, never.

Jo Wood, a man of instinct and sense, knew that something was wrong and knew that it was something inward and strange, so he didn't call me on the oddity of my behaviour as we walked along, boys now four deep between me and the revelation.

We swarmed left and along the Chocolate Block, up the steps – I could see a grace in the upstride of his right leg that was entirely new to me, and I saw too Maudsley once more nudging his neighbour and heard the Kenneth Connor, under-the-breath 'Phwoo-oo-oor . . .' that accompanied the nudge. We passed the old Victorian study block to our right and the library to our left and filed along the shining cobbles of the Magic Carpet that wound like a brown river through a field of dirty-pink asphalt until it reached the colonnade. The chapel bell tolled louder and louder in my head until I thought it might explode.

I *had* to see where he would leave his briefcase. That much I had to see.

The main entrance to the chapel was like a sort of miniature of the Lincoln Memorial in Washington DC: Edward Thring sat sternly in a stern throne, his monstrous paternalist whiskers sternly set in white marble, not a boy that walked by him but the Reverend Edward stared through his soul and despised what he saw. We passed that entrance and headed for the colonnade. The colonnade was open on two sides and, on its two closed sides, notices, posters and announcements fluttered from green baize, attached by brass drawing pins. Headman's noticeboard was first, white gnomic memoranda, then came others, Gestetnered Roneo-ed or hand-written, with their announcements of Corps Field Days ('the u/mentioned will muster at 1525 hrs ...') special matches of 'Second Fifteen Possibles v. Third Fifteen Probables' (per-lease ...), calls for volunteers to join a new Speleological Club that was being founded, 'Apply Andrews, J. G. (M)' and other such dribbling toss that Fry, S. J. (F) found insupportably dull. The purpose of the colonnade that day, so far as I was concerned, was to leave my briefcase there before entering chapel and to see where *he* left *his*.

It was a remarkable sight, on those days when one was late for chapel, to see the colonnade empty of humans, but with six hundred briefcases and a hundred duffle bags dumped at the feet of its columns or leaning against the base of its inner walls.

You could *tell* he was a new boy. Just the way he checked others to see how they left their briefcases, as a shy girl at a disco might check how the other girls are dancing. He found a spot to leave his, brand new it was and of deep tan leather. I suddenly hated mine, which was black. I had thought black was cool, but now I knew I had to get a brown briefcase. I would make a point of wanting one for Christmas.

'But darling, yours is almost brand new! And it cost the *earth*!'

I'd cross that bridge when I came to it. For the moment, I

must put my hideous black next to his glorious tan. Some
boys had their initials classily branded into the leather or
trashily attached with gold stick-on letters. He was standing
by his as I approached, but facing the other way and scanning
the crowd of boys approaching from other directions. Good
God, would he always face the other way? I plonked my
briefcase down by his with a loud but cheerful sigh, a sigh
that seemed to say, 'Heigh ho. Here we go. Another term.
Tch! Blimey!'

He turned.

He turned towards *me*.

'Excuse me . . .'

A voice that . . . it was unbroken, but it had a huskiness to it
that stopped it from piping in a childish squeak. If he sang, he
would sing alto.

'Help at all?' I found myself saying in the most cheerful,
friendly, charming, relaxed and relaxing way those words have
ever been said.

And for the first time I looked into his eyes. They were blue,
not light blue, but a darker blue. Not so dark as sapphire blue,
not so bright as china blue. They were romantically blue.
Lyrically blue. They swam and I swam in them.

'I was wondering . . .' he said, 'which is West Block?'

This was, of course, his first day. His first day, and the first
day of my life too.

'Look behind you,' I said, finding time to marvel at the calm
in my voice and the strength and the confidence that it carried.
'Think Colditz. Think Lubyanka. Behold, West Block. Got a
lesson there have you? First after chapel?'

I watched how the hair at the back of his head fell and, as it
stopped before reaching the collar, how it turned fractionally
inwards and upwards in a way that made me think for an
instant of a medieval boy king. Under it, a vee of lighter hairs
herring-boned up the hollow of his nape.

'Oh Christ help me,' I croaked inwardly. 'Christ Jesus help
me.'

He turned back and looked up at me once more. Yes, he was
shorter than average, shorter, but not *delicate*. 'And that's the

door you go in, is it?' Such a delicious caramel huskiness rising from the throat.

Let me not faint, I pleaded. Following the direction in which he pointed I nodded. Simply the act of his raising his arm caused something trapped within me to leap and pummel against the inside of my chest and beg to be let out.

'Who've you got?' I asked.

'Finch. *J. S.* Finch, is it?'

'Aiee! French or German?'

'French.'

'Ah, I have him for German. Good luck, that's all I can say . . .'

'What's he like?' I followed across his eyes the passage of a small cloud of doubt or fear and noted with joyness of joy that a smile from me at once dispelled it.

'Naa, he's okay. He shouts and he screams and he swears, but he's okay. You're in Redwood's aren't you?'

'How do you know that?' *Almost* a hint of pertness in the speed and directness of the question. New boys would usually stutter with ers and ums and excuse me's when asking something of an elder. But I liked this freshness. It fell short of cheek. It was just . . . direct. One human being to another. He wanted to know how I knew, and so he asked.

I jerked my head in the direction of his duffle bag whose regulation navy blue was piped in a dusty, crushed-strawberry red. 'Your House colours tell the story,' I said and, shifting my gaze further along, added, 'see that one? Yellow piping. That's Fircroft and that's – '

A juddering thump on my back. 'Fry, you spawn of Satan, do you realise we're in the same Latin set?'

Gunn, from School House: fancied himself an intellectual and a wit. I despised him in that cordial way people will hate those who are too like themselves for comfort.

'But I thought I was in the *top* Latin set!' I exclaimed in mock horror. 'How come I've been demoted to the derr-brains?'

Shit! *He* will hear that stupid insult and know it for what it is. He will think me arrogant. I half turned, but he had gone. I turned fully round, in time to see the last of him rounding the corner towards the rear entrance to the Chapel.

'In love are we? Where the hell did *that* pop up from?'

'Who?'

'Oh Jesus, Fry,' said Gunn grinning with hideous superiority. 'For such a good liar, you're a terrible liar.'

In chapel, the boys sat in blocks arranged according to their House. Each term the Houses would move their position within the chapel. Fircroft this term were sitting near the back and Redwood's were way up at the front. I found a place between Jo and Richard Fawcett and scanned the backs of heads until I found *his*. He sat between two boys, one brown-haired the other blond like him. Both were taller. Yet I would have known. If I had seen him for the first time just then, twenty rows ahead, his golden head smaller in my field of view than a sixpenny bit, still I would have known.

But what was his *name*? How was I ever going to find out his name? Suppose his name was somehow *wrong*? Suppose it was an average name like Richard or Simon or Mark or Robert or Nigel? That would be so dull. Suppose he were a Neil or a Kenneth or a Geoffrey, how could I bear that? Suppose, God help him, he were a *Stephen*? I always *hated* my name. Later on I was to be cheered up and resigned to it by James Joyce's use of it for his hero, and by the thought of Stephen Tennant and Stephen Spender, but at the time I thought it a stupid, styleless name, a name that only a *boy* could have and rather an uninteresting boy at that.

Then again he might have an obvious name, the sort of name that would make people giggle and think him a tart. He might be a Rupert or a Julian or a Crispin or a Tim or, Lord save us, a *Miles*, *Giles* or *Piers*.

I thought of names that I could tolerate. Ben would be about all right, as would Charles or Thomas or James or William.

Jonathan? Hm . . . Jonathan would be just about within the bounds. Nathan might be pushing it a bit though. Daniel and Samuel I could cope with and Peter, Christopher and George, but Paul was right out.

Francis was not to be entertained for a second and Frederick was just too silly for words.

Roderick, Alexander or Hugh might pass, if he was Scottish. Donald would be uninteresting, Hamish would be pushing it too far and Ian simply horrid.

David? That would be acceptable, I decided. David I could live with.

There again as Bertie Wooster had pointed out, some pretty rough work is pulled at the font sometimes, maybe his parents had had a rush of blood to the head and chosen Hilary or Vivian or Evelyn? Maybe there was some rich uncle to please and he had found himself baptised Everett, Warwick, Hadleigh or Poynton?

Then there were the Grahams and Normans and Rodneys. Impossible.

Justin, Damian and Tristram. No! A thousand times, no.

But then again, as the sun streamed in through the window and lit his hair, blinding all other boys from sight, it seemed to me that he could transform any name and make it holy, just as he transformed and sanctified his uniform and his briefcase and duffle bag. Even if he were Dennis or Terry or Neville or Keith, somehow those names would rise above the commonplace. He could probably even do something to Gavin.

The service passed in a blur of such speculation and, after we had sung the school hymn reserved for the first mornings of term –

> Rank by rank again we stand
> By the four winds gathered hither

– the whole school developing sudden joyful rhotacisms for the first line so that wank by wank again we stood, I shuffled out with the others in prescribed order and, by the time I reached my briefcase, his was gone, gone to face the perils of Finch and French in West Block. When would I see him again? *How* could I see him again for more than a few fleeting seconds?

Maybe you are not aware how difficult it was for there to be any real social congress between boys of different years in the *same House*. For there to be friendships between boys in *different* Houses . . . well, he might as well have lived on the moon.

I looked towards the West Block and Finch's formroom with a sigh, picked up my horrid, horrid black briefcase and headed for double English.

> As flies to wanton boys are we to the gods;
> They undo us for their sport.

Thus I oh-so wittily misquoted that morning. Stokes was gracious enough to smile, merely pointing out that I had played merry hell with Shakespeare's scansion. I replied tartly that 'to the gods' was bad scansion already, delivering eleven syllables and mucking up an iamb. I offered the opinion that Shakespeare had been too cowardly to write the metrically perfect:

> As *flies* to *wan*ton *boys* are *we* to *God*;
> He *kills* us *for* his *sport*.

– to which Stokes correctly replied that to singularise God, aside from courting disaster from the censor, destroying the pagan atmosphere of the play and the whole line of Gloucester's thought, would also weaken the image by mismatching with the plural 'boys' – or would I have Shakespeare ruin the rhythm again with

> As flies to *a* wanton boy are we to God

– is that what I wanted? Besides, it was perfectly possible for an actor to say 'to the' as if the words had but one syllable.

I conceded that maybe old Shakespeare had known what he was up to after all, and on we moved, leaving me to my thoughts.

Where would he go for morning break? The Upper Buttery or the Lower? Would someone have told him about

Lanchberrys' exceedingly fine cream slices?

I made my way there, scanning every fair-haired head as I went.

Fate can be kind to lovers, in her cruel, careless way. As far as the gods are concerned we are indeed as flies to wanton boys. They put us under a magnifying glass, laugh if the sun focuses its rays through the lens and burns us up with a pop; they stamp on us, squash us, swat us and collect us together in jars to be fed to favoured reptiles.

I saw him moving down the steps towards the entrance to the Lower Buttery. He was talking to a boy from his House. A boy I knew! Nick Osborne was in my German set, a creep I had always thought, but suddenly I decided that he was my best friend.

I forced my way down, not caring whom I pushed aside, not hearing the oaths, not feeling the kicks and thumps that came in riposte.

'Osborne!' I called.

He turned. They *both* turned. 'Oh Fry,' said Osborne. 'My brother,' he added, lazily flapping a hand towards the divinity.

His brother. His *brother*! His-brother-his-brother-his-brother.

'Hello,' I said, with just such a casual but polite air as one might employ when being introduced to the insignificant little brother of any friend. 'Oh,' I went on, 'weren't you the one who had Finch this morning?'

He nodded with a shy smile. He seemed pleased that I could have remembered him out of so many.

'Oh, *Finch*,' said Nick. 'I was telling Matthew not to mind him.'

Matthew then.

Matthew Osborne. Matthew Osborne. M.O. Mine Own, My Only, Miraculous One, Magical Object.

Matthew. Of course it was Matthew, I knew that. What else could it have been? Ridiculous to have speculated on the possibility of any other name. Matthew. It had always been Matthew.

'Anyway,' Nick went on. 'This is the Lower Buttery. We

have to stay this side. Only fifth and sixth formers go behind that screen. See you, Fry,' he threw over his shoulder, leading his brother through the crowd.

Such progress so fast.

Nick Osborne's brother.

Now. Regroup. Think. *Think*, man, think.

What do we like about Nick Osborne?

Not much. He's clever. We concede that. But he's sporty. Very, very, sporty. We don't like sportiness.

What were his hobbies? How was I going to get him to be a friend? I could be as close to Nick as I liked, he was in the same year, besides he was not especially attractive, no one would talk.

Hang on. How could they possibly be *brothers*?

Nick was nearly as tall as me: he had to shave once a week. He was dark-haired, greasy haired. Not ugly, not ugly at all, but surely not of the same parentage?

No, there was *something*, a look, a cast of expression, a slight downward dip of the head when it turned. They both had that. Nick's eyes were blue too, but without any lapis lazuli depths. Just blue eyes.

There was a German lesson that afternoon, I would make sure I sat next to Nick and start to cultivate him.

Back at Fircroft after lunch I went to my study and sat alone to think about things. I was magnificently, triumphantly off games for a least a week with asthma: my doctor at home had come up trumps with an unequivocal note after a bad attack in late August just after my fourteenth birthday.

I took a block from my desk and started to write down what I knew.

He was Matthew. He was Matthew Osborne. He was at Redwood's, like his brother.

Matthew Osborne (R).

I would find out his middle initials later. Osborne, M. J.? No, his brother was Osborne N. C. R., so Matthew would probably have two middle names as well. Osborne, M. P. A.?

Matthew Peter Alexander, for example? It was possible. Osborne, M. St J. G.? Matthew St John George. That was just as possible.

The most important thing to sort out was the *why*.

Why did he do what he did to me? I wrote that down.

And the *what*.

What *was* it that he did to me? I wrote that down too.

And the *how*.

How did he do what he did for me? I started to write that down until I realised it was very nearly a song-lyric. Gerry and The Pacemakers? Freddie and The Dreamers? Something like that. *Not* very dignified. 'How *do* you do what yah do for me . . .' Banal. Won't do, won't do at all. I crossed it out. Crossed it all out, screwed up the paper, ripped it into tiny shreds and started again.

In *The Liar* I compressed the whole thing jokily, like this.

> He had fallen in love with Hugo Alexander Timothy Cartwright the moment he laid eyes on him when, as one of a string of five new arrivals, the boy had trickled into evening hall the first night of Adrian's second year.
>
> Heydon-Bayley nudged him.
>
> 'What do you reckon, Healey? Lush or what?'
>
> For once Adrian had remained silent. Something was terribly wrong.
>
> It had taken him two painful terms to identify the symptoms. He looked them up in all the major textbooks. There was no doubt about it. All the authorities concurred: Shakespeare, Tennyson, Ovid, Keats, Georgette Heyer, Milton, they were of one opinion. It was love. The Big One.
>
> Cartwright of the sapphire eyes and golden hair, Cartwright of the Limbs and Lips: he was Petrarch's Laura, Milton's Lycidas, Catullus's Lesbia, Tennyson's Hallam, Shakespeare's fair boy and dark lady, the moon's Endymion. Cartwright was Garbo's salary, the National Gallery, he was cellophane: he was the tender trap, the blank unholy surprise of it all and the bright golden haze on the meadow: he was honey-honey, sugar-sugar, chirpy chirpy cheep-cheep and his baby-love: the voice of the

turtle could be heard in the land, there were angels dining
at the Ritz and a nightingale sang in Berkeley Square.

Adrian had managed to coax Cartwright into an
amusing half-hour in the House lavs two terms previously,
but he had never doubted he could get the trousers down:
that wasn't it. He wanted something more from him than
the few spasms of pleasure the limited activities of rubbing
and licking and heaving and pushing could offer.

He wasn't sure what the thing was that he yearned for,
but one thing he did know. It was less acceptable to love,
to ache for eternal companionship, than it was to bounce
and slurp and gasp behind the fives courts. Love was
Adrian's guilty secret, sex his public pride.

All very well for me to write that nearly twenty years later, but
even as I was writing it in the year 1990, seven years ago, I felt
a twinge of guilt that I could be so cavalier, so casually
sophisticated and so knowing about my former self and the
acuteness of my feeling and the depth of my confusion.

'It had taken him two painful terms' – well, I suppose those
seven words have the virtues of honesty and brevity. No
pleonasm *there*. There is a hoary old chestnut in the film
business. What is the most expensive stage direction you can
write in the fewest number of words? So far as I know the
winner, which was written into a genuine script, is still this:

The fleets meet.

'Two painful terms' is probably my equivalent in the field of
emotional budgeting.

It took my mind, which is painfully slow when it comes to
the acknowledgement of interior truths or to the achievement
of any self-perception, a long time to realise what I sensed in an
instant.

I was in love. Very well. I could use that word. It had been
translated and I understood it. All those dreary romantic plots
made sense now. Those interminable screen looks between
men and women shot in soft focus to the accompaniment of
high strings, they had a meaning. That I could grasp.

So I wrote it down that first afternoon.

I love Matthew Osborne

I instinctively knew this meant that everything was changed. It was not the same thing at all to write

I love Matthew Osborne

as it was to write

I love Paris

or

I love pizza

So I had to add

Everything is different

Even so, despite my knowing that 'everything was different' I did not realise that *everything* – each thing that existed – *was* – truly, really, positively, actually was – *different* – not the same, other, ineradicably altered.

After all, my timetable looked the same: still German at four and Maths at four-fifty, still CCF on Fridays, still Saturday compline and Sunday Qs. The study that Jo and I planned that evening to set about decorating, that looked the same. The quad outside appeared to be the same quad. The records on my shelf were the same records.

I screwed the piece of paper up once more and stared out of the window.

5

I can't remember, I honestly can't remember if the events I am going to describe happened on the same day I laid eyes on Matthew Osborne. In my imagination it has become the same day, so that will have to do.

I got up and left the study. I crossed through to the main part of the House and entered the changing room.

There were pretty boys in Fircroft too. I went to the locker of the prettiest of them and opened it. The back of my hand just touched the jacket hanging inside and I heard the clink of money.

I stole it.

I stole it all, left the House, went down the music school and conducted my favourite Rossini piece as it had never been conducted before. Not *William Tell*, or *The Barber of Seville*, but the overture to *The Thieving Magpie* and do you know, never up to this very minute has the significance of that title struck me? I knew the piece so well that its individual words had stopped meaning anything. The Thieving Magpie. It seems so neat and organised and obvious as to resemble fiction, but it is God's honest truth. Or the devil's. Maybe that should have been the title for this book. The Thieving Magpie . . . or The Devil's Honest Truth, for that matter . . .

I've slipped it on now, *La Gazza Ladra* as it calls itself in this compilation, and I am listening and jumping in my chair as I type this and I can see what I saw in it, and hear what I heard it in. For Rossini the sun always breaks out with such a joyful jerk that nothing, for a while, can ever seem bad, not even the stolen money in your pocket that chinks and clinks as you bring in the woodwinds and the brass section, thrashing like an epileptic in your *hysterica passio*, twitching with spastic arhythmic heaves and thrusts, not even the hard stone of new knowledge that was born in you that day that childhood is over and that something new has come into your being that may well unseat your reason for ever.

This now became a pattern. I had always been Bad both publicly and privately. Bad in terms of 'mobbing' and 'ragging', showing off in front of the other boys, daring to go those extra few yards towards trouble and punishment, and Bad in the realms of secret wickedness. But now I didn't care. I just did not care. My behaviour in the first year may have been judged to be purgatorial, now it became unequivocally infernal.

Sometimes it made me popular, sometimes it made me loathed. In my first year I had tried to improve my judgement of the bounds of propriety that boys set in their tribally codified way. I became better at sensing when I was going too far and risking disfavour, better at riding the bucking bronco of popularity.

Sometimes the jokes worked well and I would rise above my generation in a bubble of fame and admiration. I think it fair to say that of all my intake in my first year I rapidly became the best known in the school. Not the most liked or the most admired, but the most recognisable and the most talked about.

One great achievement was to be the Brewer affair which earned me many thumps on the back and chuckling congratulations.

The Uppingham School Bookshop, where blocks and stationery were bought as well as textbooks, fiction, poetry and other more usual bookshop fare was run on behalf of the school by a rather fussy man called Mr Brewer. Most items were bought by use of the Order Form, a chit which one got one's housemaster to sign after lunch to authorise the purchases, which would end up on the parental bill at the end of term. A typical order form might look something like this:

UPPINGHAM SCHOOL ORDER FORM

NAME......................HOUSE......................

> *6 blocks*
> *1 bottle ink (blue-black)*
> *1 bottle ink (green)*
> *1 pencil sharpener*

Signature..................Authorised...............

The Signature field, as we would say in computer jargon today, was for oneself to sign, the Authorised field was for the housemaster's initials.

'*Green* ink, Fry?'

'Well sir, for English essays. I think it's more stylish.'

'Oh Lord. Very well.'

Naturally, I was adept at Frowde's hastily scribbled 'G. C. F.' and on the rare occasion when I could lay my thieving hands on a blank order form pad I would go mad with purchase.

Something about Mr Brewer, however, some quality of fussiness and distrust, made one absolutely desperate to mob and bait the man to distraction. My first scheme was to persecute him by telephone. I had discovered, God knows how, that in those days of pulse telephony, before the introduction of the digital exchange and tone dialling, you could call a number by striking the receiver buttons in Morse code style, ten times for zero, nine times for nine and so on, a small gap left between each number. If you got the rhythm right you could tap out '350466' in a public phone-box and get through without having to pay a single penny. Today's phreaking and hacking make this look like child's play, of course, but fun could be had with it.

There was a red telephone kiosk in the market-place just opposite the High Street windows of the bookshop which meant we could call up Brewer and watch one of his assistants passing him the phone.

'Is that Mr Brewer on the line?'

'Yes.'

'Well, you'd better get off, there's a train coming.'

A feeble start admittedly, but it got better.

'Mr Brewer? This is Penguin Books here calling to confirm the order of four thousand copies of *Lady Chatterley's Lover*.'

'*What?* No, no. It's those boys! I never made the order. Cancel it! Cancel it!'

'I see. And the order for ten thousand of *Last Exit to Brooklyn*?'

Tee-hee.

Or one could get elliptical and weird, which worked best

when he picked up the phone himself.

'Uppingham School Bookshop.'

'Yes?'

'Uppingham School Bookshop.'

'What do you want?'

'I beg your pardon?'

'How can we help?'

'This is the Uppingham School Bookshop here.'

'So you keep saying, but what do you want?'

'You made the call.'

'No I didn't.'

'Well what number did you want?'

'I don't want any number. I just want to get on with my life without being pestered by Uppingham School Bookshops, whatever they might be. Nuisance calls are against the law you know.'

'But you called me!'

'Look, if you don't get off the line I shall call the police. The bishop is awaiting a very important call from one of his wives.'

'It's a boy, isn't it!'

'This particular one isn't, no.'

'I can see you out of the window! I shall report you all.'

One day I was with Jo Wood in Boots the Chemists. I had been planning to buy a bottle of aniseed liquid to sprinkle on my trouser turn-ups to check out Jeeves's theory that this would cause dogs to follow me (it didn't work, incidentally, just made them yap and howl) and I noticed Brewer in another aisle. He hadn't spotted me or Jo and an idea arose within me.

'No, it's so simple,' I said, in a sudden, artificially low whisper, the kind that causes ears to prick up everywhere. 'Brewer is so blind he never notices.'

Jo looked at me in his usual strained and constipated manner, but was sharp enough and familiar enough with my ways to realise that I must be up to something. I could tell from the sudden silence and stiffening in the neighbouring row that Brewer had frozen into a keen listening attitude.

'You just go in with your duffle bag apparently full, a pair of old plimsolls on the top, go up to the book section and stuff as many books as you like in the bag. Put the plimsolls back on top, sling the bag over your shoulder, then go up and buy a pencil or something. Best when the shop's really busy, during break, some time like that. He never, ever notices a thing. I've stolen literally *hundreds* of books that way. Come on, if you're done here, let's hit the buttery.'

I spread the word amongst a few friends and the next morning about seven of us entered the bookshop and oh-so-casually wandered up to the book section, which was on a raised level overlooking the rest of the shop. We all fell to our knees at different shelves, examined books, shot guilty glances over our shoulders and seemed to fumble about with our duffle bags, causing gym-shoes to fall out which had to be hastily replaced.

Down the steps we went, duffle bags over shoulders, towards the girl at the cash desk. We proffered order forms for the acquisition of one block or one pencil (HB), swallowing nervously.

Suddenly Brewer sprang up as if from nowhere. He had, rather pathetically, been hiding under the counter, which was enough to cause one of our number to give a premature scream of laughter that only a swift hack on the shins from me snuffed out.

'Just a moment, gentlemen!' said Brewer.

Looks of startled innocence and amazement.

'Yes, Mr Brewer?'

'All of you. Kindly empty your duffle bags on to the counter.'

'Really, Mr Brewer . . .'

'Do as I say!' he rasped. 'One at a time. Mr Fry first, I think. Yes. You first, Mr Fry.'

I shrugged resignedly and turned my duffel bag upside-down, grasping the sides so that only a pair of tattered black gym-shoes fell on to the surface of the counter.

'Everything!' said Brewer, a squeak of triumph entering his voice.

'Everything?' I repeated nervously.

'Everything!'

'If you insist, Mr Brewer.'

'I do, Mr Fry!'

I shook and shook the duffle bag and out tumbled:

- 6 very dirty jock-straps
- About 70 loose mixed Jelly-tots, Bassett Mint Imperials, Liquorice All-Sorts and Trebor Refreshers
- 12 broken Digestive biscuits
- 4 of Mr Lanchberry's best Cream Slices (three days old)
- 200 assorted fishing weights and air-pistol pellets
- Pencil shavings
- 1 leaking bottle of Vosene Medicated shampoo
- 1 brand-new copy of *Sons and Lovers* (W. H. Smith's receipt carefully tucked inside)
- 1 packet of Embassy Regal cigarettes and 1 box of matches

It was extremely hard not to fold up in a heap, but we managed to keep our faces straight and earnest.

'Get those things off my counter!' screamed Brewer, grabbing at *Sons and Lovers*, but already the other boys had started adding their own itemries, including condoms (which, with the artful addition of globs of Copydex and paste, presented the horrible appearance of having been very passionately used), a fish, rotting cheeses, a slippery heap of lambs' kidneys and much, much more.

'Stop, stop!' shrieked Brewer.

'But Mr Brewer you *said* . . .'

'You did say, Mr Brewer!'

'We heard you.'

'Gosh, look at the time, everyone!' I called in panic. 'The bell's about to go any minute. We'll be back at lunchtime Mr Brewer, I'll need the Lawrence book for an English lesson this afternoon. In the meantime do make free with anything you like the look of. I will want the jock-straps back *eventually*. You know, when you've done with them.'

And out we streamed, deaf to his protests. I was especially enjoying the possibilities of the one little ray of hope I had left him, the packet of Embassy and the matches. The Embassy pack was filled with slugs and the matchbox wriggled with a dozen spiders.

This was all part of the thirteen-year-old innocence of my first year. Coupled with my acceptance within the House by boys like Rick Carmichael, Mart Swindells and Roger Eaton and my friendships with Richard Fawcett and Jo Wood life was good. My brother Roger did not have too much cause to blush for me yet. He was getting on with life in the benign way he had, with malice to none.

Another older boy in our house who made me feel accepted was Paul Whittome, who simply exploded with paintings, drawings, surreal rock operas and poems, excellent at both the double bass and rugger. He found me amusing enough to include me in a band that he assembled with a saxophonist friend of his from Brooklands and Rick Carmichael, who played the piano superbly. We performed Jack Teagarden jazz standards, the Bonzo numbers 'Hunting Tigers Out In India' and 'Jollity Farm' and classics like 'Rock Around the Clock' and Hoagie Carmichael's 'Rocking Chair'. My party piece was to play the trumpet solo in 'Rocking Chair' with staggering physical passion and bulging Dizzie Gillespie cheeks. Meanwhile the curtain behind would accidentally rise to reveal that in fact the real trumpeter was a boy called Sam Rudder who stood there, barely moving, playing with completely serene calmness. Aside from that, I can't remember what I actually did to justify my presence in the band, apart from a little incompetent hammering on the piano when Rick was playing the guitar or singing. I suppose I just arsed about entertainingly. We did well enough to be invited to perform at the public school in Oakham, six or seven miles away. When Paul Whittome left Uppingham he almost instantly made himself a millionaire, as he had promised Frowde he would. He started by selling vegetables in a stall off the A1 and rapidly became a King of Potatoes and Potato broking. He sold his spud business and now runs probably the most successful hotel restaurant in East Anglia. I go sailing with him and his wife sometimes and had the honour of being asked a few years ago to open a new set of guest-rooms for his inn, The Hoste Arms in

Burnham Market. He would never forgive me for not giving you the name and address of his establishment for he is quite miraculously shameless and brazen when it comes to publicity. How else does a man get to be a millionaire at twenty-two? Besides, I owe it him for his kindness in believing in me enough to put me, musically talentless as I am, in a band.

My other brush with showbusiness came when Richard Fawcett and I planned our sketches for the House Supper, Fircroft's end of term Christmas party in which sixth-formers got to wear dinner jackets and drink wine, while the rest of us pulled crackers and mounted a mini-revue composed of music, songs and sketches.

Richard and I rewrote a Benny Hill skit in which a vicar is being interviewed unaware that his trouser flies are widely undone. Richard was the vicar ('I like to throw open my portals to the public'), I was the interviewer, ('I see your point, yes I do see your point.'). We rehearsed this endlessly and were astonished, as the curtain descended on our dress rehearsal, to hear Frowde, the housemaster, call out, 'Trousers down, trousers down!'

We looked at each other, utterly baffled as to his meaning (as I still am).

The curtain jerked up again and Frowde stood there, hands behind his back.

'No, no. Trousers down,' he repeated. 'It's either trousers up or trousers down. This kind of innuendo won't do at all.'

So we had to go away and hastily assemble something else.

Rick Carmichael and Martin Swindells had been censored too, so that night, at midnight in our dormitory there was seen a performance of Banned Material. Richard and I did our Vicar Sketch and Rick and Mart a dialogue playing with the St Crispin's day speech from Shakespeare's *Henry V* and its suggestive reference to those holding their manhoods, cheap.

Richard Fawcett and I had by this time become so obsessed with comedy that we wrote to the BBC who had just started a new series called *Open Door*, the pioneer of that now depressingly common programming phenomenon 'Access Television'. *Open Door* was designed to allow dyslexics, victims of injustice, support groups and others to air their grievances, but Richard and I had somewhat misinterpreted its aims and believed it to be a chance to Perform On Telly and Become Famous.

In our letter to the BBC, we pompously elaborated our pitch. Comedy, we observed, with the arrival of Monty Python, had entered a modernist phase. Would it, like the other arts, disintegrate into modes of abstraction and conceptuality? How could a 'new comedy' be formulated? All that sort of thing. We planned to show the progress of comedy over the last twenty years and compare it with the progress of music, painting and literature. Would comedy disappear up its own self-referential arse, we wondered? Ridiculous, I know, but there you are.

It was enough at least, to get us in interview in Lime Grove, Shepherd's Bush. Nothing came of the meeting, but I still have the producer's card. Mike Bolland went on to become senior programme commissioner for Channel 4 when it started up; in those days he must have been one of the BBC's most junior juniors, given the unfortunate job of weeding out the loonies who came knocking on the *Open Door*. I see him from time to time and I'm always far too embarrassed to remind him of those two public school boys babbling pretentiously about comedy and ideas.

We must, I fear, return briefly to sex (as I write this, National Sex Awareness Week is coming to a close and its thrust, I believe, is to get Britain to talk about sex in order to dispel the guilt, misery and taboo surrounding the subject: I feel I'm doing my bit).

It was towards the end of my first year that I was successfully seduced and deflowered. Now, I have never believed myself to be physically attractive. There are three reasons for this.

1. I'm not my type
2. I'm not physically attractive
3. So there

None the less, in the eyes of some, I do know that I can give off a quality that comes close to sex appeal. I was never a prettyboy, or anything like (you have the pictures to hand that prove it) but being a late developer sexually I combined a mixture of knowingness, insolently suggestive sophistication and some kind of appetisingly unspoiled quality that could, on occasion, take the people's fancy.

A red-haired sixth-former and House Polly called Oliver Derwent called me to his study one day when I was on general fagging duties.

'Close the door,' he said.

I obliged, wondering what I could possibly have done wrong this time.

'Do you play cards?' asked Derwent.

'Er, yes. Yes. I suppose I do.' The question took me completely by surprise. Maybe Derwent was starting up a House bridge club. Mine not to wonder why, however, mine but to stand patiently on the carpet and await instructions.

'I'm just so bored,' he said, languidly. 'I thought I might find someone prepared to have a game or two of cards with me.'

It transpired that the only game Derwent knew how to play was a game called Strip Poker, so strip poker was the game we played.

'Better lock the door,' said Derwent.

'Right-o,' I said.

Now, you might well be thinking: Hello! If this Derwent could play *strip* poker, then he could play *ordinary* poker. This never crossed my mind. One just didn't question senior boys. They knew.

So the pair of us knelt on the carpet and Derwent dealt. Within a very short time I was completely naked and Derwent was in nothing but his underpants. My legs were drawn coyly up to conceal what little there was to conceal and I was starting to feel a touch embarrassed.

'Fry,' said Derwent, blushing with that ferocity peculiar to redheads, 'may I feel your body?'

Those are the exact words he used. 'May I feel your body?' Rather sweet really.

'Er . . . okay,' I said.

So he felt my body. I became excited, in the way that I had been excited at Stouts Hill with Halford and the others. I could see from the prodding in his underpants that he too, was excited.

He then began a long, complicated speech about the frustration he felt at the lack of girls at Uppingham and how, in my smoothness, I was actually rather like a girl. Perhaps I wouldn't mind if he made love to me?

I had simply no idea what that phrase meant, but it sounded charming and I said that it sounded like a reasonable idea.

At this point there came a knock on the door.

'Derwent!'

'Just a minute!'

I leapt to my feet and started to scrabble frantically with my clothes. The door handle rattled.

'Ho! Wanking!' said a voice.

Derwent leaned forward and cupped his hand around one of my ears. 'Out the window!' he breathed hotly. 'I'll see you in the House Rears in ten minutes.'

I nodded, slightly frightened by this time, and not so sure that I wanted to go through with this making love business, but I climbed out of the window and dived into a nearby bush.

Dressed again, teeth chattering, I made my way to the House Rears, a set of disused Victorian lavatories round the back of the House.

When Derwent arrived eight minutes later I regret to say he had come prepared with a tub of Vaseline and a grim determination to see things through.

I remember very little about the experience. I remember being bent forward and I remember grasping my own ankles. I remember some pain, plenty of grunting from Derwent and a sliding, slippy wetness running down the inside of my thighs when I stood up. Derwent was gone by the time I had pulled up my trousers and turned round, and whenever we saw each other in the House it was as strangers, no mention made, no extra friendliness shown or expected. Just a blankness.

I would love to be able to tell you that this Oliver Derwent

is now our Ambassador in Washington or the Chairman of
ICI, but I have no idea what he's up to or where he is. Last I
heard he had children, and was working in one of the Gulf
States. I bear him no grudge and cannot believe he did me any
harm. He didn't make me queer, he didn't make me a bugger or
a buggeree, so all's jake as far as I'm concerned.

Besides, all that was BMO, Before Matthew Osborne, and
events BMO were rendered meaningless by everything AMO.

AMO, as I said, I went loopy. Everything I did publicly and
privately became more extreme. Publicly, the jokes and the
wildness intensified, privately the stealing became more and
more regular.

At this time, the only salvation and sense in my life came
from reading. It was then that I started on Douglas, Firbank
and Forster. It was then that I discovered the novels and
autobiographies that reflected my own emotional turmoil and
my own circumstances, sometimes so exactly that I alternated
between a triumphant feeling of being vindicated and endorsed
by the Masters and a deflated sense of being nothing more than
a living cliché: *The Flannelled Fool*, by T. C. Worsley; *A
Separate Peace*, by John Knowles; *Sandel* by Angus Stewart;
Lord Dismiss Us, by Michael Campbell; *Escape from the
Shadows* by Robin Maugham; *Autobiography of an
Englishman* by 'Y'; *The World, The Flesh and Myself* by
Michael Davidson (with its famous opening line: 'This is the
life-history of a lover of boys.'); *The Fourth of June* by David
Benedictus; *Special Friendships* by Roger Peyrefitte, and many,
many others, which in turn guided me towards the notorious
Book Twelve of the Greek Anthology; *The Quest For Corvo*
by A. J. A. Symons (the unexpurgated edition complete with
Baron Corvo's infamous *Venice Letters*); the novels of Simon
Raven (happily still then being produced in profusion); the
works of Jean Genet, Oscar Wilde, Edward Carpenter and the
Uranian school, the paintings of Eakins and Tuke, and that
wonderful, syrupy slew of pre- and post-First World War
sentimental school love stories like *The Hill, David Blaize,
Jeremy at Crale* and Alec Waugh's *The Loom of Youth*.

So, stolen money in my pocket and nothing but Matthew on

my mind, that is how I would spend my afternoons, either in the library or howling to Rossini and Beethoven.

The Lower Buttery was perched halfway between the steps that led down from the Magic Carpet to the Music School, so I would leave the record library and climb up, as other boys were coming down, their hair still wet from showers, their faces pink from exercise, and I would avoid their eyes as I went in. My eyes were only for Mrs Lanchberry as she broke more eggs into her vat of boiling lard, money stolen from the pretty and the athletic clutched in my hands, and of course my eyes were for Matthew in case he might come in too. But I had discovered a terrible truth about Matthew.

He was healthy.

He was

Good at games.

In fact, he was *brilliant* at games. He was going to be a star. We hadn't seen nothing yet, apparently. You think he's a fine hockey player? You wait till you see him on the cricket field in the summer term. You just wait, his brother said.

We already had a cricket hero at Uppingham, in the shape of Jonathan Agnew, who went on to play for Leicestershire and England and as Aggers now comments wittily and (thus far) without ego and derision for the BBC's *Test Match Special*.

Whether the stealing in earnest really did start the day I first saw Matthew Osborne I cannot, as I say, be sure, but they are connected. Falling in love is not an excuse because, as I have shown you before, this was by no means the first time I had stolen. But now it gripped me like a demon. It became an addiction, a necessity and, perhaps, a revenge. A revenge against beauty, order, healthiness, seemliness, normality, convention and love. To say that *I* was the victim of these crimes, that I was punishing myself, that is hardly fair. There must have been dozens and dozens of boys whose lives were temporarily screwed and savaged by the sudden disappearance of their money. It's hard for even the most Christian and temperate soul not to be enraged by theft. And that old complaint about the sense of violation, of invasion, of tainting that is felt by the victims of theft: maybe that is part of what I was doing – leaving a foul kind of urine trail, an anti-social territorial marking, or unmarking, wherever I went, wrestling with Hassan's Anti-Hero's 'problems of estrangement and communion, sincerity and simulation, ambition and acquiescence.'

Yeah, yeah, yeah – you were a thieving little tosser, we get the picture, we will draw the conclusions, thank you.

My behaviour too, as I said, my general social behaviour, that went to hell in a handcart. Poor old Ronnie Rutter who taught me French. He had joined the school aged seventeen, just after the First World War and was so gentle, so pliable, so plain sweet that he had never even been made a housemaster. Temporarily he had taken charge of Meadhurst for a term during the Second World War, that was the greatest career height he had ever scaled. I used to mob him up, as the school slang had it, so thoroughly, so completely, so *humiliatingly* that I blush cardinal red at the memory of such cardinal sin. I once stood on top of my desk, took out a gat gun (one of those air pistols that fires pellets but looks to the uninitiated to be a deadly automatic weapon) and shouted in a hysterical Cody Jarrett voice, 'I've had it. Had it, I tell you! Just one move, and you're dead. You're all *dead*.' Everybody pissed themselves and Ronnie did the best he could.

'Put it down, there's a good fellow, we've *so* much to get through this period.'

I made up a letter once that purported to come from a female 'pen-friend' in France and filled it with every dirty, disgusting sexual French word I knew or could find out. I approached him at the end of a lesson and asked if he could help me with it, as I found some of the vocuabulary rather difficult.

'I'm so pleased to hear you have a French pen-friend, Fry,' said Ronnie. And he proceeded to translate the letter for me, replacing the obscenities with innocent little phrases of his own as he went, pretending for all the world that it was the most ordinary communication in the world. 'I would like to suck your big fat cock' became, 'I look forward so much to visiting your country' and 'Lick my wet pussy till I squirt' emerged as, 'There are so many interesting things to do and see in Avignon' and so on throughout the letter.

The word he used in his school report to my parents at the end of term was, I think, 'exuberant'. 'Sometimes a little more exuberant than is good for him.' None of that 'bad influence', 'rotten apple', 'thinks he's so clever' stuff the others off-loaded. He invited me to tea with his wife. It brings a lump to my throat to think of such absolute sweetness of nature, such tenderness.

He hadn't *given up*, either. We used to say sometimes, in our sneering way of schoolmasters, that after more than ten years they had turned into cynical time-servers or unworldly eccentrics. Ronnie was neither cynic nor sentimentalist, and he put all of himself into every lesson. Utterly ineffectual as a disciplinarian maybe, but I cannot think of a life that was less of a failure.

There's a passage in *Portnoy's Complaint* (which I had read greedily and joyfully, *loving* the daring of those jerk-off scenes in the bathroom):

> . . . society not only sanctions gross and unfair relations among men, but encourages them . . . Rivalry, competition, envy, jealousy, all that is malignant in human character is nourished by the system. Possessions, money, property – on such corrupt standards as these do you people measure happiness and success.

Scarcely fresh news I suppose, but then the Gospels aren't either, yet they too contain ideas that bear repetition. Only a fool dismisses an idea because it has been heard before.

'Man will become better when you show him what he is like,' Chekhov thought. Maybe Ronnie tried to show me what I was like. He did so more effectively than many masters who tried to *tell* me what I was like, which is not the same thing at all. I used in the end to feel a kind of sickness, a feeling of nauseous surfeit after a Ronnie Rutter French lesson, a sickness that I soon identified as self-disgust. After a while I gave up and became sanctimoniously fierce in my refusal to allow others to mob him up. Anybody else was fair game, but Ronnie was exempt.

Maybe Ronnie *saw*, that was the other thing. Maybe it was written all over me, this agony of love that I was enduring.

We're in the second term of the year now. I've got to know Matthew a little better, partly by getting to know Nick better, partly by following the promptings of unrequited love, which train you exquisitely well in the art of accidental meetings.

When you love you plan your day entirely according to the movements of your loved one. I knew Matthew's timetable by heart. I knew the places he was likely to visit. I knew the matches he played in – he was already in the Colts First XI – I knew the clubs and societies he had joined and I joined them too. I knew what sort of music he liked, when he was likely to be visiting the Thring Centre and when he was likely to be in his House.

And every day he grew more and more beautiful. He was still climbing the gentle slope to his peak of perfection. He never succumbed to acne, greasy hair or gawkiness. Every day he grew and grew in grace towards the completion of his beauty.

I was subtle, Christ Jesus, was I subtle. He could never have imagined for ten seconds that I had any interest in him at all, not from the accident of our endless meetings, nor from the coincidence of our mutual interests. I never looked *unpleased* to see him, but neither did I show any pleasure. I took a kindly interest and . . .

I *entertained*.

For the joy of it was . . .

He found me funny

and, like Elizabeth Bennett, Matthew was one who dearly

loved a laugh. He was talented. He played the piano like an angel, his athleticism was outstanding and he was academically competent. I don't remember what degree he later took at Cambridge, but it was either a First or a 2:1 as well as an inevitable triple haul of sporting Blues. Verbally however, he was ordinary. He had no rhetoric, no style, no wit nor any easy companionship with words. Since I seemed to him to have all these things, he looked on me as extraordinary and would roll and roll about with laughter whenever I wanted him to, which was often, a kitten on the end of my verbal balls of wool. Never too far ... I learned early on that like a kitten he could suddenly bore of a game, suddenly appear to think it all rather facile and beneath his dignity. Often then, just when I sensed that moment might come, I would stop the joking at its still pleasurable height, shake my head and express some deep thought of frustration, anger at the political injustices and criminal stupidity of 'this place' as the school was mutteringly called by all.

Once, I remember, I was in the Thring Centre, typing out the whole of a P. G. Wodehouse novel on one of the big IBM electric typewriters. *Frozen Assets*, the book was, I recall. I did this sort of thing a great deal, I adored the feel of typing, watching the keys leap and smack the paper, making words appear with such clean magical clarity; I loved too the way I could monitor my noticeable improvement in accuracy and speed and God how I gloried in the admiration when boys clustered around gasping in amazement at the rapidity with which my fingers could fly over the keys without my even looking down. Today's qwerty generation would think me abominably slow, of course, but in those days typing proficiency was a most eccentric and enviable attainment.

I was alone however in the typing and Gestetner room, that February evening, just clacking away at the keyboard.

I didn't hear him come in, but a fraction of a second before he cleared his throat to speak I felt a presence in the room, a presence that I later convinced myself I had known was *his* even before I heard his voice.

'What are you doing?'

A great surge went through me that tingled my cheeks (still does, you know, to remember it) as I heard that voice. Something else there was too. Something that alerted me to the possibility that all was not well with him.

'That you, Matteo?'

I called him Matteo: it was *my* nickname for him. I scorned the 'Ozzie Two' that had become 'Ozziter' as far as the rest of the school was concerned. To be given a private nickname, even if it is carelessly, almost disdainfully given, is a massive compliment; successful nicknaming is an absolutely essential weapon in the armoury of any romantic seducer. I had discovered that his middle initial (unlike his brother he turned out to have just the one) was A for Anthony, which made him M. A. O. I had experimented with the idea of calling him the Chairman, as in Mao, but that seemed obvious. Then it struck me that Matt. A. O. sounded like the Italian for Matthew, so Matteo it was, from me and me alone. I once walked on air for a week when I overheard him ticking off a contemporary, Madeley-Orne, who had dared to call him that.

'Matteo is *not* my name,' he had said hotly.

'I've heard Fry call you that.'

'Yes, well Fry calls everybody weird things, but that doesn't give *you* the right. He calls *you* Makes-Me-Yawn, if it comes to that.'

The real reason I came on Monday evenings to the Thring Centre was because I knew that Monday was Matthew's pottery day. This was one activity I had not tried to join him in, since I had queered my pitch with the pottery department my very first term by contriving to burn out the motor that drove one of the throwing wheels and then, the very next week, breaking one of the pug-mill dyes. A pug-mill, in case you haven't been introduced, is a sort of potter's mince-making machine. You shove all the spare offcuts of slip and old clay into a hopper at the top, squeeze them down with a lever and pure, consistent clay comes out the other end, either in one great thick sausage, or – if you fix a template or dye over the exit hole – in smaller little wriggly snakes that can be used to make those coil-ware mugs, vases and pots that are still

produced in woundingly huge quantities to this day, much to
the distress and embarrassment of all. Fearing that during the
third week I might do even more damage I was pronounced
persona non grata by the staff, the pot-it-buro, as I liked to call
them, and so filled my Mondays, while Matthew was there, in
the Thring Centre too, by typing or playing with the gerbils
that scuttled about in transparent perspex conduits and pipes
all round the building, citizens of their own Fritz Lang Rodent
Metropolis. The system was designed – like almost everything
else in Uppingham from the theatre up the road that was even
now rising from the skeleton of the old Victorian gymnasium,
to the chairs and light fixtures of the Thring Centre – by the
remarkable master in charge, Chris Richardson, who is today
supremo of the Pleasance Theatre, the organisation which
seems ever more to dominate the Edinburgh Festival Fringe
and which now has permanent habitation in London too.
Richardson was known, for no reason I can tell, as Trog –
perhaps because his Hogarthian features resembled the work
of the *Punch* cartoonist Trog. He carried the smell of pipe
tobacco about with him and tolerated my arsiness, frivolity
and absolute incompetence and lack of common sense in those
fields of endeavour which came so naturally to him,
draughtsmanship, planning and construction, because 'at least
I made use of the bloody place' even if my idea of making use
of such a 'resource', as it would be called today, was pointlessly
to tip-tap away like a temp in a typing-pool.

So there I am, doing just that, and I hear behind me the voice
that is my reason for being.

'That you, Matteo?' As if I didn't know. And said as if I
didn't really care too much, so absorbed was I in my Important
Typing.

'Mm . . . You writing something?'

'No just typing practice really. Bored of the potting-shed?'

'Got something in the kiln.'

'So . . . just kiln time then, are you?'

'Tsserh!' That is really the best way I can render his polite
giggle at my dreadful pun.

I swung round in my seat to look at him.

I was right. He *was* in distress. I suppose I had sensed it because the way he had asked 'What are you doing?' had set up some chime in me, had reminded me of the way I would ask my mother precisely the same question when I knew perfectly well what she was doing but wanted her to stop because I had a grievance to air.

'You all right, old crocus?' P. G. Wodehouse was seeping deep into my language.

'Oh it's nothing . . .'

There was a fierce disconsolacy in his expression. I have described him to you as beautiful, which is a senseless description, a space that you will have to fill for yourself with your own picture of beauty; also I have told you he was below the average in height. There was a *hint*, no more than that, of stockiness about him, a solidity that prevented, despite such overwhelming beauty of countenance and body, any suggestion of the porcelain, any pretty delicacy that might de-sex and sanitise. It was enough to turn sensuousness into sensuality, but not enough to detract from his liquid grace. It was even more marked, this grounded solidity now, I noticed, as he defiantly attempted not to look unhappy.

'How long have you got to wait before the dinner's-ready bell goes in your oven?' I asked.

'Oh, about forty minutes. Why?'

'Let's go for a walk then. All this typing is no good for my back.'

'Okay.'

He waited while I squared the typed sheets, switched off the typewriter, threw on its silvery dust cover and perched a scribbled note next to it: 'Leave alone or die bloodily.'

This was the era when military greatcoats were the innest thing to wear. I had a WW2 American Air Force coat that was the envy of the world, Matthew an RAF equivalent: he had also, perhaps on account of his older brother, managed to get one of the old school scarves, striped in knitted wool like a Roy of the Rovers football scarf, unlike the scratchy new college-style black and red that I wore. With his wrapped warmly about his neck he looked so divine and vulnerable I wanted to scream.

It was a cold night and just beginning to snow.

'Yippee, no games tomorrow by the looks of it,' I said.

'You really hate sport, don't you?' said Matthew, vapour steaming from the hot mystery of his mouth and throat.

'I don't mind watching it, but 'Is this the man who has lost his soul?' I misquoted: 'The flannelled fool at the wicket and the muddied oaf at the goal.' I had just read Cuthbert Worsley's autobiography and it had sent me into quite a spin.

'Is that what you think of me as then? A muddy oaf?'

'I wouldn't have said so,' I said, a little surprised. 'I mean, I don't mean to be rude, but I'm not sure I think of you as anything, really.'

'Oh.'

We walked on in silence, while I tried to work out where this was leading.

'You don't . . .' he blurted in some confusion, '. . . you don't *like* me then?'

'Well of course I like you, you daft onion. I'm not in the habit of going for walks with people I dislike.'

'In spite of the fact that I'm a flannelled fool and a muddy oaf?'

'I'll let you into a secret, Matteo. The reason I hate games so much, and don't you dare tell anyone this, is simple . . . I'm no bloody good at them.'

'Oh,' he said again. Then. 'Why do you like me then?'

'Christ, Osborne,' I said, getting a bit senior in my panic at the direction all this seemed to be going in, 'I like *most* people. You seem harmless. You're polite and most importantly of all, you laugh at my bloody jokes. You fishing for compliments here or what?'

'No, no. I'm sorry. It's just that. Well. It was something someone said to me.'

Oh fuck here we go, I thought. His brother has been warning him off. Some jealous son of a bitch has been whispering. The game is up.

'Who said what to you?' I asked, trying to smother the swallowing nervousness I felt.

'It doesn't really matter who it was. Just someone in my

House. I was sweeping the corridor, you know, and he started
. . . he started trying stuff.'

'He made an advance you mean?' I said. *Advance*? Well what
other word could I have used?

Matthew nodded, looked away and out it all came in a hot,
indignant tumble. 'I told him to leave me alone and he called
me a *tart*. He said that everyone could see the way I played up
to certain pollies and to people like Fry who I was always
hanging around with. He said I was a prettyboy pricktease.'

In my head, even as I winced at hearing such words from
him, I rapidly ran through a list of possible names that might
fit the picture of this bungling, asinine, spiteful brute from
Redwood's and at the same time just as rapidly selecting, from
a whole suite of possible reactions, the right stance for me to
take on this choked and miserable confession: outrage,
indignity, tired man-of-the-world cynicism, fatherly admoni-
tion, comradely sympathy . . . I considered them all and settled
on a kind of mixture.

I shuddered, half at the cold, half at the horror of it all. 'This
place!' I said. 'This fucking place . . . thing is, Matteo, it's a
hothouse. You wouldn't think so with the snow falling all
around us, but it is. We live under glass. Distorting glass.
Everything is rumour, counter-rumour, guesswork, gossip,
envy, interference, frustration, all that. The secret of survival in
a place like this is to be simple.'

'Simple?' It was hard to tell whether the clear swollen globes
of moisture that glistened at the end of his lashes were melted
snowflakes or tears.

'In a way simple. Rely on friendship.'

'Yes, but . . .'

'If you've got a good friend, you've never really got any
reason to worry. You've always got someone to talk to,
someone who'll understand you.'

'Like you and Woody, you mean?'

It wasn't what I meant, of course. It was far from what I
meant.

'Yes. Like me and Woody,' I said. 'I could tell Jo anything
and I know he'd see it in its right proportion. That's the trick

in a place like this, proportion. Who would you say is your best friend?'

He shrugged his shoulders. 'Don't know,' he said, almost sulkily. 'You see, thing is, I know, because my brother told me . . .'

'Know what?'

'You know, that I'm . . . you know, *pretty*.' He got rid of the word as if its presence had been souring his mouth like a bad olive.

Pretty! God I hated that word. Pretty boy, pretty boy . . . only a lumpen, half-witted heterosexual would think Matthew *pretty*. He was beautiful, like the feet of the Lord on the hills, he was beautiful. Like the river, like the snow that was falling now more thickly than ever, like nothing on earth, like everything on earth he was beautiful. And some roaring hairy-pizzled Minotaur had dared to grab at him and call him a prettyboy pricktease. Even his own *brother* had used that word.

'Pretty?' I said, as if the idea had never struck me before. 'Well you're exceptionally good-looking, I suppose. You've got regular features, unlike me with my big bent nose and my arms ten foot long. But pretty isn't a word I would have used. *Morgan* is pretty, I would say.'

Morgan was a Fircroft new boy, on whom many eyes had fallen.

'Thomas Morgan?' said Matthew in surprise. 'Oh.' Was there just a *touch* here, the merest *hint* of wounded vanity in his reaction or was that my imagination?

'If you go in for that sort of thing, that is,' I added hastily. 'Personally, as I say, *friendship* is my credo.'

He nodded dumbly and I took a chance.

'Look,' I said, and I put my arm round his shoulders and squeezed. 'That's what friends do in a natural world. It's affection and support in a universe where we all need affection and support. But in this place it's "queering" and it makes people point and sneer. You and I know it's friendship, but when someone like that vile cunt in your House tries it on with you, he kids himself that it's *your* fault. Always remember that he's the one who's scared. He may insult you but secretly he's terrified that you're going to tell your brother or your housemaster or the whole House. That's why he's trying to kid himself that you led him on. It's the old, old story. Just like Potiphar's wife and just like every rejected rapist the world over. But don't let what your brother said worry you. He meant well but he's obviously made you doubt everyone's motives towards you. Those millionaires who are convinced that people only like them for their money, you know the type? Well, you don't want to become the equivalent, do you? Someone who only believes that people like you because you're good-looking. You wouldn't want to live like that. That's nothing but the lack of confidence trick.'

He had allowed my arm to stay around him without protest. It was dark. No one could see us.

It was the finest achievement of my life so far, arrived at with bluff, deceit, hypocrisy, manipulation, abuse of trust and a few exploitative elements of gimcrack wisdom and genuinely good advice. Good advice, like a secret, is easier to give away than to keep.

I let my arm drop and returned it to the warm interior of my greatcoat pocket. 'Do *you* think you're pretty?' I asked.

He shook his head.

'Well there you are then. You can't live your life in the shadow of other people's opinions, can you? As I say, keep it simple.'

'Thanks, Fry,' he said. 'I wish I knew how you know all these things.'

'Hey, come on. You're only in the second term of your first year. You're thirteen years old. You're not expected to know the secrets of the universe.'

'I'm fourteen actually,' he said. 'It was my birthday last week.'

Jesus, he was only . . . what, six months younger than me?

'Well, fourteen, then. Still, you can't . . .'

'The same age as you. But you just seem to know everything.'

The bass-line to the badly produced dance-track of my life.

'How come you know everything, Fry?'

I want to reply, 'How come you think I know everything? Or, how come you think *I* think I know everything? How come that?'

Well, I must be honest, I do have some idea how people might believe it.

Take for example the selection of photographs to accompany this book. What a job. To find a single photograph of me in which I don't look like a smug, self-satisfied creep who has just swallowed a quart of cream and knows where he can get his complacent paws on another. That photograph of me, standing next to my brother dressed for his first day at Chesham Prep, my smugness there qualifies for swagger, pride in him at least. You should see the photographs I had to discard.

Every time I pose for a photograph I try and smile a friendly smile, a sort of 'Hello there! Gosh! Crumbs! Isn't this jolly!' sort of smile. Every time the photograph comes out I see a silken smirk on my face that makes me want to wail and shriek.

Vanity of course, as the preacher saith, all is vanity. Maybe I should have let you see my graduation photograph and a few other pictures that would have sent you doubled-up to the vomitorium.

So that *look*, that oh-so-pleased-with-himself look, combined with a lamentable propensity to explode with unusual words, to spout like a thesaurus and to bristle with look-at-me-aren't-I-clever general knowledge ... I'd be the fool of the world if I didn't see how that might give others the impression that I thought I knew all the answers. But then you see, I *am* the fool of the world.

Matthew was no exception to the general view of me. He looked up to me, physically because I was a foot taller and intellectually because he sincerely believed that I had access to wisdom and knowledge that were denied him. I did a lot of reading, and I had a good memory, everyone knew that of me. He thought that this knowledge gave me power, *even* when he knew, as everyone knew, that I was *always* getting into trouble, getting into more and more trouble all the time: he couldn't have known that so much of that was on account of him or that I was on the verge of getting into the most serious trouble of my life so far that very week.

Still this persists. Enough people know by now what a mess my life has always been, yet they continue to believe *either* that 'It's all right for you, Stephen, you've got it sorted' *or* that *I think* it's all right for me and that *I think* I've got it sorted, neither of which – however many times I scream it and how-ever many times history and circumstance prove it – is true.

This whole thread somehow started with my speculating about the gentle kindness of Ronnie Rutter and wondering whether maybe he *saw*. Perhaps it was written all over me, this agony of love, I wondered.

That has been the big cleft stick of my life. It was around this time that I started punstering like a maniac, mostly dreadful nonsense, but I do remember being struck by discovering the happy accident of this:

Compromise is a stalling between two fools.

It's sort of too neat and too perfect (perfect in the wrong way) to be amusing or even interesting, just another example of the weirdnesses thrown up by our extraordinary language, but the two stools that *I* fell between, and daily fall between still, are best described as being defined by the circumstance that I was and am both transparent *and* opaque, illegible *and* an open book.

Sometimes I wonder what is the point of all my dissembling and simulation if so many friends, acquaintances, enemies (if I have any) and perfect strangers are able to see through my every motive, thought and feeling. Then I wonder what is the point of all my frankness, sharing of experience and emotional candour if people continue to misinterpret me to such an extent that they believe me balanced, sorted, rationally in charge, master of my fate and captain of my soul.

My guess is that the instinct of Ronnie Rutter was that I was an 'unhappy boy' and that he was too scrupulously well mannered or too trusting in the benevolence of time and fate as to enquire into the whys and wherefores.

Matthew, the source of all my misery and all my joy, all my feeling and all my inability to feel, was completely blind to my absolute need for him, too lacking in imagination to be able to see that my happiness was entirely contingent upon him, and I blamed him for that without being able to see that I was trapped in a hole that I had dug. How could he possibly have known? How could he possibly have guessed? Until someone has loved they cannot possibly know what it might be like to *be* loved.

Such then was the spin of my madness. I expected the illegible and the deeply buried in me to be read as if carved on my forehead, just as I expected the obvious and the ill-concealed to be hidden from view.

When I wrote the phrase, many pages back now, 'unrequited love' I giggled to myself, for at the first go I committed the Freudian keyslip of typing 'unrequired love'.

It is, I know, for I have experienced it perhaps twice in my life, an awful privilege to be too much loved and perhaps the kindest thing I ever did in my life was never to let Matthew know to what degree he had destroyed my peace and my happiness. He, after all, was to prove brave enough . . . but that is jumping the gun.

The real Matthew Osborne is reading this now and laughing. Maybe he is groaning. Maybe he is writhing in embarrassment. It might fall out that one day in the future he will say to his wife or his children (for he is a family man now) that if they happen upon *Moab is my Washpot* in a library or second-hand bookshop they might be interested to know that *he* is Matteo. If they do read this book they will look at his grey, thinning hairs and his paunch and his faded blue eyes and they will giggle and shake their heads.

We walked back to the Thring Centre, Matthew thinking – what? Pondering my advice on friendship, ruing the snow that might cancel tomorrow's match, hoping that his vase hadn't cracked in the kiln, I could not guess. I walked by his side, everything inside me crying out to make this speech:

'Come on, let's just turn on our heels and leave this place. What does it hold for you? There's nothing here for *me*. We'll walk along the road to the end of town and, in the end, someone will give us a lift to London. We will survive there. Whom else do we need but each other? Me with my quick wits, you with your quick body. We could find work doing something. Painting, decorating, stacking shelves. Enough to buy a flat. I would write poetry in my spare time and you would make pots and play the piano in bars. In the evenings we could lie by each other's side on a sofa and just *be*. I would stroke your hair with my fingers, and maybe our lips would touch in a kiss. Why not? Why *not*?'

Instead, we made the rather awkward farewells of those who have just exchanged intimacies – exchanged? I had taken, he had given – and he returned to the pottery shop. With no stomach left for the keyboard I trudged my way back through the snow to Fircroft. I had a horrible feeling if I went to my study I might open my heart out to Jo Wood, so I decided to seek out Ben Rudder, the House-captain and ask his permission to have an early bath and go to bed with a book. I needed to clear it with him so that I could be absent from evening call-over. Rudder could be a stickler: strange to think that such an efficient public school authoritarian should go to Cambridge, get a degree, then a doctorate in zoology, and suddenly transform himself into a committed and far left socialist, ending up as editor of *Frontline*, the newspaper of the Workers' Revolutionary Party. Strange, but true. I've lost touch however, so maybe now he's changed again. I hope so, not because I disapprove of the WRP, but because people who can change and change again are so much more reliable and happier than those who can't.

Rudder consented to my request and I went upstairs. That's when it happened.

Everyone has their own story. With some it's a deliberate and concerted attempt to get things moving, with others it might be the result of a friend's assistance. A common one is sliding down a rope, I believe. With me it was the old cliché of soap in the bath.

Well, it gave me the shock of my life, I can tell you. I've described the slight revulsion of watching that boy's penis at Stouts Hill suddenly sick up with semen, so I was prepared for the appearance of the stuff itself *qua* stuff; what I had no inkling of was the physical sensation. I don't suppose anyone will be able to forget the head-swimming power of their first orgasm. Still, you don't want to hear any more on that subject. We've all been there, unless we're female in which case we've been somewhere else, but I dare say it amounts to more or less the same thing, but in different colourways.

I am certain, certain as I can be, that this breakthrough of mine was a mechanical response to idle lathering and nothing to do with Matthew and my having had my arm round him. At least I think I am certain.

Once I realised, at any rate, that I was not going to swoon into a dead faint or see hairs sprouting from the palms of my hands, I tidied things up and went to bed feeling rather pleased with myself. A good day.

6

The next day was a bad day. They really don't come much worse. Like all bad days it started well and full of promise. The world was wedding-cake white, there would be no games. What is more I had no PE on Tuesdays, so it looked like a day of gentle trotting about from lesson to lesson, followed perhaps by a nice fat pigout at the Lower Buttery.

For which, it goes without saying, money would be required. My Post Office account book showed that I had five new pence in credit, not enough even in those far-off days for much more than a slice of bread, a glass of water and a Trebor Refresher. I had recently happened upon a new source of money however: Matron's handbag.

After lunch, Matron had coffee with the Frowdes and their guests, and this, I discovered, provided me with a marvellous opportunity to sneak into her flat, which was just off an upstairs corridor, dive into her handbag and snaffle what could be snaffled.

So that lunchtime I was back at the House, after a morning's Latin, English and horrid, horrid Maths, looking forward to the joys of a splendid afternoon. How was I to find out what Matthew might be doing? That was the only question that really concerned me. His match would be cancelled. There was talk of tobogganing down the slope that ran down from the Middle – Redwood's was the nearest House to that area, maybe I would take the path a long way round and see if Matthew was to be found there.

I was still high on my breakthrough in the bath too. For a moment I had wondered if maybe I wasn't whole. There is some absurd steroid that floats about inside the male and makes him feel ten foot tall just because he's been able to come. It is founded no doubt on the soundest evolutionary principles, but it is ridiculous none the less. Since I was already close to being ten foot tall without the help of the steroid anyway, its effect may have been weaker on me than on many others, but there was still a great spring in my stride as I climbed the stairs after lunch and headed for Matron's flat. I should have known better, it was a Tuesday in February. Many of my life's most awful moments have taken place on Tuesdays, and what is February if not the Tuesday of the year?

I walked casually up and down the corridor a few times to make certain that it was as deserted as usual and then opened the door and went down the little passageway that led to her flat.

There, on her bed was the handbag. I opened it, reached for the purse and then, with terrible swift suddenness, a cupboard swung open and Matron stepped out.

There was nothing I could do or say.

'Sorry' I think was the only word I managed. I said it perhaps a dozen times, rising in trembling tones.

'Go to your tish and wait there.'

It seems Matron had noticed the continual disappearance of money and had worked out when it was going. She had set a trap and I had walked straight into it.

There was no possibility of escape nor any suggestion of an excuse. It was plain that I was the Thief. No hand was ever caught redder, no cash register drawer ever slammed shut on more palpably guilty fingers.

By this time Fircroft knew there was a House Thief and most people guessed it was me, which is why, I suppose, I had diverted my attention away from the House changing rooms and confined my thieving to Matron's handbag or the Sports Hall and swimming-pool changing rooms down in the school.

Rudder the Captain of House himself came to escort me down to Frowde's office. The dear man was simultaneously distraught and furious.

'Damn you, Fry!' he cried, slamming the table. '*Blast* you!'

The decision had already been made. Rustication until the end of term. Rustication meant temporary banishment home, only expulsion was worse. The camel's back was beginning to bend and creak.

My father was already on his way. In the meantime I was to go upstairs and wait once more in my tish.

The drive home was monumentally quiet, but I knew that words would come. My father's analytical mind would not be content to know that I had erred and strayed from my ways like a lost sheep, nor would he simply forgive, forget, judge, punish or exhort. It would be far worse than that. He would need to *understand*. I did not want him to understand, no adolescent ever wants to be understood, which is why they complain about being misunderstood all the time, and most passionately of all I did not want him to know about Matthew.

I am not sure that I thought then that Matthew was the root of the thieving. I am not sure that I know it now. I *am* sure, however, that he was at the root of the recklessness. He was at the root of all my emotions and I was not going to share *them* with anyone, least of all my parents, lest they somehow lead back to the truth.

There was the inevitable analysis in the study, like the scenes that came on the mornings of the school report's arrival, but more intense. Father at the desk in a dense fog of tobacco smoke, Mother on a sofa, alternately hopeful and tearful. I would become transfixed by the amount of smoke Father could inhale: after puffing and puffing at the pipe and ejecting the clouds from the side of his mouth, each cloud thicker than its predecessor, he would finally give one enormous puff and in one huge inhalation the thickest cloud of all would disappear, fractions of it emerging from his mouth and nostrils over the next minutes as he spoke. Sometimes a full ten minutes after this one massive inhalation he might laugh or snort, bringing up from the very bottom of the lungs one last wisp of smoke that had lingered there all that while.

How he coped with the sullen 'Don't know', 'Don't know' that answered every question asked I cannot guess.

He had perception enough to see that there was something there lodged deep within me that he could not reach with reason, cajolement or threat. He continued to analyse and theorise like Holmes, of course, but like Holmes he knew that it was a cardinal error to theorise without sufficient data.

One of his hypotheses was that he and I were very alike, an idea which I rejected as monstrous, nonsensical, absurd, unthinkable, insane and intolerable. I see the similarities now. His brain is better, his standards are higher and his capacity for work is far greater: he is, as a John Buchan hero might say, in almost all respects, the better man, but we do share characteristics. A particular colour of pride, a particular need to analyse. From my mother I have inherited qualities he lacks: an optimism, a desire to please, to cheer up and to gratify others, to make them *feel good*, and an ability to glide superficially, both where superficial gliding is actually a more efficient means of going forward than thrashing through murky waters and where superficial gliding is a kind of moral cowardice. I lack my mother's goodness and ability to subsume her ego and I lack too her capacity to make everyone feel warmed by the radiancy of good nature. I think with my parents the old irony obtains: my mother is the practical one, my father the sentimentalist. I can far more easily imagine my mother coping with life on her own than my father. I don't ever underestimate my father's capacity to surprise and to solve problems, but nor do I forget that his very capacity to solve problems has burdened him with the propensity to find problems where none exists. We all know the ancient story of the Gordian knot, a tangle so complex that it was said he who could untie it would rule the known world: Alexander simply slashed it open with his sword. My father could never, never cut a Gordian knot – he might complicate it further and eventually solve it, but by the time he did so the known world would have moved on. Michael Ramsay, Archbishop of Canterbury during my childhood and during my religious phase a hero and profound influence, was once accused by an interviewer of being wise.

'Am I?' he asked. 'I don't think so really. I think it is probably just the impression given by the absurd fecundity of my eyebrows.'

'Well, your Grace,' the interviewer persisted, 'how would you define wisdom?'

'Wisdom?' Ramsay chewed the word around in his mouth. 'Oh, I should say that wisdom is the ability to cope.'

On that definition, one with which I wholeheartedly concur, I should say my mother is the wiser of my parents.

One inherits or absorbs just so much: my sneakiness, slyness and my wit, in its senses of funniness and of native wit, are all my own. My parents have wit in both those senses too, but it is not the same wit as mine, and best of all for them, each fits the other like teeth into a cog-wheel. From an early age I would watch them do *The Times* crossword each night. There was and is a type of clue that my father would always get and a type that my mother would always get, and between them they would, as it were, lick the platter clean. Occasionally they can complete a puzzle on their own, but I think they get infinitely more pleasure from doing it together. I could finish it by myself from a fairly early age and *hated* sharing it with anyone else, stiffening into cardboard if someone looked over my shoulder or asked for a clue. This is indicative of my need for independence, I suppose, proof that I didn't need anyone in the way my parents needed each other, more than that, proof that I positively needed *not* to need, proof in other words, of fear.

My father also feared the kind of mind I possessed. He knew

I was a clever clogs. A smart-arse. He saw a *Look & Learn* kind of a mind, eagerly competitive with a pastichey, short-cutting brain and a frantic desire to see its name in print, its knowledge praised. It won't surprise you to learn that I had once begged my parents to apply to be on Robert Robinson's television quiz programme, *Ask the Family.* Yes, I really was that dreadful, that insupportably, toweringly, imponderably, unpardonably naff. By good fortune and sense my father would rather have sawn off his legs with the sharp edge of a piece of paper than gone anywhere near such a repulsive proceeding and he made that clear from the outset with a great snorting cloud of pipesmoke. My mother, God love her, may well have been prepared to bite the bullet on my behalf and go through with the horrid thing, but I suspect that even she, loyal to me ever, cheerfully relied on the blank certainty of my father's absolute and categorical refusal.

We know the type, and he knew the type, that's the point. *Blue Peter, Look & Learn, The Guinness Book of Records*: facts, facts, facts. I exploded with facts much as contemporaries exploded with blackheads and Black Sabbath. Dates, capitals, inventors, authors, rivers, lakes and composers. I begged to be asked questions, begged to show off how much I knew, begged, like that little robot in the *Short Circuit* films, for Input . . . Input . . . Input . . .

There's nothing so desperately strange about this. It was perhaps rather more suburban a style than one might expect from a boy of my upbringing: my brother preferred to dream of farming and flying and other pursuits more usual amongst the country-bred, but none the less I was one of the millions and millions of fact-collecting, did-you-know-ing, apparently-ing, it-is-a-little-known-fact-ing little shits that the world has put up with since Gutenberg first carved a moveable letter 'a', which, as every schoolboy tick like me knows, he did in Strasbourg round about 1436.

Such a brain was not consonant with my father's idea of intellect, work and the mind. The first and most urgent problem to be tackled however, was this incessant thieving.

It was decided that I should see a psychiatrist and the man

chosen was Gerard Vaughan, later to become a Government Health Minister, and already I think a Conservative Member of Parliament by this time. I believe he had been recommended by a parental friend, Tommy Stuttaford, then a doctor and MP himself, but now the man hired by *The Times* to add footnotes to every news story that carries the slightest medical implication: *Private Eye* makes merciless fun of him in their 'A Doctor Writes . . .' column. The Stouts Hill School Magazine would have described him as an "Expert" in as many double inverted commas as their printer could spare.

Vaughan had his surgery at Guy's Hospital in London and thither my father and I repaired.

I completed some Bender Gestalt tests, interpreted a Rorschach blot or two and chatted. The thieving was a little puzzling to Vaughan, who felt that I should really be the offspring of a diplomat or a soldier. Teenagers who stole often did so, it appeared, because they came from families who were constantly uprooting. It peeved Vaughan that I should come from such a stable background.

Nevertheless, my problem was diagnosed as 'developmental delay' – academic maturity combined with emotional immaturity: a sixteen-year-old's brain and a ten-year-old's mind warring with each other inside a confused fourteen-year-old boy, resulting in an inability to concentrate, conform or settle. Nowadays a lot of what was wrong with me would no doubt be ascribed to Attention Deficit Disorder, tartrazine food colouring, dairy produce and air pollution. A few hundred years earlier it would have been demons, still the best analogy I think, but not much help when it comes to a cure.

Vaughan's cure came in the shape of an attractive yellow capsule called, if I remember rightly, Lentizol. The only effects, so far as I can remember, were a very dry mouth and terrible constipation. Perhaps this was part of the pill's clinical function: they can't steal if they're on the bog kneading their stomach all day.

Meanwhile, there was the problem of my academic work. If I was rusticated, it meant that I was at home for the rest of term. The following term, the Summer, was my O level term and my father was not about to let the grass grow under my feet, especially when it came to Maths, a subject I was absolutely certain to fail. Failure in Maths O level was disastrous because you couldn't go on to do any A levels without it. I had passed English Language, the other essential, in November: why one sat an exam such as that so early I've no idea – simply to get it out of the way I suppose.

Unfortunately for me, as I thought at the time, my father was as proficient in French, German, Latin and English Literature as he was at Physics, Chemistry and Mathematics.

It was maths that he concentrated on however. He was to become my private tutor.

This was the deepest hell imaginable. The man I most feared and dreaded in the world, in whose presence all intelligence, coherence and articulacy deserted me, teaching me *mano a mano, tête à tête* the subject I most feared and dreaded in the world.

How could he possibly understand how difficult maths was for me, he for whom mathematics was a language he spoke as a Norwegian speaks Norwegian, a Spaniard Spanish and a musician music?

Worse was to come. He looked at the GCE Oxford and Cambridge Board O level maths syllabus and found it wanting. It was, in his judgement, weak, cheap, and Fundamentally Unsound. Mathematics was beautiful, he believed. It should be part of the arts and humanities side of a school, not the science side, he believed. Unlike a science, you did not have to *know* anything to engage in mathematics, merely how to count, he believed. Even that could be discovered from first principles, he believed. Calculus could be taught to a six-year-old, he believed.

There were some French lessons too: he would take down an old copy of a favourite book of his, Daudet's *Lettres de Mon Moulin* and we would go through it together after a day's mathematics. Yes, a *day's* mathematics, day after day after day.

When he grasped the completeness of my ignorance and my incompetence he did not gulp or gasp, I'll give him that. He stuck by his own beliefs and went right back to the beginning.

He taught me something that I did not understand: the equals sign.

I knew what $2 + 2 = 4$ meant. I did not understand however even the rudimentary possibilities that flowed from that. The very thought of an equals sign approximating a pair of scales had never penetrated my skull. That you could do anything to an equation, so long as you did the same to each side, was a revelation to me. My father, never once flinching at such staggering ignorance, moved on.

There came the second revelation, even more beautiful than the first.

Algebra.

Algebra, I suddenly saw, is what Shakespeare did. It is metonym and metaphor, substitution, transferral, analogy, allegory: it is poetry. I had thought its a's and b's were nothing more than fruitless (if you'll forgive me) apples and bananas.

Suddenly I could do simultaneous equations.

Quadratic equations I pounced on because there was a formula you could remember for solving them. My father was not interested in my remembering formulas. Any fool can remember a formula. He wanted me to see *why*. So we went back to the Greeks, to Pythagoras and Euclid.

Oh shit. Geometry. I *hated* geometry.

He decided that we would set out together, as if we knew nothing, to prove the suggestion that, so far as right-angled triangles were concerned, the square on the hypotenuse might well turn out to be equal to the sum of the squares on the other two sides.

Proof?

How *could* you prove such a thing? The whole idea was completely alien to me. I suggested spending an entire day drawing right-angled triangles of different sizes and checking. If they all conformed to this theorem then that would suit me.

Ho-no.

I don't remember the proof, I remember it took in circles and segments and sectors and angles which were temporarily designated the value Theta. But I remember that we got there and that I had followed it all the way and I remember too that when the final, triumphant QED! was written on the bottom of the page I felt a thrill of genuine joy.

We moved on to trigonometry and some very baffling propositions concerning, sin A equalling something and cos A equalling something else, a pair of propositions that were on the A level pure maths syllabus and nothing to do with basic O level mathematics at all.

I can't claim my father made a mathematician out of me. I still speak only stumbling, schoolboy maths with an atrocious English accent. I never quite got the hang of vectors. I have damned Descartes eternally for the foul things. My father can vectorise anything from Dutch Elm Disease, to a sunrise, to the act of opening a tin of beans. Plotting things against things, writing $4x = (x^2 - y^2)$ on a graph line, that sort of runic weirdness – absolute mystery to me.

It was a breakthrough, a breakthrough that enabled me to pass Maths O level and a breakthrough in my relationship with my father. It was a permanent breakthrough in that I never hated him again (feared and dreaded, never hated) but temporary in as much as it altered nothing once I was back at school for the summer. Matthew Osborne still walked the planet, still inhabited almost every waking moment of my life, still gazed at me from every tree, every dawn, every brick in every wall. Indeed so brilliant a teacher was my father that he awoke a fire in me which was extrinsic to mathematics and which, amongst other things, I used to fuel my greatest love, poetry. Novels meant less to me (unless they were stories about my kind of love) and rightly too, for while the novel is an adult invention, the poem is universal but often most especially charged in the mind of the adolescent. The most common betrayal the literary-minded make as they grow up is to abandon their love of poetry and to chase the novel instead. To find oneself believing, as I did when in my twenties, that John Keats for example was strictly for moonstruck adolescents is as stupid and ignorant as to think that grown-ups shouldn't ride bicycles. More stupid, more stupid by far. John Keats may not seem as sophisticated a paperback for the hip pocket of a self-conscious student as Beckett, Bellow or Musil, for example, but his greatness is not something that can be diminished by the stupidity of the newly adult. You can't outgrow Keats any more than you can outgrow nitrogen.

That isn't what I was trying to say, however: you've got me off the point again. The very act of my father's teaching inspired in me a love of the act of teaching in and of itself, *that's* the point. I don't suppose he had ever taught anyone anything before, but he taught me how to teach far more than he taught me how to 'do maths'. I was so fascinated by my own progress that I became more excited by that than by what I was progressing *in*. Part of it may have been connected again (of course it was) to Matthew. I fantasised awakening *his* mind to something in the same way. Not in order to be admired, not in order to win affection, but for the sheer pleasure of the thing, the sheer love of Matthew and the sheer love, the gardener's love, of watching an idea germinate and blossom. I must suppose that my father, for all his apparently cold, Holmesian practicality, was motivated by love too, love of ideas and love of me. Self-love too, but self-love is fundamental to any other kind. *Amour propre* can also mean *proper* love, after all.

My father had believed that I did not know how to think and he had tried to show me how. Showing, again, not telling, had proved efficacious. He knew that I was a natural mimic, intellectually as well as vocally and comically, but he knew that Mimesis is not the same as Reason.

I had had good teachers. At prep school an English master called Chris Coley had awoken my first love of poetry with lessons on Ted Hughes, Thom Gunn, Charles Causley and Seamus Heaney. His predecessor, Burchall, was more a Kipling-and-none-of-this-damned-poofery sort of chap, indeed he actually straight-facedly taught U and Non-U pronunciation and usage as part of lessons: 'A gentleman does not pronounce Monday as Mon*day*, but as Mundy. Yesterday is *yest*erdi. The first 'e' of interesting is not sounded,' and so on.

I remember boys would get terrible tongue lashings if he ever overheard them using words like 'toilet' or 'serviette'. Even 'radio' and 'mirror' were not to be borne. It had to be 'wireless' and 'glass' or 'looking-glass'. Similarly we learned to say *form*idable, not form*i*dable, *pri*marily not pri*mar*ily and *circum*stance not circum*stance* and never, for a second would such horrors as cirumst*ah*ntial or subst*ah*ntial be countenanced. I remember the monumentally amusing games that would go on when a temporary matron called Mrs Amos kept trying to tell boys to say 'pardon' or 'pardon me' after they had burped. The same spin upper-middle-class families get into to this very day when Nanny teaches the children words that Mummy doesn't think are quite the thing.

'Manners! Say "pardon me".'

'But we're not allowed to, Matron.'

'Stuff and nonsense!'

It came to a head one breakfast. Naturally it was I who engineered the moment. Burchall was sitting at the head of our table, Mrs Amos just happened to be passing.

'Bre-e-eughk!' I belched.

'Say "pardon me", Fry.'

'You dare to use that disgusting phrase, Fry and I'll thrash you to within an inch of your life,' said Burchall, not even looking up from his *Telegraph* – pronounced, naturally, Telly*graff*.

'I *beg* your pardon, Mr Burchall?'

'You can beg what you like, woman.'

'I am trying to instil,' said Mrs Amos, (and if you're an *Archers* listener you will be able to use Linda Snell's voice here for the proper effect, it saves me having to write 'A am traying to instil' and all that), 'some manners into these boys. Manners maketh man, you know.'

Burchall, who looked just like the 30s and 40s actor Roland Young – same moustache, same eyes – put down his Telly*graff*, glared at Mrs Amos and then addressed the room in a booming voice. 'If any boy here is ever told to say "Pardon me", "I beg your pardon", or heaven *forfend*, "I beg pardon", they are to say to the idiot who told them to say it, "I refuse to lower myself to such depths, madam." Is that understood?'

We nodded vigorously. Matron flounced out with a 'Well, *reelly*!' and Burchall resumed his study of the racing column.

I can't call such a teacher an inspiration, but there was certainly something of him in the mad general I played in *Blackadder*, and any teaching that drew attention to diversity in language, even the most absurd snobbish elements of it, was a delight to me.

At Uppingham Stokes inspired in me a love of Jonathan Swift, William Morris, George Orwell and those two great Victorians, Tennyson and Browning. In fact my mother had already given me a great reverence for Browning. She, like my father and myself, has a prodigious memory. Hers is especially remarkable when it comes to people and to poetry. She used to reel off a lot of Browning when I was small. No one, sadly, has ever inculcated in me the slightest admiration for the novels of Thomas Hardy or D. H. Lawrence, although I adore the poetry of both, the first being quite magisterially great, the second being charming and often very funny.

So although, as I say, I have been lucky enough to have had some good teachers at the various schools I've inflicted myself upon, none of them came close to my parents. Someone once said that all autobiography is a form of revenge. It can also be a form of thank-you letter.

I returned to Uppingham for the summer term of 1972, better at sums, more fired up by ideas and the idea of ideas, but not fundamentally chastened. I was chastened by the shame and disgrace of having been found and proved a thief, but boys, as Frowde had told me they would be, are limitlessly generous, and they were inclined to treat the subject with immense tact, as if I had been the victim of an unfortunate illness, just as the citizens of Samuel Butler's *Erewhon* treated their criminals. I was probably in my greatest period of physical growth too, shooting up an inch a fortnight it seemed to me. Pubescence was kicking in strong, making up for lost time. I never, thank God, was prey to spoes, as acne was called, but my hair became a little lank, and my eyes took on that strange adolescent brightness that lives under a film of sullenness. They were eyes that looked out, but never want to be looked into.

Summer term was Matthew's term because it was cricket

term. I had always disliked summer, a hot, sticky, asthma-inducing time. It looked pretty, but it bit and it stung. I had a terror of insects, moths in particular, horrible scaly moths which flew through open bedroom windows and fluttered about the light bulb as I tried to read. I could not rest or relax in any room which contained a moth. Butterflies were fine during the day, but moths disgusted and terrified me.

For Matthew's sake, I tried to become good at cricket. Just so that I might occasionally find myself in the same nets as him, or be able to talk about Brian Close or Hampshire's prospects for the Gillette Cup and other such crickety arcana.

It is impossible for me to separate Matthew and cricket, so my current passion for the game must have much to do with him. As I write, it looks as if Australia will at least retain the Ashes at Trent Bridge (today is the Saturday of the 5th Test) and you have no idea what it is costing me to keep away from the television and radio – *wireless* I do beg Mr Burchall's *pardon*.

There is only one story to tell of this summer term and it is the story of the small act of physical consummation that took place between me and Matthew. Consummation is perhaps not the right word: it did not endorse or set the seal on our relationship, it did not fructify or sanctify it. It was a quick and sweet sexual act between two (from Matthew's point of view) friends. At least I can say that it did not *ruin* the relationship or change my feelings for Matthew. It did not fortify them, for sex was never, as I have said, the point. Come to think of it I don't know that love *has* a point, which is what makes it so glorious. Sex has a point, in terms of relief and, sometimes procreation, but *love*, like all art, as Oscar said, is quite useless. It is the useless things that make life worth living and that make life dangerous too: wine, love, art, beauty. Without them life is safe, but not worth bothering with.

It was after a late 'net', as we cricketers call practice. Matthew had asked if he might bowl at me for a while. His chief glory was his batting, but he bowled too. He was left-handed for both batting and bowling and had just taken an interest in wrist spin, which meant that he was experimenting with that peculiar ball, the chinaman. I was by no means a good enough batsman to deal with any kind of spinning ball: anything bowled on a good length at any pace, in fact, had me in trouble, but I was pleased to be asked (indeed had hung around casually all afternoon talking to others, his brother principally, occasionally to Matthew, being amusing and charming, simply in the hope that there might be such an outcome) and did my best.

After a while we stopped and looked around. We were almost the only two on the Middle by this time, the whole wide sward was deserted. Two or three late games of tennis were going on at the Fircroft end, otherwise we had the place to ourselves. Tennis was despised by Garth Wheatley, the master in charge of cricket and by the professional, an ex-Leicestershire player whose name, I am ashamed to say I have forgotten. They both called it, disdainfully, 'woolly balls'.

'Too many promising cricketers are being lured away from the game by the effeminate glamour of woolly-balls,' I heard Wheatley say once, with a disparaging sniff.

Matthew closed his cricket-bag and picked up his blazer. 'Oh, I love summer,' he sighed, looking around.

'Me too,' I said. 'Hang on, what am I talking about? I hate it.'

'What do you mean?'

We started to walk, aimlessly it seemed, in a direction that took us away from both our Houses, away from the school, towards nothing but fields.

I explained my hatred of insects, my asthma and my inability to cope with heat. 'Let's face it,' I said. 'I'm made for the winter. The more clothes I keep on the better I look. In shorts I'm a mess. And unlike you, I don't look glamorous in cricket whites.'

'Oh, that's rubbish,' he said and then after the briefest of pauses. 'I quite fancy you, for a start.'

'Oh yeah?' I said, and gave him a push. 'Trying to seduce me are you?'

'Yeah!' he said, pushing back and knocking me over.

It was all that quick and that silly. Nothing more than rolling and tickling in the long grass that turned into rubbing and sliding and finally angrily rapid mutual masturbation. No kissing, but at least plenty of giggling and smiling. Sex without smiling is as sickly and base as vodka and tonic without ice.

He left me there, lying in the grass. I leaned up on one elbow and watched him go, until his shape, cricket cream-coloured against the grass, disappeared from view. He never once turned back.

I lay back, stared at the sky and fell asleep.

I passed Maths O level, not with distinction, but I passed. The only exam I failed was Physics, a determined cock snooked at my father to remind him that I was still myself. He had not made me his creature, his good science boy. For physics, above all, was what father was about.

I did not just fail Physics, I ploughed it spectacularly. Such was my pride that I could not bear to be seen to fail anything unless it was quite deliberate.

There had been a question in the examination paper which asked about something called EMF. To many of you reading this, EMF probably means that Forest of Dean combo whose excellent single 'Unbelievable' had us all foot-tapping five or six years ago, to Mr Pattinson the poor sod whose job it was to try and get some physics into my head, EMF meant Electro-Magnetic Force, or Field or something vaguely similar, please don't ask me to elaborate.

The question read:

Describe the EMF of a bicycle torch battery.

Well, I hadn't the faintest idea what they were on about, so I spent the entire physics exam drawing a bicycle. I wasn't bad at this, Object Drawing was the part of the Art O level that I was best at, my painting had never again reached the heights of the IAPS award-winning *Unforgettable Character*, but copying, I could always *copy*.

The bicycle I drew had a crossbar, saddle bags (an open cross-section of which revealed the presence of a Tupperware box containing an apple, a Mars bar and some cheese and chutney sandwiches) and, naturally, torches front and rear.

My last act, at the end of the exam was to rule a line towards the front torch and write at the other end:

'This is the torch that contains the battery that contains the EMF that the questioner seems so desperate to know about.'

O levels in those days came in Grades 1 to 6, which were passes, and then 7, 8 and 9 which were fails. I achieved none of these. I achieved something far more magnificent. I was awarded an Unclassified, which included a letter to the school.

I don't think my father was hugely surprised when the results came through in the summer holidays. At least I had passed Maths, that was the great thing.

I decided, as my third year began, my Sixth Form year, that I would do English, French and Ancient History for A level. My father tried, with half-hearted idealism to suggest that there would be more of a challenge to me intellectually if I chose Maths, but my choice prevailed.

Some two or three weeks after my fifteenth birthday, therefore, I was a member of Lower VIA. I was far too young to be a sixth former. Too young literally, and much too young if one believed Gerard Vaughan's diagnosis of 'developmental delay'.

I had the joy of Rory Stuart, a remarkable teacher. Actually a Cambridge classicist of distinction, his enthusiasm (and he was the living embodiment of that divine Greek quality) had turned to English Literature. He went on to become head of English at Westminster and then, on the death of a plants-woman aunt whose cottage and grounds he inherited, he altered direction once more, this time reinventing himself as a landscape gardener. He calls himself, with splendid im-pudence, RHS Gardens (using his genuine initials but infuriating the pompous arses of the Royal Horticultural Society in Wisley) and does a little teaching still at the nearby Cheltenham Ladies' College. He co-wrote a book about making a garden with the novelist Susan Hill, a book I thoroughly recommend. His pupils are spread wide around the world and feel themselves to be part of a special club. Sometimes I will bump into someone in the street who'll say,

'Excuse me, weren't you taught by Rory Stuart?' and we will stand there together swapping stories about him and what he did for us. Like me, there was something immensely distant and aloof about him in private, he was very unknowable there, but once his metaphorical teaching cap was on, he was energetic, charged and boundlessly creative. Anything that was said he could open like a flower, examine as a geologist might examine a stone or a squirrel a nut: a stupid and flippant remark could be as excitedly chased down as serious. Every remark or thought from any boy came to him as if it was utterly new and vibrating with possibility.

Given what I have already said about my parents, Stuart was *the teacher* that some are lucky enough to have in their lives. Others will always blame the lack of such a being on their failure to progress. Maybe they are right to do so, but I have always disbelieved that Sicilian saying about revenge being a dish best served cold. I feel that – don't you? – when I see blinking, quivering octogenarian Nazi war criminals being led away in chains. Why not *then*? It's too late *now*. I want to see them taken back in time and punished *then*. There were pictures of Pol Pot last week, tremblingly enchained: again, too late one feels, too late. Blame, certainly, is a dish only edible when served fresh and warm. Old blames, grudges and scores congeal and curdle and cause the most terrible indigestion. There were those who *might* have been able to save me from myself. It is possible that somewhere in the chain of events from Chesham Prep to prison I could look back and say, '*He* failed, *she* failed, *they* never tried,' but where would that get me *now*? Off the hook? I don't feel that I'm *on* one. 'If my devils are to leave me, I am afraid my angels will take flight as well,' said Rilke in sharp defiance of the future industry of TV and self-help-book exorcism.

Maybe it's my mother's side in me that makes me one who would rather look to people to thank and praise than people to blame and damn. Don't get me wrong, unlike my mother, I've a wicked tongue in my head and when it comes, for example, to that pallid, fraudulent, dangerous twentieth-century version of true mysticism, the charlatanism of runes, tarot, horoscopy, telepathy, rootless opinion, stale second-hand 'open-minded-ness' and all that shite. I get blisteringly unforgiving and furious. I am capable of being horribly polemic and culpatory in many arenas, but in the arena of the past I see no point. Had I been palpably abused in any senses of that much (ha!) abused word, then maybe I would think differently – as it is and as I have never tired of restating, *I* am the one who did most of the abusing: I abused trust, love, kindness and myself.

As a sixth-former life was, technically, more relaxed. As a fifteen-year-old it was, naturally, growing more complex every day. My feeling for Matthew had not altered. We never repeated the allegro rapture of our one sexual experiment, and we never referred to it. I still don't know why it happened. Maybe he had guessed the depth of my feeling for him and had thought it was founded in lust and had as a result wanted to get all that out of way because he valued my friendship. Maybe he was being kind. Maybe he was just a *healthy* fourteen-year-old who fancied a quick bit of nookie. Maybe he felt for me what I felt for him. I'll never know and that is as it should be. I'll always have that memory at least . . . the heat of him, the heat of him from his day's exercise, the heat that radiated from the base of his throat, the heat under his arms, the heat-of-the-moment heat of that moment. Oh dear, will these memories never lose *their* heat?

I acted in a play in Trog Richardson's brand new Uppingham Theatre, being amongst the first three to step on its stage. Patrick Kinmonth, Adrian Corbin and I were the weird sisters (none weirder, believe me) in the theatre's baptismal pro-duction of *Macbeth*. I had read David Magarshak's translation of Stanislavsky's *Art of the Theatre* and had decided that acting was my destiny.

The director, Gordon Braddy, wanted the witches to design their own costumes, a decision he came to regret, since I announced that I wanted my costume to hang with fresh livers, lungs, kidneys, hearts, spleens and other innards, all bound by intestines. And why not, I argued, produce *real* eyes of frog and *genuine* tongues of newt from the cauldron?

This was considered too much, but my offal-trimmed costume was permitted. The costume itself was constructed of strips of PVC. Kinmonth, who is now a highly respected painter anyway so it wasn't fair, designed something excellent. Corbin too managed to snip something out of plastic that was at least wearable. The Christine-Keeler-meets-the-little-red-murderer-from-*Don't-Look-Now* nightmare that I threw together haunts me still and, I swear to you, for I have returned many times, the smell of rotten guts still informs the under-stage dressing-rooms.

I returned to that Uppingham Theatre for the first time, as it happens, in 1981, just after leaving Cambridge, with Hugh Laurie, Emma Thompson, Tony Slattery and the rest of our Footlights troupe, to perform prior to Edinburgh. Uppingham had become, because of Chris Richardson, a common stop-off place for comedians. It had started with Richardson designing the set for Rowan Atkinson's original one-man-show. Rowan always tried out his new material at Uppingham and the Footlights followed.

I have since been back to give little talks and readings and so forth, Old Boy on the Telly, Sleb Speaker, all that, but every time I stand on that stage I see Richard Fawcett as Seyton and Third Murderer, Tim Montagnon as Banquo, David Gaine laying on as Macduff and above all Rory Stuart as Macbeth. Like most actors I forget the lines of any play a week or so after the run is over, but I have forgotten hardly a single word of *Macbeth*, from 'When' to 'Scone'. It is too far distant to recall Rory's performance in any detail, but I was thrilled, simply entranced, by the way he delivered the climax to the great 'If it were done when 'tis done' soliloquy –

> And Pity, like a naked new-born babe,
> Striding the blast, or heaven's cherubim, horsed
> Upon the sightless couriers of the air,
> Shall blow the horrid deed in every eye,
> That tears shall drown the wind.

Hoo-werr . . . I still shudder at it. I may have felt guilt and fear of punishment in my day, but it was never quite that bad. A few people whispering in corners, the soul of my dead grandfather, the sad-eyed Christ, those things have bothered and shamed me, but I never imagined heaven's cherubim blowing the horrid deed in every eye or Pity, like a naked new-born babe, striding the blast. God where *did* he get it from, that man, that Shakespeare?

None the less, nemesis was drawing up her skirts ready to charge, and as always with that fell dame, I wasn't looking for her in the right places.

My parents, with as much realism, I fear, as generosity, had made it plain that if *ever* I was short of money, I was to go to Mr Frowde and he would advance me enough to buy as many of Mrs Lanchberry's lard-fried eggs and her husband's cream slices as I could eat. It must have been something more than slightly sickening and slightly frightening for them to know that the most efficient way to stop me stealing was to let me have as much money as I wanted. It's like proving Pythagoras by drawing and measuring as many different right-angled triangles as you can.

I had more or less stayed out of trouble for the first month or so of that sixth-form term. The work was fun: I liked Anouilh's *Antigone*, the first French set text we had reached, and I liked Ancient History too, which was actually a cop-out: I should have chosen Latin and Greek, but I saw Ancient History as a good dossy compromise.

I developed around this time a mania for climbing around the roofs of the school buildings. Any psychologist who can interpret this convincingly for me will earn my thanks. The School Hall, a great Victorian building with onion domes at each corner and the Chapel itself, both yielded wonderful runs of leaded channels and strange platforms from which one could survey the school beneath. I knew where Biffo Bailey, the school porter kept the keys to everything and had become a master at the art of this particular form of non-theftual cat-burglary.

> ('Did he just say *non-theftual*?'
> 'He did, you know.'
> 'I thought so. Shall I, or will you?'

'Best let it pass I think.'
'Really?'
'Mm. Only encourage him otherwise.'
'Well, if you say so. Personally I've half a mind to call the police.')

Both the Chapel and the Hall also contained two enormous Walker organs, with gigantic thirty-two-foot wood diapasons. If you stuck a piece of paper over the vent of one (I'm sure there's a better name for it than 'vent', but I've lost Howard Goodall's telephone number) a single one-second blast on a bottom A would break the paper in two. Best of all, the lectern could be raised to reveal a huge array of presets. Between each of the three keyboards, you see, were buttons numbered one to, I think, eight. The organist, instead of having to grab at and pull out a clutch of different stops while in mid-Toccata, could just press Button 3 say, which would automatically push out a preset combination of, for example, viol, tromba and clarion. I discovered, one Saturday afternoon while the rest of the school was thrilling to the excitements of the Oundle match or whatever frantic tourney was being enacted on the field of battle, that I could *alter* these presets, and I did so. All you needed, with the lectern lifted and balanced on your head, was to use the tip of a biro to flick a series of dip-switches, as I believe they're called. I changed every preset which was loud and thunderous to a preset that used one feeble oboey wail and every preset which was dulcet and faint to a great combinatory blast of the very loudest, most thundering pipes.

The following morning, Sunday, as we walked down to the Chapel I explained to Richard Fawcett, Jo Wood and a few others what I had done.

'You wait,' I said. 'You just wait.'

The organ on Sundays was usually played by one of the music staff rather than a boy. It would either be Dr Peschek, whose son Dickon was at the school and a friend, or by Mr Holman who had wild dark curly hair and looked like Professor Calculus from the Tintin books.

As we reached the Magic Carpet, I saw Holman hurrying

along with sheaves of music under his arms. Splendid, I thought. Splendid.

The result was indeed splendid.

The moment for the entry of the choir arrived and Holman, as he improvised the quiet preludey music that organists favour while congregations settle, was beginning to look a little rattled already. A huge blasting fart had emerged in the middle of one of his gentle, meandering doodles and blown back the hair of the first two rows of School House who were sitting in front of the diapason array and had directed at him the most indignant looks. This had unnerved him and we could see, between peeping fingers, that he was beginning to lose faith in his beloved presets. But there was no time for him to do anything about it, the chaplain and servers were there at the back with the choir and candle-bearers, it was time for action and the procession. Holman raised his two hands, a tiny knuckle crack was heard as he bent his fingers and –

'Neeeeeeeeee . . .'

Handel's stirring anthem 'Thine Be The Glory', instead of roaring the faithful to their feet, peeped like a shy mouse from the wainscoting. Headman at the back of the procession, shot a look up at the organ loft, and Holman's wild face, reflected in the mirror for us all to see, turned a bright shade of scarlet. The fingers of one hand flew around the stops, pulling frantically, while the other hand vamped ineffectually and the feet trod up and down the pedals which gave out tiny squeaking thirds and fifths, the kind of waily wheeze someone produces when they pick up a mouth-organ for the first time.

The school rose uncertainly to its feet, all save Jo Wood, Richard Fawcett and I, who were under the pew, biting hassocks and weeping with joy.

Further stabs of delight assailed us when we saw, during sermons and lessons, Holman furtively lifting the lectern and trying to make adjustments, looking for all the world like the form's bad boy peeping at a porn-mag in his desk.

A few weeks later the school had the excitement to look forward to of a Day Off. The kingdom was to celebrate the excitements of the Silver Wedding of the Queen and the Duke of Edinburgh and had declared a Monday Bank Holiday in its patriotic fervour. Jo Wood and I had even more to look forward to, for Geoff Frowde had given us permission to go to London.

I had a meeting of the Sherlock Holmes Society to attend, and had invited Jo to come along as my guest.

For many years now I had been a member of this harmlessly dotty sodality. I had been the youngest member for a long while, though by now some snot-nosed little creep had limbo-danced under me to that distinction. The organisation was run by eccentric men like Lord Gore-Booth, the President, who dressed up as Holmes every year when the Society went to Switzerland to re-enact that final, fateful tussle between Moriarty and Holmes by the Reichenbach Falls. Gore-Booth's wonderful daughter Celia who died way before her time, (I *think* she was his daughter, not niece) I got to know many years later when she was one of the many remarkable actors in the troupe known, slightly embarrassingly, as *Théâtre de Complicité*.

Another leading light was the editor of the *Journal*, the Marquess, or possibly Marquis (I have no Debrett's to hand, I fear) of Donegal. The *Journal* ran fierce articles on hot Holmesian topics and ran a correspondence page calling itself 'The Egg Spoon', in honour of the item of cutlery that Watson wagged petulantly at Holmes one breakfast very early in their relationship, Watson using the splendid phrase, if I remember rightly, 'Ineffable twaddle!' to describe an article he was reading, which turned out of course, to be have been written by Holmes himself.

The usual meeting room was the old Royal Commonwealth Club in Villiers Street, off the Strand (deemed propitious I suppose, since Holmes made his first appearance in *The Strand Magazine*).

Anyhoo, as Ned Ryerson likes to say in *Groundhog Day*, Frowde had consented to our attendance of a Saturday evening meeting of the Society. We had booked hotel rooms for ourselves in Russell Square and were due to return on Monday afternoon, which gave us almost three days of London.

Only it didn't, because we had rushes of blood to the head and went to the cinema and watched *A Clockwork Orange*, *The Godfather* and *Cabaret*, over and over and over and over and over again for four days in a row. Hell of a year for cinema, 1972. All the films were X-certificate of course, but both Jo and I looked as if we just *might* pass as eighteen.

I don't know what it was that possessed us. It was as if we were gripped by some uncontrollable force. We simply could *not* move away from those films. I think we took in *Fritz the Cat* four or five times as well, but it was that trio that slammed us amidships like three gigantic icebergs. We could hardly have chosen better, I will say that for ourselves.

I don't know if our respective parents thought the other child was to blame, or constituted a Bad Influence on the other (I'm not sure my parents ever *quite* got the point of Jo) but I think we would both agree that it was a simple case of compulsion. If either had left to go back to school, the other would probably have stayed. We were completely mesmerised by an utterly new world and all its possibilities. Art had gripped me, poetry, music, comedy, cricket and love had gripped me and have me in their grip still, but *cinema*. Films have a peculiar power all their own. Maybe we had found a rock and roll for ourselves, something that was neither solipsistic, tragic and sublime like music, nor egocentrically bullying like comedy. I can't explain. Until that moment, I had been content and perfectly delighted to watch *The Guns of Navarone* and *You Only Live Twice*; now films suddenly seemed to have reached a puberty like mine and were the Real Thing. It was *me*, of course, not films that had really changed, though there is no doubt that it *was* a good crop and that there was something new about their style and their treatment of subject matter. As every scene of *The Godfather* unwound in front of my disbelieving eyes, from the wedding to the final famous closing of the door and the shot of the leather chair, Uppingham School looked smaller and smaller and smaller.

I think I even forgot about Matthew.

I remember feeling the desire to see the films with him, the need to *show* them to him, but while I was watching them, neck up, front row, over and over and over again, I forgot everything except the world of each film.

When we returned to Uppingham, still blinking at the light and at the dawning realisation of our madness, all was up. In my case the camel's back had been snapped completely in two by this final straw and I was instantly expelled, not even given the chance to say goodbye to a single friend.

In Jo's case, punishment came in the form of rustication until the end of term.

I shall never forget my father's only words in the car as he, yet again, drove his infuriating, ungrateful, monstrous middle child home.

'We will discuss this sorry business later.'

We did discuss it later, this sorry business, of course we did. One aspect, however that we never discussed, oddly enough, was the films. To my father, and I can see why, this was disobedience, rebellion, wildness, attention-seeking ... all kinds of things. He saw the urge to self-destruct, but he did not choose to examine the weapon I had selected. I think that is a fair and a reasonable thing for anyone, but it is strange that we never spoke about the films.

One could argue that there was something in each of them that spoke directly to me.

In *Cabaret* there was homosexuality in the form both of divine decadence and of guilty, smothered English shame; there was guilty, smothered *Jewish* shame too; there was the tension and love between a stuffy Englishman unable to scream or express himself and the fantasising, romantic Sally Bowles, each equally doomed and equally in pain, each one half of me.

In *A Clockwork Orange* there was the bad, uncontrollable, rebellious, intolerable and intolerant adolescent, with his mad romping love of Beethoven (even Rossini got a look in too) and society's need to constrain and emasculate him, to drive both away his devils *and* his angels and stop him from being himself.

In *The Godfather* there was ... hell, this is pointless, there is everything in *The Godfather*.

Didn't Woody Allen say that all literature was a footnote to Faust? Perhaps all adolescence is a dialogue between Faust and Christ. We tremble on the brink of selling that part of ourselves that is real, unique, angry, defiant and whole for the rewards of attainment, achievement, success and the golden prizes of integration and acceptance; but we also in our great creating imagination, rehearse the sacrifice we will make: the pain and terror we will take from others' shoulders; our penetration into the lives and souls of our fellows; our submission and willingness to be rejected and despised for the sake of truth and love and, in the wilderness, our angry rebuttals of the hypocrisy, deception and compromise of a world which we see to be so false.

There is nothing so self-righteous nor so right as an adolescent imagination.

Breaking Out

I

THE REPLACEMENT FOR Uppingham that my parents chose was The Paston School in the Norfolk market town of North Walsham. A direct grant grammar school (there *had* been some point to that Eleven Plus after all, it seemed) its greatest claim to fame was its old boy, the 'Norfolk Hero' as he is known around these parts, Horatio Nelson.

Having been expelled from Uppingham ('asked to leave' is the proper expression) in November 1972 I naturally had to start at Paston in the Spring Term of 1973. The school, which was not accustomed to fifteen-year-olds in the Sixth Form, suggested that I retake all my O levels in the summer of 1974, when I would be sixteen, only *then* might it be appropriate to think about A levels.

Well I mean, what? The blow to my pride was immense; never had a pride been that so deserved a great blow, but that was not how I looked at it. On hearing this news, I instantly, before I had so much as crossed its threshold, detested and despised all things Pastonian.

By this time I think my parents were beginning to worry about any influence I might have on my sister, Jo. She turned eight years old about the time of my expulsion and had remained entirely devoted to me. Being a girl, it was not considered so necessary, according to the curious logic of these things, for her to board, so she attended Norwich High School for Girls, a private school which involved the snazziest green

uniform you can imagine. Now that I was starting at The
Paston, a day school too, Jo and I would breakfast together·and
spend evenings together every single day. My bus went from
Cawston to North Walsham, Jo was enmeshed in a complex
network of school runs with the parents of other girls around
the Booton area, but essentially we were in the same boat now.
Roger naturally stayed at Fircroft, where he was to go on to
become a House Polly and then School Polly and Captain of
House and I would see him only in the holidays.

Paston School lived up to all my prejudices, as things always
will to the prejudiced. I did not take to the place one bit. I can
remember barely anything about it, except that it was there
that I started to smoke and there that I learned to play pinball:
not within the school grounds, but within the town of North
Walsham. For within a very short space of time I started to cut
the school dead. I would get on the Cawston bus and dismount
at either Aylsham or North Walsham and then head straight
for a café and spend the day pinballing, listening to records by
Slade, the Sweet, Wizzard and Suzi Quattro and smoking
interminable Carlton Premiums, Number Sixes and Embassy
Regals.

The Paston took this insolence for about a term and a half
before suggesting to my parents that maybe I might be happier
somewhere else.

I wish I could write more about the place, but I simply do
not remember a thing. I drive through North Walsham
sometimes, on my way to visit friends in the old wool town of
Worsted, and I see the school but I wouldn't be able to tell you
what any of the buildings were used for. I suppose there were
assembly halls, sports fields and all the rest of it, but the entire
establishment is a vacuum in my mind. My whole being was
concentrating entirely on Matthew Osborne and nothing else
in the world existed.

I thought of writing to him, but could not begin to express
my thoughts, or if I did, I did not dare to communicate them.
So I did the next best thing and wrote poetry.

Once The Paston had dislodged me, my ever patient parents
thought that perhaps what I needed was the more mature

atmosphere of a Sixth Form College, a place where pupils were called students, lessons were called lectures, where smoking was not against the rules, where independence of mind and eccentricity were tolerated. The place available to me, which could take me on as a weekly boarder, was the Norfolk College of Arts and Technology in King's Lynn, known as Norcat. I remember visiting the vice-principal, and my mother enquiring about Oxbridge entrance. The VP gave a kind of derisive snort and said that, looking at my record he *really* didn't think that this was an option we need consider. I shall never forget the indignant flush that suffused my mother's face, the closest to fury I had seen her come for a very long time.

I had the summer of 1973 to fill then, before starting on a two-year A level course of English, French and History of Art. I took a job at the Cawston Winery, a little plant that produced kits for home brewing and home wine-making. My job involved making cardboard boxes, millions of the bastards. The rest of time however, was spent writing poems and starting novels. Always the same subject. The subject of most of *The Liar* and the subject of this book.

There was always a Me and there was always a Matthew. If I were to quote now extensively from any of these (I have just spent a very bloody seven hours going though them) it would hurt you, dear reader, and me, too much.

Most of the shorter poems have angry, pompous teenage titles like 'Song of Dissonance and Expedience' and 'Open Order: A Redress', a punning title this, which will only make sense if you've ever drilled in the CCF or armed services.

This was too the summer in which I wrote these words.

To Myself: Not To Be Read Until I Am Twenty-Five

I know what you will think when you read this. You will be embarrassed. You will scoff and sneer. Well I tell you now that everything I feel now, everything I am now is truer and better than anything I shall ever be. Ever. This is me now, the real me. Every day that I grow away from the me that is writing this now is a betrayal and a defeat. I expect you will screw this up into a ball with sophisticated disgust, or at best with tolerant amusement but deep down you will know, you will know that you are smothering what you really, really were. This is the age when I truly am. From now on my life will be behind me. I tell you now, THIS IS TRUE – truer than anything else I will ever write, feel or know. WHAT I AM NOW IS ME, WHAT I WILL BE IS A LIE.

I can dimly, just dimly, recall writing it. A whole condition of mind swims back into me every time I look at it, and swam back all the more strongly when I typed it out for you just now. I won't go so far as to call it a Proustian *petite madeleine*, one of those epiphanic memory revivifiers, for the memory has always been there, but it still has the power to create a feeling like hot lead leaking into my stomach, a feel-good pain that was both the dreaded demon and the welcome companion of my adolescence. It was a strange piece of writing to happen upon as I did recently, going through all my old papers, writings, poems and scrapbooks, and it's a strange thing to look at now. What would you think if you read such a message to yourself?

The past is a foreign country, they do things differently there. *The Go-Between*, the novel whose celebrated opening words those are, has long been a favourite of mine. Actually, they were filming Harold Pinter's adaptation of it in Norfolk round about the time I wrote that letter to myself. I had read the book and bicycled off to Melton Constable to see if they needed extras. They didn't, of course.

I knew that the past was a foreign country, and knew too that it followed logically that the future must be abroad; in other words I knew that it was my destiny to become a foreigner, a stranger to myself. I was passionately patriotic about my own age, a fierce believer in the rightness and justness of adolescence, the clarity of its vision, the unfathomable depths and insurmountable heights of its despair and its joy. The colours that shone and vibrated so strongly through its eyes were the true colours of life, this I knew.

Because I had read a great deal I knew as well that one day I would see things in different colours, take up citizenship in a different country, the country of the adult, and I hated my future self because of it. I wanted to stay behind in adolescence and fight for its rights and I knew that the moment I left it I would care only for the rights of my new age, my adulthood with all its falsities and failures.

In those days loyalty to youth usually meant loyalty to ideas, political ideas chiefly. Ageing was seen as compromise and hypocrisy because it seemed inevitably to entail a selling out of ideals, environmental ideals now, but political then. For me, however, all this meant nothing. I was not even remotely interested in politics, the environment, the bomb or the poverty of the Third World. Only one thing counted for me then, Matthew, Matthew, Matthew, and I suspected, quite rightly, that one day love would count for less. I did not suspect, however, that one further, finer day far, far forward, love would come round to counting for everything again. A lot of salt water was to flow down the bridge, the bent bridge of my nose, before that day would come.

I had fully determined, you see, to Do My Best at Norcat, and I believed that this would involve a number of fundamental alterations to my nature. I believed it meant I must subdue my sexuality and become heterosexual. I believed it meant I must bury all thoughts of Matthew and convince myself they were part of 'a phase' one of those 'intense schoolboy friendships' that you 'grow out of' and I believed it meant that I would get my head down and *work*.

My writings then, were an attempt at expulsion, catharsis, exorcism, call it what you will. They were a farewell. I knew, or thought I knew, that I was about to betray my former self and plunge into a world of good behaviour, of diligently completed homework, punctual attendance and female dating. A tangle of briar might as well persuade itself that tomorrow it will become a neat line of tulips, but I had thought it was my destiny. At the same time I knew, absolutely *knew* that there some quality in me, foul, ungovernable, unmanageable and unendurable as I was, that was *right*. The perception of nature, the depth of emotion, the brightness and intensity of every moment, I knew these faded with age and I hated myself in advance for that. I wanted to live on the same quick Keatsian pulse for all time. Perhaps Pope was right to suggest that a little learning is a dangerous thing, for it may be that had I read much, but I had not read all: I had read enough to *connect* my experience with that of others, but I had not read enough to *trust* the experience of others. So when, for example, Robin Maugham in his autobiography *Escape From the Shadows* wrote of his schoolboy loves and passions and his hatred for his father and his relationship with his famous uncle and his desperation to find a role for himself in an alien word, I connected with that, but when Maugham reached his twenties, became a writer of sorts, fought in tanks in the desert war, and then looked back at the 'Shadows' from which he had gratefully escaped, I thought him a traitor. He should have stayed and fought, not just in England, but in the republic of adolescence. He should not have committed the crime of growing up. I prefigured in my mind my future self being just so treacherous and it appalled me and angered me.

The only 'work' and I use the word ill-advisedly, which I can give you a few lines from is an epic poem I began that summer, an epic in which I grandly decided to ape the structure and ironic style of Byron's masterpiece *Don Juan*, which involved grappling with the complexities of *ottava rima* which, as you shall see, is a verse form which I did not do any justice at all. It suited Byron well, but then Byron was Byron; Auden excelled at it, but then Auden mastered all verse forms. I . . . well, I floundered.

The Untitled Epic (that, I grieve to confess, is its title) which I have just reread completely for the first time since writing it, much to my great embarrassment, seems to be much more directly autobiographical than I had remembered it to be. The scene I will inflict on you is the poetic version I attempted of that red-headed Derwent's ravishing of me. I call him Richard Jones in this instance and make him House-captain. As Isherwood was to do in *Christopher And His Kind* I refer to myself in this epic as 'Fry', 'Stephen' and occasionally, like Byron, 'our hero'.

We are at verse fifty something by now, I had planned twelve Cantos, each of a hundred verses. Richard Jones has sent Fry down to his study ostensibly to punish him for being in bed late. Fry waits outside the door in his dressing-gown and pyjamas, hoping he isn't going to be beaten too badly. I apologise for the completely show-offy and senseless semi-quotations from everything from *Anthony and Cleopatra* to *The Burial Of Sir John Moore at Corunna*. The painful polysyllabalism of some line-endings was in deference to Byron's much more successful comic use of hudibrastic rhyming. I was fifteen, it's my only excuse.

> He stood outside the Captain's study door,
>   And prayed to God to toughen his backside
> Against the strokes of Jones's rod of war.
>   For hours he waited, rubbing that soft hide
> In fear. He kicked the wainscot and tapped the floor,
>   Examined the plaster on the wall, eyed
> The ants that weaved around the broken flags
> And cursed the day that God invented fags.
>
> At last, as he began to think that Jones
>   Would never come, he heard the crack of steel-
> Capped heels around the corner. He froze
>   And felt within his veins the blood congeal
> To ice. The boots were sparking on the stones,
>   So in the darkening passage the only real
> Sound, rang in deaf'ning pentametric beat
> In flashes from the pounding leathered feet.
>
> The Captain halted and threw wide the door:
>   Inside his study glared the gleaming trophies
> The rackets, balls and instruments of war,
>   Sops to culture – some unread Brigid Brophies
> And Heinrich Bölls. All these our hero saw,
>   And Deco posters for Colmans and Hovis.
> But above the window, sleekly like a ship,
> Lay harboured there a deadly raw-hide whip.

But Richard Jones, it appears, is not going to inflict punishment. He tells our hero to calm down. This is going to be a brotherly chat.

> "I take it you drink coffee? Good. And cake?
>   That's it, relax! Now look, Stephen – I may
> Call you that? – I'm not here just so's to make
>   Your life hell, you know. If, in any way,
> I can help you to settle down and take
>   Your place at Brookfields House, then you must say.
> As for your being late for bed – it's quite
> Okay, for you'll be later still tonight."
>
> Those blue, blue eyes to Stephen now appeared
>   Fraternal, not so Hitleresquely bad,
> And all those fearful doubts at last were cleared.
>   Those eyes that gazed so picturesquely had,
> When he misjudged him, been loathed and feared:
>   Fry saw him by the little desk he had
> The tea-cups on, affectionate and kind,
> The best-intentioned prefect one could find.

There follows a bit of coffee spilling business which means they have to share the same chair. Richard gives Stephen a cigarette, which makes him choke and splutter and go dizzy . . .

> And meanwhile Richard gently rocked the chair
>   They sat in (like a tarnished throne) and gazed
> At Stephen, softly, as he gasped for air,
>   His mind befogged, his body numbed and dazed.
> But Richard only saw the glowing hair
>   And soft and hairless skin. He was amazed
> That such a vision could assail his eyes,
> From satin locks to silk-pyjama-ed thighs.
>
> He stretched his arms towards our hero's head:
>   "What hair you have . . ." he whispered, "may I stroke it?"
> 'How lovely,' Stephen thought, "Yes please," he said.
>   A blissful silence fell, and Stephen broke it,
> "If only – " he stopped, turning red.

"I know, I know," breathed Richard. As he spoke it
He swung one leg over the other side,
And, straddling the two arms, he faced his bride.

I will excuse you the pain of the actual scene, but there follows
what we might call an Act of Carnal Violation, ruthlessly
enacted by Jones on Fry, who is deeply hurt by the experience.

He picked himself up and hobbled about:
    He dressed in silence choking back the tears.
He carried inside him the seeds of doubt
    That had exchanged his new-fired hopes for fears
So Jones had hurt him after all, and out
    Of joy and smiles there came forth grief and leers.
Passions to passions, lust to lust shall pass:
Life's a bugger and a pain in the arse.

Not a word was passed not a parting shot,
    As Fry to his dormitory hurried.
He hit the mattress of his iron cot
    And his face in his pillow he buried.
"He's used me like you'd use a woman, not
    A friend." said Fry, hot and hurt and worried.
Thus was this boy, now sadly laid in bed,
Quite robbed of comfort, sleep and maidenhead.

I have to confess that it upsets me that extract (literary shame
aside): upsets me because it seems to indicate that I had been
more devastated by my deflowering at the hands (hands? –
hardly the right word) of Derwent than I had supposed. There
again, reading further on, I think it possible that dramatic and
poetic licence were laying the ground for more tender, lyrical
scenes that follow with the arrival of the Matthew of the poem.
The *Don Juan* form and tone, although unrealised and clumsily
done was probably the right choice, for Byron depends hugely
on undercutting emotion and lyricism with bathos, poly-
syllabic rhyming and ironic juxtapositions of the grandiose
with the banal. Since for me Matthew was a literal and living
ideal, this comic style stopped me from descending into too
much self-pity and idealising what was to my mind already

ideal, lyricising what was already lyrical and poeticising what was already poetic: it allowed me some kind of objectivity. The odd thing, and I suppose I ought to be ashamed to admit it, is that I am not sure that I could now write anything close to those verses, doggerel as they are. I wouldn't try, of course, my embarrassment glands would explode. Which is precisely what my fifteen-year-old self dreaded and predicted would become of me.

Whatever the literary defects of the poem it serves now to remind me just how completely my mind, soul and being had stayed behind at Uppingham, not just during that summer following my expulsion from Fircroft and then from The Paston School, but later on too. For I retyped and amended this poem a year afterwards (changing Stephen to David throughout) and continued to work on it until I was eighteen.

My only contact with Uppingham was with Jo Wood, who proved an amusing correspondent. I had, at one point towards the end, blurted out to him my passion for Matthew. I think I had been desperate to show someone, anyone, a section of a team photograph I had managed to steal, cutting Matthew's face into an oval and clamping it into my wallet like a schoolgirl's pressed flower. Jo had grunted sympathetically, he had never been attracted in a boyward direction, but he was good-hearted and perceptive enough to glimpse the sincerity of my passion behind the loose, self-indulgent wank of my rhetoric. Jo's return to Uppingham had gone serenely and he was heading towards A levels and Cambridge, continuing, as always to read and read and read. Occasionally in his letters he would slip Matthew's name into some piece of news, carefully and without emphasis: I wonder if he knew that just the sight of the name written out still made my heart leap within me?

My first year at Norcat was spent in digs, with an elderly couple called (you'll have to take my word for it) Croote. Mr and Mrs Croote 'took in' students once a year. There was one bedroom with two beds. I shared with a boy called Ian from Kelling, near Holt, whose passion was motorcycles. Just as I was drifting off to sleep he would awaken me with an excited cry of 'Kawa 750!' as a distant engine note drifted through the night.

Mrs Croote had three passions: the strings of Mantovani, her Chihuahua, Pepe, and natural history programmes. Each night that Mantovani's orchestra appeared (they had a regular BBC2 slot at this time) she would tell me solemnly that every member of his orchestra was good enough to be a concert soloist in his own right and I would say, 'Gosh,' and nudge Ian, who would say 'Golly!' and I would add, 'Goes to show,' and Ian would say, 'It does, doesn't it?' and Mrs Croote would be satisfied. When a wildlife programme was on we would wait with baited breath until the moment Mrs Croote would turn to us and say, at the sight of a dung beetle rolling dung up-hill, a lemur feeding its young or an orchid attracting a fly, 'Isn't nature wonderful, though?' We would nod vigorously and she would say, 'No, but isn't it, though?'

I never quite understood the 'though'. It is hard to parse. I suppose it serves the office of what the Germans call a flick word. It does *something* to the sentence, but it is hard to tell precisely what. I do know that Mrs Croote could no more say, 'Isn't nature wonderful?' without adding a 'though' on the end than Tony Blair, bless him, could reply to a journalistic question without prefacing his answer with the word 'Look'.

Mr Croote's twin passions were a bright red Robin Reliant and the King's Lynn Speedway team, which allowed him and Ian to talk about motorcycles a great deal, while I made appreciative noises about Mrs Croote's cooking, which was unspeakable.

Norcat itself hovered between the status of school and university very successfully. They had good teaching staff in the English, French and History of Art departments, but as well as A level courses they offered a large number of 'sandwich courses' and 'day release' courses for those learning trades in catering and engineering and so forth. The social mix was something I had never encountered before. I found there to be no difficulty with the differences of background, I was accepted by everyone there without any of the inverted snobbery I had dreaded.

The place was also, it must be pointed out, full of girls. Two girls, Judith and Gillian, I made friends with very quickly. Judith adored Gilbert O'Sullivan and wanted to be a novelist: she had already created a Danielle Steele, Jackie Collins type heroine called Castella, and would give us excerpts of work in progress. Together we pooled resources to buy Terry Jacks's 'Seasons in the Sun' which one-off single smote us both deeply. I *think* Judith might have suspected my sexuality, for she was the kind of naturally simpatica, thickly red-haired girl who makes a natural confidante for gay men. Gillian, on the other hand, for a short time became a girlfriend of mine, and there were disco moments of ensnogglement and bra-fumbling which came to very little.

It was in King's Lynn that I swam into the orbit of a most extraordinary circle of intellectuals who met regularly in the bar of a small hotel and discussed avidly the works of Frederick Rolfe, the infamous Baron Corvo. The very fact that I had heard of him made me welcome in the circle. These men and women, who were led by a bespectacled fellow called Chris and a glamorously half-French Baron called Paul, held regular Paradox Parties. Instead of a password or a bottle, the only way to gain entry to such a party was to offer at the door a completely original paradox. Paul, whose father was the French honorary consul (for King's Lynn is a port), could play the piano excellently, specialising in *outré* composers like Alkan and Sorabji, although he was also capable of delighting me with Wolf and Schubert Lieder. He was planning, like Corvo, to become a Roman priest. Also like Corvo, he failed in his attempt, unlike Corvo however he did not descend into bitterness and resentment but became finally an Anglican priest, which suited him better, despite his ancestry. He died unpleasantly many years later in his London parish. This group regularly produced a magazine called *The Failiure Press* (the spelling is deliberate) to which I contributed a regular crossword. A deal of *The Failiure Press* was written in the New Model Alphabet, which would take up far too much space for me to explain, but which nearly always looked like this 'phaij phajboo ajbo jjjbo' and took a great deal of deciphering to the initiated. The rest was filled with Corvine material (relating to the works of Corvo) and latterly, after I had long since moved on, it plunged into a weird libertarian frenzy of polemical anti-Semitism, gall and bitterness: the title had ever been a hostage to fortune or self-fulfilling prophecy. In its early days it was light-hearted, occasionally amusing, and always self-consciously intellectual. In a town like King's Lynn, such spirits were rare and it was amongst this group that I found my temporary best friend, and indeed first and only real girlfriend, whom I will call Kathleen Waters, to spare blushes all round.

Kathleen was in many of the same lecture sets as I, and she had the advantage of having her parents' house just across the road from college. We would spend a lot of time there, playing records and talking. She had entered the phase of smoking Sobranie cigarettes, using green and black nail polish, wearing fringey silks and delighting in that strange mixture of the Bloomsbury and the pre-Raphaelite which characterises a certain kind of girl with artistic temperament and nowhere to put it. For my sixteenth birthday she gave me a beautiful green and gold 1945 edition of Oscar Wilde's *Intentions*, which I have to this day, and a damned good fuck, the memory of which is also with me still.

We were up in her room, listening to Don Maclean's *American Pie*, as one did in those days, marvelling at the poetry of 'Vincent' and how it spoke us, when she remarked that it was odd that we had never screwed. I had told her early on that I was probably homosexual, but she did not see this as any kind of impediment at all.

It was a perfectly satisfactory experience. It was not as I had imagined from that horribly misogynistic scene in Ken Russell's *The Music Lovers* which seemed to suggest that because Tchaikovsky was attracted to men he must also have vomited at the touch of women. I could not, afterwards, deny that the design features of the vagina, so far as texture and enclosing elasticity were concerned, seemed absolutely made for the job – ideally suited in fact. We remained friends and tried it again once or twice, in a field and in a car. My heart was never in it, but my loins were very grateful indeed for the outing and the exercise.

The summer after my first year at Lynn I earned enough as a barman at the Castle Hotel (sixteen years old, but what the hell, they didn't ask questions in those days) to buy a Raleigh Ultramatic Moped, which I now used to shuttle me the weekly thirty-something miles between Booton and King's Lynn. For my second year I bade farewell to the Crootes, Pepe and Mantovani and took up accommodation in a hostel in college. I had two very good friends there, Philip Sutton and Dale Martin, both highly entertaining, charming, funny and resourceful. I must confess too that Dale was almost my first betrayal of Matthew for I found him terrifically cute. He looked like a seventeen-year-old Brad Pitt, which surely no one will deny is a wholly acceptable appearance to present. Matthew still burned a hole in my heart, but Dale was most comely to look upon. We lived on the top floor of the hostel which had a kitchenette, and Phil and Dale patiently taught me over many weeks how to fry eggs and heat up baked beans, a skill I retain to this day to the sick envy and admiration of my friends.

Both Phil and Dale were Norfolk down to their socks, but again they forgave me my background and treated me as one of them. Our idea of a really, really, *really* good time was to spend hour upon hour in a back parlour of The Woolpack, the pub next door to the college, playing three-card brag for money. Not huge sums, but enough to annoy us if we kept losing. I wasn't in the least interested in alcohol and usually drank long pints of bitter lemon and orange juice, a St Clements I think the drink is called. I discovered that I absolutely loved the company of completely heterosexual men, where the conversation ranged endlessly between sport, jokes, pop-music and the card game. There was a reluctance to talk openly of women, not out of shyness but I think out of the same graceful good manners that is more stuffily enshrined amongst the smarter classes in all those College sconcing rules and admonitions never to 'bandy a woman's name'. Phil and Dale got me a job at Christmas as a waiter at the Hotel de Paris in Cromer. In a week I earned a hundred pounds, and by Christ I earned it. I think I must have walked two hundred miles between kitchen and restaurant, silver-serving from breakfast to late, late, dinner. The money was spent on cannabis, cigarettes and still (I blush to confess) sweets.

I had been elected in my second year at Norcat on to the committee of the Student's Union. I came upon this clipping the other day which I had proudly cut from the pages of the *Lynn News & Advertiser*.

West Norfolk not to ban 'Exorcist'

Members of the environmental health committee of West Norfolk District Council exercised their powers as film censors for the first time on Wednesday.

They watched the controversial film "The Exorcist," and then approved it.

The committee members attended a private showing of the two-hour film at the Majestic Cinema, King's Lynn, to decide whether they were prepared to accept the recommended certification of the British Board of Film Censors.

COMPLAINTS

At a committee meeting afterwards the committee agreed that the film which has an X certificate, could be shown in West Norfolk.

Since April the committee has had the power to prevent cinema licensees from showing a film. "The Exorcist" was the first film they had viewed and they did so after receiving three complaints about it.

Three co-opted members of the committee also saw the film – Canon Denis Rutt, vicar of St Margaret's Church, Dr M. D. O'Brien, a consultant psychologist at Lynn Hospital, and Stephen Fry, representing the Student's Union.

Canon Rutt said he saw no reason why the film should be banned on ethical grounds.

Dr O'Brien said: "It is a film which would worry susceptible people – but you cannot protect the susceptible. A proportion of hysterical girls will faint and be carried out but it will not kill them. Presumably they want the thrill of being frightened and I would not regard this as serious."

Mr Fry said: "Far from being disturbing, it made me more appreciative of goodness, I am not in favour of even considering banning it."

But committee chairman Mr H. K. Rose who did not vote, disagreed with their views. "I would have thought it was very offensive to the good taste of many people, I was horrified, but I am obviously in the minority.

CRITERIA
"If we approve of a film like this I see no point in having any censorship at all. If people are titillated it makes them go and see something to see if we are right or wrong," Mr Rose said.

Canon Rutt commented: "This whole operation is giving the film the wrong sort of publicity."

The committee's decision is based on the question of whether the film is offensive, is against good taste and decency and whether it could lead to crime or disorder.

With its X certificate the film can only be seen by adults.

Still a self-righteous little prig. I must have been jeeyust seventeen when I was co-opted on to this committee. Why they felt a seventeen-year-old would make a good judge of a film which was legally available only to those aged eighteen and upwards, I have no idea. My role on the Students' Union was Officer in charge of Films. This was in the days before video cassettes and it was my job to order reels of film from Rank and show them in the assembly hall of the college. I suppose that's why I was chosen to represent the students for the Great Exorcist Debate. I remember the screening well. I had already managed to see the film twice before in London, so it hardly came as a surprise. The expression on Councillor H. K. Rose's face when the possessed child played by Linda Blair growled to the priest in a voice like a cappuccino machine running dry, 'Your mother sucks cocks in hell, Karras,' was wonderful to behold. His hand was still shaking as he dunked ginger nuts into his coffee in the committee room for the discussion afterwards, poor old buster. What he would have made of *Crash* or *Reservoir Dogs* one can only guess at . . .

At this time at King's Lynn I began to dress, in accordance with the latest vogue, in suits with very baggy trousers, their cut inspired by the Robert Redford version of *The Great Gatsby* which had just been released. I wore stiff detachable collars and silk ties, well-polished shoes and, occasionally, a hat of some description. I must have looked like a cross between James Caan in *The Godfather* and a poovey Chelsea sipper of *crème de menthe* and snapper up of unconsidered rent.

Drama was taken care of at Norcat by a talented enthusiast called Robert Pols. He cast me as Lysander in *A Midsummer Night's Dream* and Creon in a double bill of Sophocles' *Oedipus* and *Antigone*. Somewhere inside of me, I was still certain that I was going to be an actor. My mother used to explain to me that *really* I wanted to be a barrister, which, as she pointed out, is *much* the same thing and I had played along with this idea. In my heart of hearts however, and in hers too I suspect, it was acting that mattered. My writing I considered infinitely more important, but so private as to be impossible to show or publish. I thought that acting was simple showing off and that writing was a private basin in which one could wash one's sins away.

It is strange that although I spent two whole academic years at Norcat my memories of it are so much more vague than my memories of Uppingham at which I spent only a month or so longer.

By that second year at King's Lynn I reached a terrible low.

I was seventeen now, no longer anything like the youngest in my class, no longer the fast stream clever boy, no longer the complex but amusing rogue, no longer the sly yet fascinating villain, no longer in some people's eyes excusable through adolescence. Seventeen is as good as grown up.

Everything and everyone I cared about was growing away from me. Jo Wood was bound for Cambridge, Matthew would be trying for there the following year. Richard Fawcett was going up to St Andrews, my brother was going to an officer's training course in the Army. I was a failure and I knew it.

Some argument with my father in the holidays between the fifth and sixth and final terms at Norcat resulted in an attempt at suicide. I cannot recall the reason for the argument, but I determined absolutely that it was the end of everything. I had nothing to get up for in the morning, nothing at all. Besides, what pleasure, what exquisite, shivering delight, to picture my father's devastation when my body was discovered and he and everyone would know that it was *his* fault.

I took a huge selection of pills, principally Paracetamol but also Intal. Intal was an encapsulated powder that was supposed to be 'spinhaled' into the lungs to help prevent asthma. I reckoned the devastating admixture of those two, with a little aspirin and codeine thrown in, would do the job. I can't remember if I wrote a note or not, knowing me I must have done, a note filled with hatred and blame and self-righteous misery.

If ever I have been a total prick, a loveless, unlovable prick in my life, this was the time. I was horrid to look upon, to listen to, to know. I didn't wash, I didn't take interest in others, I was argumentative with the two people who were most unconditionally prepared to show me their love – my mother and my sister, crushing their every enthusiasm with cynicism, arrogance and pride; I was rude and insulting to my brother, to everyone around me. I was the cunt of the world, filled with self-loathing and world-loathing.

I missed Matthew, I wanted him and I knew he had gone. He had literally *gone*, that was the Pelion on Ossa, madness on madness that tipped me over the edge. *My* Matthew had disappeared, Matteo was no more.

I saw a photograph of him in a school magazine in Roger's bedroom. Matthew's face in a cricket photograph, a hockey photograph and a photograph taken from the school play. Three pieces of evidence to prove irrefutably that he had gone. The features had *coarsened*, he had grown in height and build and stockiness. He was now descending from the peak which, while I had known him he had always still miraculously been making towards. Maybe that late afternoon in the field outside the Middle, in his cricket whites, rolling and panting and fiercely jerking with me. Maybe that had been the summit. For us both.

Now the only Matthew who really existed, existed in my mind. Which left me nothing, nothing but a burst wound of bitterness, disappointment and hatred and a deep, deep sickness with myself and the world.

Any argument on any subject with my father, therefore, could have caused me to make this *geste fou*. Anything from a refusal on my part to pump up the water when it was my turn, to a solemn talk about 'attitude'.

Choking with dry tears and raging, raging, raging at the absolute indifference of nature and the world to the death of love, the death of hope and the death of beauty, I remember sitting on the end of my bed, collecting these pills and capsules together and wondering why, *why* when I felt I had so much to offer, so much love, such outpourings of love and energy to spend on the world, I was incapable of being offered love, giving it or summoning the energy with which I knew I could transform myself and everything around me.

'If they only knew!' I screamed inside. 'If they only knew what I have within me. How much I can pour out, how much I have to say, how much I have inside. If they only *knew*!'

I used many times to touch my own chest and feel, under its asthmatic quiver, the engine of the heart and lungs and blood and feel amazed at what I sensed was the enormity of the power I possessed. Not magical power, not all that Carrie teenage telekinetic wank, but *real* power. The power simply to *go on*, the power to endure, that is power enough, but I felt I had also the power to *create*, to *add*, to *delight* to *amaze* and to *transform*. Yet I was unwanted, rejected and unthought of. My *mother*, yes, she believed in me, but everybody's mother believes in them. No one else believed in me.

Principally of course – oh how one sees that now – myself. Principally, *I* did not believe in me. I believed in *ghosts* more than I believed in *me*, and take my word for it, I never believed in ghosts, I'm far too spiritual and emotional and passionate to believe in the supernatural.

I did have a friend. One friend. He was the local rector: he looked, oddly enough, exactly like Karras in *The Exorcist*, but his own life was so emotionally difficult and his own struggles with faith, family and identity so intense that it was, in his case, a question of Physician, heal thyself. He did me good by asking me to teach his daughters maths, which was psychologically smart and very touching. He knew maths had come hard for me and he knew too that there was a teacher in me raging to get out. He *nearly* tipped me (certainly not by trying to, he was no evangelist) into religion and I had made a quiet visit to the Bishop of Lynn, God's representative in Norfolk of a mysterious body called ACM, the church's vocational testing instrument, which accepted or declined applicants for ordination. We talked awhile, this Bishop, Aubrey Aitken, and I and he had given it as his booming opinion that I should wait awhile until God's Grace became clearer to me. He boomed because he had no larynx and spoke by means of one of those boxes that Jack Hawkins was forced to use towards the end of his life. The ceremony of 'switching the Bishop on' when Aitken came to preach was an accepted addition to local services within the diocese.

The Bishop was right of course, I had no vocation at all, merely the kind of vanity of a Henry Crawford in *Mansfield Park*, the vanity that made me think I would make a better preacher, a more stylish preacher than the kind of soggy, incoherent priest that was beginning to proliferate all over England. I knew I couldn't believe in God because I was fundamentally Hellenic in my outlook. That is the grand way of putting it, I was also absolutely convinced, if I want to put it more petulantly, that if there was a God his caprice, malice, arbitrariness and sheer lack of taste made him repulsive to me. There was a time when he had on his team people like Bach, Mozart, Michelangelo, Leonardo, Raphael, Laud, Donne, Herbert, Swift and Wren: now he had awful, drippy wet smacks with no style, no wit, no articulacy and no majesty. There was as much glory in the average Anglican priest as you would find in a British Home Stores cardigan. Of course what I didn't know was that – looked at in the right way – there is as much glory in a British Homes Stores cardigan as can be found in St Peter's, Rome, the Grand Canyon and the whole galaxy itself, but that is because I looked at nothing in the right way. When I had first caught sight of Matthew I saw the beauty in everything. Now I saw only ugliness and decay. All beauty was in the past.

Again and again I wrote in poems, in notes, on scraps of paper.

My whole life stretched out gloriously behind me.

If I wrote that sick phrase once, I wrote it fifty times. And believed it too. In a phrase from *Dirty Harry*, I had been flopped lower than whaleshit. I was at the bottom with no way up. If Ronnie Rutter saw me now, what would he think? His school reports had been generous, but there had been a kernel of truth in that word, whatever my woes at Uppingham, that word he used, 'exuberant'. Exuberance now was something gone from me for ever, something I could never recapture.

Which brings us back to the heap of pills and capsules and the glass of water. With one last vile and violent curse against the world, the world that had turned back into a rotting mole, an uncaring cycle of meaningless, wearisome repetition and decay, I swallowed them all, turned out the light and fell asleep.

I awoke in a flickering strip-lit world of whiteness and to a grotesque pain in my throat and cheeks. A tube was being forced down me, while a nurse slapped my cheeks and repeated and repeated and repeated:

'Stephen! Stephen! Come on, Stephen! *Come on*. Stephen,

Stephen! Stephen! *Stephen*! Come on now. Try! Come on. Come on. Stephen!'

It seems that at about midnight my brother had been awoken by the noise of my vomiting. When he entered the room he saw me arc a huge spray that he swears reached the ceiling. The ceiling in my bedroom was very high. I remember nothing of this, no ambulance rides, nothing. Nothing between switching out the bedside lamp and the sudden indignity of rebirth: the slaps, the brightness, the tubing, the speed, the urgent insistence that I be choked back into breathing life. I have felt so sorry for babies ever since.

It seems that the very mixture that I had thought would truly put an end to me was what saved me. I have given up puzzling over whether I subconsciously knew that or not. I am just grateful to the luck, the subliminal judgement (if there was any), the care of the gods, the sharp ears of my dear brother and the skill and ceaseless implacability of the Norfolk and Norwich Hospital nurses and doctors.

Little was said about it all at home. There was little *to* say. One of the men who worked for my father, who had worked for him since Chesham days, stopped me two days later and gave me the most vicious ticking off I had ever been given in my life. He was a frighteningly strong man called Tyler, who looked like a weather-beaten Malayan planter and whom I suspected of extreme right-wing politics (probably on account of his Mosley moustache): whether he thought he was doing psychologically the right thing or not I have no idea. The burden of his tirade was the worry that I caused my poor mother and my poor father. Had I *any* idea?

'Did I make them unhappy?' I asked.

'Of course you did, you young bastard,' he snapped.

'Unhappy enough to end their own lives?'

'No,' he called after me as I fled, 'because they've got more *guts.*'

I think my father may have guessed that love was at the root of this, for I remember him coming up to my room (for almost the first time in his life) and telling me some complicated story about how he had consulted a tarot reader who had said that I was unhappy in love. I believe this was his way of indirectly indicating that he was ready to listen to anything I had to say. I had nothing to say of course. Maybe I've made this memory up. Tarot and my father don't seem to go together.

I can't think what all the stampings and yellings and sobbings must have done for my poor sister Jo. We don't talk often about this time, except with rueful smiles and raised eyebrows. How grateful my parents must have been when it was time for me to go back to Lynn for my last term, my A level term. Grateful that I was out of the way, for all that they knew it was a pointless exercise, my returning. They knew, they knew that I was all played out.

Between the three-card brag at The Woolpack, life and more pinball in the Students' Union, the Paradox Parties, Kathleen and my own misery, I had given up any pretence of academic work. Towards the end of my second year it had become apparent to me and to everyone else that I would fail everything. I cannot recall my mental state, by 'recall' I mean just that, I cannot summon it up into me, the way I can so exactly feel again the earlier emotions that led up to the pitiful suicide attempt. I have memories of Kathleen and the Corvo set, I have memories of Phil and Dale and cards, I have memories of organising films to show for the Film Society. I have memories of trying to dance to Slade and Elton John at Union discos. I remember the unknown band Judas Priest coming to give a concert. I remember the little acting I did.

The greatest educational stimulation at this time, oddly, seemed to come from History of Art. I became obsessed in particular with architecture, the Greek orders, the Gothic orders, Michelangelo, and then the English House, the Gothic revival and the Victorians. My bible was Bannister Fletcher and my God was Inigo Jones. I am ashamed to say I cannot even remember what texts were set for English or for French. Hold up . . . for French it was Anouilh's *Antigone* again. That's it, I fear, that's the sum of my memories of King's Lynn in my second year there.

I sat the A levels – most of them, ducking out of the final

papers of French and English. Fear of failure again:

'Of *course* I failed! I didn't even bloody turn up!'

And then, in the phoney period of awaiting results that we all knew would be disastrous, the stealing began again in greater earnest. My mother had been used to the raids on her handbag, God knows how she could bring herself to look at me sometimes, and I felt sick myself then, not as sick as I feel now, but sick all the same.

I was still stuck at home, knowing that by the end of August, my eighteenth birthday, I would be without A levels, without friends, without purpose, without anything but the prospect of a winding down into permanent failure and lost opportunity. I had started, in King's Lynn, occasionally visiting the public lavatories, cottages as they are known in the gay world, and I saw a future for myself, at best, as an assistant librarian in a mouldy town somewhere, occasionally getting a blow job in a public bog. Arrested once or twice every four or five years and ending up with my head in an oven. Not so uncommon a fate in those days, or today. Life, that can shower you with so much splendour, is unremittingly cruel to those who have given up. Thank the gods there is such a thing as redemption, the redemption that comes in the form of other people the moment you are prepared to believe that they exist.

I remember an episode of *Star Trek* that ends with Jim turning to McCoy and saying, 'Out there, Bones, someone is saying the three most beautiful words in the galaxy.' I fully expected the nauseous obviousness of 'I love you'. But Kirk turned to the screen, gazed at the stars and whispered:

'Please, help me.'

Strange, the potency of cheap television.

I had no concept of such a thing as seeking help. I had successfully signed up on the dole, to the distressed resignation of my parents, and I headed, that July, with my Giro cheque to King's Lynn, for one last Paradox Party, which would be followed by my meeting up with Jo Wood for a camping holiday in Devon.

When I next returned to Booton, it would be as a convicted felon.

2

One of the most shameful of many shameful acts that were to follow was the theft of pension money from the handbag of the grandmother of the young man who was hosting the Paradox Party. There are few crimes lower and nothing I write in this paragraph will mitigate, deaden or palliate the pain and fury it must have caused that family.

I caught a train to Devon, arranged some humiliating business to do with Giro cheque forwarding by telephone with my mother and wandered with Jo Wood around Chagford and other beauty spots until it was time for Jo to go home to Sutton Coldfield.

I accompanied him there. The next two months were to see me moving around the country searching for some element of my past that might give me a clue as to my future.

That is a very strange way to describe what happened.

A very strange way to describe it indeed.

But it is true, for over the next two months I found myself making my way towards Chesham, desperate to see a town again that I barely remembered, a town that I had not seen since I was seven years old, but which pulled me like a magnet. I went to Yorkshire and stayed with Richard Fawcett's family. I went to Uley and saw Sister Pinder and the Angus girls and Cloud the pony, still alive, her grey milky belly now all but brushing the ground. I made my way to the Reading rock festival because I had heard a rumour that Matthew might be there. I knew Matthew wasn't the same Matthew, the real Matthew, but I wanted to search for the traces and I wanted perhaps at last to *tell* him, to let it all go.

A less strange way to describe what happened is to report that I went about Britain stealing, stealing, stealing and stealing until the police caught up with me.

Jo's place was in Sutton Coldfield where he lived with his mother, sister and two brothers. I stole some money from the hosts of a drinks party I had been invited along to and headed to Sheffield, where I stayed a while with Richard Fawcett and his parents. They were kind to me: Richard and I chatted and caught up with each other, but my feet were itching, the desire to return had gripped me, I wanted to go right back, right back to the beginning. I don't *believe* that I stole from the Fawcetts, but maybe I did.

My next destination was Chesham and the Brookes and Popplewells. Amanda Brooke, Florence Nightingale yellow, lambswool V-neck and straight brunette cut had been my girlfriend when we were five and six. The Popplewells were a family of four boys, all of whom were horrifyingly good at cricket and everything else. At Christmas the Popplewells traditionally sent, instead of cards, general letters that delineated their sons' enviable records of shining academic and athletic distinction – 'Alexander has won a scholarship to Charterhouse, Andrew achieved Grade 7 in the viola, Nigel had a successful trial for Hampshire Seconds, Eddie-Jim's prep-school composition "What I Did In The Holidays" has been shortlisted for the Booker Prize . . .' that kind of thing. Our family, in moments of rare collective humour would wryly compose the equivalents that the Fry family might send: 'Stephen has been expelled from his third school and continues to lie and steal. Jo has defiantly smeared mascara all over her ten-year-old eyelashes and looks a mess, Roger's CO describes him as too considerate and pleasant to make a successful career officer. The house temperature has now plummeted below anything an Eskimo would tolerate.' We knew that the Popplewell Christmas Letter was never designed to crow or gloat, but its effect on us was none the less that of lemon on a paper-cut.

Margaret, to whom I owe an eternal debt of gratitude for presenting me with my first Wodehouse book, had been at school with my mother. Her husband Oliver, a team-member along with Peter May and Jim Prior of the Charterhouse XI immortalised by Simon Raven, won his Blue at Cambridge and then turned to the law. He kept in touch with the cricket establishment however and only last year completed a two-year term as President of the MCC: he now judges away full-time in the law courts. One of the greatest regrets of my life was to turn down his offer to put me up for MCC membership.

I don't know why I declined, a kind of embarrassment I suppose. Two years later I changed my mind but by then the waiting list had gone supernova and the opportunity was lost. Whether coaching me in cricket as a tiny tot along with his sons, or later as a skipper trying to teach me the rudiments of sailing, he always presented the image of a bluff, Hawk's Club, won't-put-up-with-any-of-this-intellectual-nonsense hearty, which belied a deep intelligence and very real sensitivity – as we shall see. The oldest son Nigel, closest in age to me, was also to become a Cambridge Blue, double Blue in fact, and went on to play for Somerset, in the cup-winning side that included Ian Botham, Joel Garner and Viv Richards. He too is now a lawyer.

My mother tells me that, aged five, I once returned from an afternoon in the Popplewell garden, bowling and batting and fielding and said to her, 'Mummy, are you allowed to choose your husband?'

'Why of course, darling.'

'Do you mean you picked *Daddy* when you could have chosen Mr Popplewell!' I exclaimed in outrage and disgust. For years the Popplewells symbolised to me everything that was successful, integrated and marked down by the gods for effortless achievement. What is more, they were impossible to dislike: they proved to me that it was feasible to conform and to excel without losing integrity, honour, charm or modesty. I had always believed that my father, with his irksomely onerous integrity and pathologically intense distaste for worldly rewards could have been like them if only he hadn't escaped to the remote defensive fastness of rural Norfolk.

Maybe I believed that the failures I associated with Booton and with Uppingham could be wiped out by this return to Chesham. If I had not been taken from Chesham to Norfolk in the first place, I could have been a glowing success like the Brookes and the Popplewells, I would automatically have joined in. I would have grown up healthy, sensible, talented, law-abiding and decent, instead of being transformed into the mess of madnesses that I had become. I don't know if that is what I thought, but the Brookes and Popplewells were immensely kind and welcoming, either swallowing the story that I was just holidaying around England before A level results and university or tactfully choosing not to probe. The Popplewells had two of the Australian test side staying with them, Ross Edwards and Ashley Mallet, whom I met in a lather of dripping excitement: cricket by now had entered my soul for keeps. Ashley Mallett told me something that I did not want to believe, something that troubled me deeply. He told me that professional cricket was ultimately hell, because the pain of losing a match was more intense than the joy of winning one. Edwards disagreed with him, but Mallett stuck fast to his belief. It was, I see now, simply a personal difference of outlook between the two of them, but to me it was fundamental. One of them must be right and the other must be wrong. Was the pain of failing a deeper feeling than the joy of success? If so, Robert Browning and Andrea del Sarto were wrong: a man's reach exceeding his grasp did not justify heaven, it vindicated hell.

After a week or so of cheerful, tumbling, merriness in the Brooke household I left, brimming with charm and gratitude.

I took with me Patrick Brooke's Diner's Club card and the insanity really took hold.

In those days any credit card purchase under the value of fifty pounds was a simple matter of signature and a roller machine. There was no swiping and instant computer connection. I took some self-justifying comfort in the thought that as soon as the loss of the card was reported Mr Brooke's account would not be debited, only that of Diner's Club Inc. But what does that mean? I had stolen from a pensioner's handbag and from anyone who had money, I can't claim that the smallest scrap of decency, altruism or respect lay behind any of my actions.

The next few weeks passed in a kind of cacophoric, if there is such a word, buzz – which is to say a state of joylessly euphoric wildness, what a psychiatrist would call the upswing of manic depression or bi-polar cyclothymia or however they choose to designate it now. The functional opposite, in other words, of the listless misery that had caused me to scoop up a suicidal bowlful of pills a few months earlier. I know that I went to London and transferred my possessions, such as they were (books mostly) from my rolled up sleeping bag to a brand-new suitcase. I stayed for a while in the Imperial Hotel in Russell Square, applied for a job as a reader of talking books for the blind and made regular visits to the American Bar of the Ritz Hotel where I had become friends with the barman, Ron, whose passion was renaissance painting. He could remember P. G. Wodehouse sipping a cocktail in the corner, and F. Scott Fitzgerald leaping over the bar, drunk as a skunk, snatching up a bottle of whisky that he brandished like a woodman's axe, all kinds of juicy and wondrous moments. But these were as nothing to Ron when compared to a Duccio or a Donatello. He would show me slides of Mantegnas and Correggios and of Masaccio and Giotto fresco cycles that he kept under the bar, light-box and all, and speak to me of the great book in his life, the greatest book about art ever written he told me, Reitlinger's *The Economics of Taste*. He fed me free peanuts, olives and cornichons as he talked, enthused and displayed and I listened. I drank glasses of tomato juice and smoked Edward VII cigars in my new blue suit and felt for a while, that this is where I belonged. The American Bar of the Ritz is now a casino club to which, strangely enough, I do belong. Sometimes Hugh Laurie and I will go in there and lose fifty pounds at the minimum stake blackjack table. I once went in with Peter Cook who was solemnly handed a pair of shoes to replace the white trainers he was wearing.

'What,' said Cook, 'take off my lucky Reeboks! Are you mad?' and we had gone to Crockford's instead.

London palled however. A rather unsavoury man of fifty with a perpetual giggle had tried very hard to pick me up in a pinball arcade in Piccadilly and I had hated the experience, hated, that is, how close I had come to accepting his offer of accompanying him home. We had walked together towards a taxi rank in Regent Street and I suddenly ran off, streaking up Sherwood Street and deep into unknown Soho, convinced he was following me all the way and that every sex-shop owner was a friend who would lay hands on me and return me to him.

He probably, poor soul, rattled home in the taxi in a fever of terror, quite as convinced that I had marched straight into West End Central and was even at that moment furnishing the police with a detailed description.

I decided that really my destiny lay in a visit to Uley. Maybe that is where I would find some kind of something, any kind of anything. A clue. An opportunity to lay an unknown ghost.

What I believed I was looking for I cannot say. I can only assert that, as in a novel, the locations with which this story climaxes are the same as the locations with which it begins. Life is sometimes novel-shaped, mocking the efforts of those authors who, in an effort to make their novels life-shaped, spurn the easy symmetry and cheap resonance of reality.

So I arrived in Uley and saw those members of staff who chose to remain there during the summer holidays, staying a few nights with Sister Pinder in her little cottage and drinking pints of beer in the pub with Paddy and Ian Scott-Clarke. There was nothing for me in Uley of course. They must have known that I had been expelled from Uppingham and they must have wondered what I thought I was up to now. The crushing humiliation engendered by such unquestioningly, such unconditionally kind treatment sent me on the move again, this time towards the Cotswold villages of Boughton-on-the-Water and Moreton-in-the-Marsh.

It was in a Bed and Breakfast hotel in Moreton-in-the-Marsh that I happened upon my second piece of plastic; it lay snugly in the inside pocket of a casually hung jacket in the hallway, just sitting there for anyone, anyone like me, to steal. It was an Access card this time, much simpler to use, and with a signature that I could more easily reproduce than that of Patrick Brooke.

I had a suitcase, a suit I had bought in London, a few other clothes, some books and unlimited spending power. It was time now to head for the Reading Festival and the thrillingly shocking possibility of a meeting with Matthew.

My journey to Reading was broken in a town whose name I cannot even remember. I stayed overnight in as dreary a Post House Hotel as you have ever seen, even in your worst nightmare. Your worst nightmare, of course, is the precise inspiration for designers of this species of hotel. They steal your sleeping fears like a succubus and drop them down beside the ring-roads of dying towns.

It was only as I was finishing my dinner of steak and salad and beer in the dining room of this soulless assembly of melamine and artex that I realised that the date that day was the twenty-fourth of August 1975. My eighteenth birthday.

It was my eighteenth birthday. I had come of age here, in this place. I was eighteen years old. Not a fifteen-year-old discovering poetry, the beauty of algebra and the treachery and terror of growing up. Not a tormented fourteen-year-old whose life has exploded into love. Not a naughty twelve-year-old who broke school bounds to visit sweet shops. Not a grown up eight-year-old who put a new boy at his ease on a train. Not a funny little boy who cried when his mole was upstaged by a donkey and didn't dare go into the Headmaster's classroom because he was frightened of the big boys. Not a wicked little imp who pulled down his trousers and played rudies with a boy called Tim. An eighteen-year-old youth on the run. A somewhat less than juvenile delinquent. A petty thief who ruined people's lives with theft, betrayal, cowardice and contempt. A man. A man wholly responsible for all his actions.

Alone in my room, I ordered a half bottle of whisky from room service and for the first time in my life I made myself completely drunk. Drunk in the most dismal, appalling and lonely conditions conceivable. A concrete and smoked glass travelling salesman's shake-down, an apocalypse of orange cushions, brown curtains and elastic-cornered nylon sheets. Hardly had the whisky gone down my throat in heavily watered gulps than I added to the bathroom sink heave after heave of sour sick.

My sister told me later that this was the worst day, the very worst day of all at Booton, this day of my eighteenth birthday. My first ever birthday away from home and, at that, my eighteenth. My parents had no idea where I was or what I was doing. Since I had left the Brookes' house they had had no news of me from anybody. I had been filed as a missing person, but they knew in this England of *Johnny Go Home* and fresh waves of missing teenagers reported every hour, they knew that they may as well not have bothered. When August the twenty-fourth came round however, when it was my birthday, my eighteenth birthday, so Jo tells me, my mother was inconsolable all day, weeping and sobbing like a lost child, which is, I am afraid, how I am weeping as I type this. I am weeping for the shame, for the loss, the cruelty, the madness and again the shame and the shame and the shame. Weeping too for mothers everywhere, yesterday, today and tomorrow, who sit alone on the day of their child's birth not knowing where their beloved boy or their darling girl might be, who might be with them or what they might be doing. I am weeping too for grown-up children so lost to themselves and to hope that they squat in doorways, lie on beds, stare in stupors high or wired, or sit alone all eaten up with self-hate on their eighteenth birthday. I am weeping too for the death of adolescence, the death of childhood and the death of hope: there are never enough tears to mourn their passing.

The whisky had done its work with me, as whisky will. It blanked my mind enough to stop it wandering to the raspberry canes at Booton, banned it from conjuring a picture of Jo and Mother stripping clean the gooseberry bushes and denied me the image of the raw red hands of Mrs Riseborough rolling dough, stewing pears and shredding suet. Scenes from a childhood that I loathed and which sent me mad with longing, as did the tattered photograph of the loathed familial prison that still I carried with me everywhere I went – the oval loveliness of Matthew pasted on the obverse side. Without the numb wall of whisky between my head and my heart, all these would have buffeted me with such howling waves of grief that I and all the concrete foulness about me would split apart.

The following day this eighteen-year-old arose and took his headache and his suitcase and his credit cards to Reading. The Festival was too vast and frightening to penetrate, but there was a rumour of something happening on Salisbury Plain later, a rumour that Steeleye Span might be performing in the shadows of Stonehenge. If Matthew went anywhere he would go where Steeleye Span and Maddy Prior were.

I see from irrefutable documentary evidence that it was a full two weeks later before I arrived in Swindon on my way to Salisbury. It seems in my memory to have been only a day or so later, perhaps those two weeks were whiskied into one long stupor.

There was a grand looking hotel in Swindon, calling itself, I think, The Wiltshire, or the Wiltshire County. Four stars I counted on its marquee: four stars was no more than I expected as my due from life.

I checked in, that sunny morning of the ninth of September, well used to the procedure by now.

'Edward Bridges,' I said to the receptionist, 'would you have a room for the night?' Edward Bridges was, let us imagine, the name of the man whose Access card I had stolen: the real Edward Bridges, innocent victim as he was, does not need to have his name dragged into this sordid tale.

The usual procedure was gone through: the signing in, the flexible friend slapping into the bracket beneath the roller, the keys handed over with a beaming smile.

'Charming,' I said to the porter who came up with my suitcase, as I surveyed the room. 'Quite charming.' I slipped him fifty pence and laid down on the bed.

Tomorrow Stonehenge. Somehow I knew, because the god of love is capricious and insolent, that this time I would bump into Matthew there. A Matthew with sideburns no doubt, a Matthew thick with muscles, but Matthew none the less. I would probably get stoned with him and, at some propitiously giggling moment, let him know, in a bubble of hilarity that I had mooned after him this four years or more.

'Crazy man, or what?' I would drawl, and we would laugh and joke and laugh again.

Yes, that is how I would play it tomorrow.

I frowned as I crossed and uncrossed my feet.

Those shoes. Really, those shoes! The one little luxury I had not been able to obtain with all my stolen money and all my stolen credit was a decent pair of shoes. Being size twelve and half it had never been easy. Perhaps Swindon might provide where others had denied. One never knew. I hauled myself up to my feet, straightened my smart blue suit, winked to myself in the mirror and left the room.

'There you go!' I said in that silly, cheerful, English way as I dropped my key on the reception desk.

And would you believe it, the first thing I come across is a damned good shoe shop where they have, as if awaiting my arrival, a pair of thunderingly sound black semi-brogues in a perfect twelve and half? Excellent. Capital.

I walked up and down and inspected them in the angled mirror.

'Do you know,' I said, handing over my Access card, and casting a rueful glance at the cracked old pair that lay on the carpet looking for all the world as if they were waiting for Godot, 'these fit so well I think I'll wear them home!'

I passed a little jeweller's shop next and the idea struck me that the wristwatch I wore was commonplace and ill-favoured.

The assistant was most helpful and showed me first a smart young Ingersoll, charming in its way but worth less than ten pounds.

'Maybe you have something a little more *stylish*?' I ventured. The little man dipped down below the counter to find a tray and I ran from the shop with the Ingersoll clutched to me.

A very satisfactory morning's shopping, I thought to myself as I flew from the shopping centre, but trying on the nerves. Time now, I think, to return to the hotel for a spot of television and a plate of club sandwiches.

I picked up my key from the reception desk and bounced cheerfully up the stairs. I may be eighteen, I conceded, but that did not mean I was in need of electric lifts. There was spring in me yet.

I unlatched the door and was surprised to see that there was a man in my room.

'It's all right,' I said as I entered. 'If you can come back and clean later? I'll leave the room free for you in about an hour.'

Another man appeared, stepping sideways out of the

bathroom. Two men in my room. Both wearing grey suits.

'Mr Bridges?' said the first.

'Yes.'

'Mr Edward Bridges?'

'That's right . . .'

God how stupid can a man be? It never for a minute crossed my mind, until they revealed themselves, that they were anything other than strangely dressed and gendered chambermaids.

'We are police officers, sir. We have reason to believe that you may be using a stolen credit card, the property of a Mr Edward Bridges of Solihull.'

'Ah,' I said and smiled.

All at once a hundred thousand gallons of acid poison poured out of me and a hundred thousand pounds of lead fell from my shoulders.

'Yes. Yes,' I said. 'I'm afraid that you are absolutely right.'

'If you wouldn't mind coming with us, sir? I am arresting you now and will shortly make a formal charge at the station.'

I was so happy, so blissfully, radiantly, wildly happy that if I could have sung I would have sung. If I could have danced I would have danced. I was free. At last I was free. I was going on a journey now where every decision would be taken for me, every thought would be thought for me and every day planned for me. I was going back to school.

I almost giggled at the excitement and televisual glamour of the handcuffs, one for my right wrist the other for the policeman's left.

'If you'll just put your hand in my jacket pocket, sir, like so . . .'

Of course, the *hotel*. The sight of a criminal youth being led away in handcuffs was no kind of happy advertisement for the Wiltshire Hotel, Swindon. Cuffed together then, each of us with a hand in the his left pocket, the two of us, followed by the silent other who carried my suitcase, descended the stairs.

The two receptionists stood on tiptoe to watch me go. I gave them a small, sad, sweet smile as I left. And do you know what? One of them, the elder of the two, perhaps a mother herself, smiled back. One of warmest smiles I have ever been given.

I expected to be pushed into a waiting police car, but no, we walked on and soon I saw the reason why. Directly opposite the hotel doors, not thirty yards away, was a huge building with a blue sign.

WILTSHIRE CONSTABULARY

'I hope I get special consideration,' I said, 'for being easy on the legwork.'

The policeman not attached to me smiled. I was smiling, everyone was smiling. It was a glorious day.

'Special consideration for being such a prannett as to commit a crime within sight of a police station?' said the policeman. 'Special extra sentencing more like. We do like a challenge, you know.'

The most important consideration, the *only* consideration so far as I was concerned, was to keep my identity a secret. They could charge me as a John Doe, or whatever the British equivalent might be – not Fred Bloggs surely? – and I would be happy. But they must never find out my real name. There was no reason that they should, I argued. I had been travelling for some weeks now as Edward Bridges. How could they connect this non-person to Stephen Fry of Booton, Norfolk?

I sat in my little police cell and hummed a hum to myself. I imagined that once they had totted up all the depredations made on the Access card I would serve at least two years in prison. Two years in which I could do some serious writing, perhaps even apply to retake my A levels. I would emerge, newly qualified, write a postcard to my parents to let them know that everything was all right, and then start life again. Properly.

In the interview room, the same two officers, a detective constable and a detective sergeant, played that fiendish role game in which each of them adopts a different stance towards the accused. The version they played was Nice Cop and Even Nicer Cop, each competing with the other for the part of Even

Nicer Cop. It is hard not to crumble under such a cunningly vicious approach.

'I mean you're a young lad, you're well spoken,' said Nice Cop.

Ah, that wonderful English euphemism, 'well spoken'. I was well spoken, certainly, but not well spoken of.

'You could only be the son of very understanding parents,' said Even Nicer Cop. 'They'll be so worried.'

'Maybe you're on the missing child register,' said Nice. 'It would take us a bit of time, but we'd find out in the end.'

'Try one of these,' said Even Nicer, offering up a pack of Benson and Hedges. 'Not quite so rough on the throat as those Embassys, I think you'll find.'

'It's just that I've given my parents enough grief already,' I said. 'I'm eighteen now and I'd like to take responsibility for this on my own.'

'Now that,' said Nice, 'is very commendable. But let's think it through for a moment. I reckon if you want to stop giving your parents grief, you'll let us call them up straight away. That's the way I see it.'

'But you don't know them!' I said. 'They'll descend in a swoop with lawyers and things and I . . . I just couldn't face it.'

'Hey up, I reckon it's time for a cup of tea,' said Even Nicer. 'Let me guess . . . white, two sugars? Am I right?'

'Spot on. Thank you.'

Nice and I chewed the fat awhile.

'See,' said Nice. 'If we don't know your name it's very hard for us to charge you. We know that you have dishonestly obtained a pecuniary advantage for yourself by using a stolen credit card, but for all we know, you are wanted for murder in Bedfordshire or rape in Yorkshire.'

'Oh but I'm not!'

'Technically,' said Nice, 'you have also been guilty of forgery. Every time you sign one of those credit card vouchers you forge a signature, isn't that right?'

I nodded.

'Well now you see, it's more or less up to us. If we charge you for forgery, you'll go to prison for at least five years.'

'Five years!'

'Woah, woah, woah . . . I said *if*. If, mind.'

I chewed my lower lip and pondered. There was a question that had been bugging me since my arrest. 'I wonder if you mind me asking you something?' I said.

'Ask away, son.'

'Well, it's just this. How did you find me?'

'How did we find you?'

'Yes. I mean, there you were in my hotel room. Was it the wristwatch, had you followed me from the jewellers?'

'Wristwatch?' Nice frowned and made a note.

Oops. They had known nothing about the Ingersoll.

'What then?'

'It was your shoes, son.'

'My *shoes*?'

'When you checked into the hotel, the girl at reception, she noticed how your shoes were very tatty, see? "A tramp's shoes" she called them. After you'd gone up to the room, she thinks to herself. "A young man like that, nice suit, but tatty shoes. Something not right, there." So she calls up the credit card company and they tell her that the card you gave her when you checked in, that was a stolen card. So she rings us up, see? Simple really.'

'And what was the first thing I went out and bought?' I moaned, looking up at the ceiling like a rabbi at prayer. 'A nice new pair of shoes.'

'Smart girl. Always look at the shoes first,' Nice said approvingly. 'Didn't Sherlock Holmes say that very thing once?'

The door opened and Even Nice popped his head round, 'Oh, Stephen, one thing I forgot to ask . . .'

'Yes?'

'Ah,' said Even Nicer. 'A*ha*! so it is Stephen, then? Stephen Fry.'

What a *pratt*, I mean, what a *gibbon*. Not since Gordon Jackson replied to the German guard's English 'Good luck' with an instant 'Thank you!' as he and Dickie Attenborough climbed aboard the bus to freedom in *The Great Escape* has anyone been so irretrievably, unforgivably, slappably, *dumb*.

'Oh,' I said. 'That was a bit silly of me, wasn't it?'

'Well frankly, Stephen, yes it was,' said Even Nicer. 'Stephen Fry was the name on three of the books in your suitcase, see.'

'But,' said Nice, 'knowing your name does make our lives easier and when our lives are easier, your life is easier.'

I was on the register of missing children, having been placed there weeks before my eighteenth birthday so within minutes my parents had been telephoned. Within minutes of that I had myself a brief, as we lags call them. My godmother and her husband lived near Abingdon, and he was a lawyer. My parents acted swiftly.

The first night was spent in the police cells. I was in a fever of worry about seeing my parents in the magistrate's court the next morning. I didn't want to break down, I wanted to show them that I, and no one else, was taking responsibility for all this. I thought that if they heard through the police that I had refused all thought of bail, it might send them the signal that I was prepared to face my music alone. Nice and Even Nicer, once they began to get some picture of the full extent of my travels, told me that it might take a long time for my case to come to trial, for there was a great deal of paperwork to be gone through from several English counties. These things always took time.

The morning passed in such a rush that I barely remember anything about it, except that I was marched up from the cells, placed in a dock, a policeman beside me, and asked my name and age.

'The question of bail?' the magistrate asked.

'Your honour, bail is not requested in this case,' said my lawyer.

A look towards me from the magistrate as of a camel inspecting a blow-fly and a note was made.

There was muttering talk from the police solicitor concerning the collation of paperwork at which the magistrate grunted and placed me on remand to reappear in another two weeks, by which time the police solicitor should have framed a complete set of charges to which it would be possible for me to plead. Straight from the police court I was led, daring to look up just once to see if I could spot my parents in the gallery, into a van and towards prison.

They had been there. I had seen my mother's anxious face, desperate to catch my eye and give me a warm smile. I had tried to smile back, but I had not known how. That old curse again. How to smile. If I smiled too broadly it might it look like triumphalism; if I smiled too weakly it might look like a feeble bid for sympathy. If I smiled somewhere in between it would, I knew, look, as always like plain smugness. Somehow I managed to bare my teeth in a manner that expressed, I hope, sorrow, gratitude, determination, shame, remorse and resolve.

There again, why should I have to *design* a smile or an expression? If I felt all those things, which I did, why should I have to *act* them? Did normal people question their smiles and looks, did *they* go into lathers of insecurity about the impressions they gave, the figures they cut? If I *truly* cared about what people thought, surely I would alter not my reactions, but my actions. I would change my behaviour, not the nuance of my smiles. Or did I think that style was parent, not the child of substance? And was I right, deep down, ultimately right, to think so?

The van, in which I was the only prisoner, sped along the motorway until we crossed the border into the brand-new county of Avon, passing by the Chippings – Chipping Norton, Chipping Hamden and Chipping Sodbury. Hadn't there been a boy called Meade at Stouts Hill who lived at Chipping Sodbury? A dim memory returned to me of us all once crowding round Meade and teasing him about his buck-teeth and of him fighting back with the gloriously pre-war riposte, 'You're rotters, all of you. Nothing but utter rotters!' I had immediately taken his side because 'utter rotter' was a phrase my mother used – still uses to this day on those rare occasions when she is moved to disapproval – and this made me feel that Meade must be a good thing. Strange the ways in which loyalty to one's parents can show itself: never when they are there and when they would cut off a finger to see the tiniest scrap of evidence of filial devotion, but always when they are miles away. I visited a boy's parents one Sunday for tea when I was eight or nine and saw that they used Domestos in their lavatory, not Harpic which we used at home and I remember thinking poorly of these people because of it. We were Vim, Persil Fairy Liquid and RAC, other families were Ajax, Omo, Sqweezee and AA and one pitied them and felt slightly repelled: didn't they realise they had got it all wrong? Fierce pride in one's parents' choice of bathroom scourers, withering contempt for their opinions on anything concerning life, the world and oneself.

The van stopped at a large set of gates.

'What's this place called?' I asked the policeman cuffed to me.

'Didn't they tell you, son? It's called Pucklechurch.'

'Pucklechurch?' I said.

'Ah. Pucklechurch.'

'But that's so friendly! It sounds so sweet.'

'Well, lad,' said the policeman, getting to his feet. 'I don't think that's precisely the idea.'

Pucklechurch was a prison for young offenders on remand. I think all the inmates were between sixteen and twenty-five, and either awaiting sentencing or allocation to major prisons.

You will find that there are two states of being when you are placed on remand. Con and Non Con. A non con is technically innocent of any crime: he is confined because bail has been denied him or because he cannot afford it. He has either pleaded not guilty or else, as in my case, he has not yet had a chance to plead: either way, the law regards him as guiltless until proven otherwise. The cons, however, the cons have pleaded guilty and await their trial and sentencing.

Non cons wore brown uniforms, could receive as many visitors a day as they pleased, have as much food brought in as they could eat and were not obliged to work. They could spend their own money, watch television and enjoy themselves.

For the first two weeks, that then, is more or less what I did. I settled down in B wing, very happily, with a cell to myself. The only moment of pity and terror came when my parents visited on the third day.

I pictured them trying to decide which day might be best for a visit. Not the very first day because I would still be finding my feet. The second day too, that might still look too quick and swoopy. The fourth day would perhaps give the impression of indifference. They wanted to show that they cared and that they loved me: the third day was the best day.

You have all seen prison visiting rooms on television or in the cinema. You can picture the distress of parents, sitting on one side of a glass cage and watching their son being led forwards in prison uniform. We did our best. They smiled, they gave straight-lipped nods of firm encouragement. There was no questioning, no recrimination, no overflow of emotion.

The moment that tried me the most sorely came when, as the interview drew to a close, my mother took from her handbag a fat wadge of crosswords neatly clipped from the back page of *The Times*. She had saved the crossword every day since I had been away, removing the answers from the previous day's puzzle with completely straight, careful scissor strokes. When she pushed them under the window and I saw what they were I made a choking noise and closed my eyes. I tried to smile and I tried not to breathe in, because I knew that if I breathed in the choke would turn into a series of huge heaving sobs that might never end.

There was more love in every straightly snipped cut than one might think was contained in the whole race of man.

I watched them go and lurched dumbly towards the prison officer who turned me round and led me back to my cell.

Prison officers, known of course as screws, found themselves at this point at an embarrassing sartorial mid-point. The older guard still wore the black of Mr McKay in *Porridge*, their proud chests glistening with a whistle chain that led from a silver tunic button into a pleated breast pocket, while the newer officers had to bear the indignity of a sort of light blue suiting that made them look something between Postman Pat and a mimsy Lufthansa steward. They felt it keenly, you could tell.

The prison currency then was tobacco, called 'burn'. I dare say drugs are now the gold standard, but in my day I never heard of any drugs proliferating at Pucklechurch. My parents had given me enough money to buy cigarettes, so all was fine for that first two weeks, which passed in a blur of letter-writing and crossword solving. I was left very much to myself, as were all non cons.

The day came however, when I had to ride back in a police van to Swindon to make my plea. The police solicitor had decided, in the light of the dozens and dozens of uses I had made of the credit cards, that four specimen charges would be presented. You can see a photocopy of the Memorandum of the Court Order in the picture section of this book.

I pleaded guilty to all four charges, one of the straight theft of a watch, contrary to Section 7 of the Theft Act of 1968 (which raises the question, what on earth could be the offences covered by sections 1–6?), the other three charges being that I did, by deception, obtain a pecuniary advantage for myself contrary to that same Theft Act, Section 15. The Clerk of the Court in Swindon, you will notice, has rather sweetly typed 'pecunairy' in each instance.

The moment the fourth 'guilty' had mumbled from my lips I was instantly a con, convicted not by the court, but out of my own mouth and my status at Pucklechurch was to change.

For this second appearance in Swindon was by no means my trial. A probation officer was appointed by the court to look into my case, my history and my future. The trial was set for November the first, a whole month and a half away. I still stoutly refused bail and, returning in the van, resigned myself to the prospect of seven weeks of 'real bird'.

The first thing to change was the colour of my uniform. Next, my accommodation. I was marched to A wing, shouted at nose to nose every time I slowed down or looked from left to right, and told that I had better get used, pretty fucking quick, to being treated like the shitty little villain that I was.

The only burn to be got now was from work. If you worked every day you might get just enough to buy a half ounce of Old Holborn tobacco to last you the week and two packs of cigarette papers, these were standard Rizla+ rolling-papers, but presented in buff coloured packaging with HM PRISONS ONLY printed at an angle across the flap.

Work was assigned: you either mopped and polished the floor (a great treat because you got to use the electric floor polisher) or you worked in the 'shop', painting toy soldiers. I sometimes tried to imagine the children who received for Christmas a set of Napoleonic plastic soldiers, hand-painted by prisoners and how they would react if they knew the provenance. Now, of course, one knows that most children's toys, from Barbie dolls to the latest Disney fashion imperatives have been constructed under conditions often a great deal worse than those of Pucklechurch, in which young men sat, tongues out, happily plying the Humbrol in a well-heated room, like enthusiastic members of the Stouts Hill Model Club, with Simon Bates and Radio 1 blaring out good fun pop. After four weeks spent in this dozily lulling routine work, I was promoted to floor mopping, what we used to call at Uppingham 'lav fag'.

That's the key to my contentment at Pucklechurch. I've said it before in interviews and it's been taken as a witty joke, but life in prison was a breeze for me, because at that point I had spent most of life at boarding school. I didn't mean to suggest by that, as was supposed, that boarding schools are like prisons, I meant that prisons are like boarding schools. I knew how to tease authority enough to be popular with the inmates and tolerated by the screws; I knew how to stay cheerful and think up diversions, scams and pranks. I knew, ironically, given my inability to do so in real boarding schools, how to *survive*. Some of the sixteen-year-olds at Pucklechurch had never left home before. Nearly all of them were inside for TDA or TOC-ing, which is to say 'Taking and Driving Away' or 'Taking w/out Owner's Consent' – there must be some difference between the two offences, but I'm dashed if I know what it is. Also, the vast majority of them were from South Wales and the West Country. I found something immensely endearing about that. I had been trained by television to believe that all lags are either Scottish, Liverpudlian, or, most especially, Londoners. I had expected Sweeney accents and Glaswegian brogues, not Devonian burrs and Chepstow lilts.

There was little free time. Up at six, fold up all the bedding material, pick up one's potty and slop out in the lavatories.

'It is not a potty! It is a slop-pail!'

'Well, I prefer to think of it as a potty, sir.'

'You can fucking think of it what you fucking like. You will not call that cunt a fucking potty, you will call that cunt a fucking slop-pail, got it?'

'Very good, sir. It shall be as you wish.'

After slopping out (a practice that Oscar Wilde, a hundred years ago had written to the newspapers to protest about and which the Howard League for Penal Reform has *finally*, I believe, managed to push into desuetude) one would be handed a safety razor (in my case a fruitless offering, since I was still so testosterone light that I had not even the faintest traces of down on my cheeks or upper-lip) and the ablution ceremonies would be performed, just as at school only conducted in complete silence, save for the rhythmical brushing of teeth and scraping of stubble. Next, we were marched down to breakfast for a completely familiar (to me) prep-school tea of tinned tomatoes and grey scrambled egg on fried bread. Then we were led to work.

In the evenings there came Association. Association was the prison's major carrot and stick.

'Right! You, off Association for a week.'

'First one to clear up this fucking mess gets an extra ten minutes' Association.'

Association took place in a large room, where there was a television, a dartboard and a ping-pong table. To me it resembled exactly the games room of a French youth hostel, only without the appalling smell. It was on my second night's Association that a large con put his hand on my knee and told me that I was cute.

'Ere, why don't you fuck off and leave 'im alone,' a Bristolian car-thief next to me said.

There was no fight. That was it. No terrible moment later in the showers when I was told to bend down and pick up the soap. Just a hand on the thigh, a squeeze and a shy withdrawal.

Later that evening someone came up to me and said, 'Two's up then!'

'Sorry?' I said.

'Two's up with you!'

I agreed with him pleasantly and wandered off. As I was finishing my cigarette another con approached and said, 'I'll take that off you, mate.'

'Fine, help yourself,' I said, handing him the weedy little butt of my roll-up.

'Oi!' a thump on my back. 'You said you'd go two's up with *me*!'

'I'm terribly sorry,' I said. 'But I had absolutely no idea what "two's up" *meant*.'

Those who had run out of their supplies of burn lived on the fag-ends of others, going two's up with the smallest, thinnest butts, collecting dozens together to make new roll-ups or burning their fingers and lips by smoking each one down to a millimetric strip.

My accent and vocabulary endeared me to everyone. Again, I had expected nothing but jeering cries of 'Oh I say! How absolutely topping, don't you know?' and similar inaccurate mockeries, but I think the inmates enjoyed the confusion I caused to the screws who found it difficult to talk to me without thinking of me as Officer Class or suspecting me to be some Home Office official's son, planted to keep an eye on things.

'Don't think me some awful antinomian anarch, sir,' I might say to one of the screws, 'but is the rule about drinking hot cocoa in precisely forty seconds not perhaps dispensable? The ensuing scalding of the soft tissues about the uvula is most aggravating.'

Pathetic, I suppose, pathetic, vain and silly, but in circumstances where survival is the key any human characteristic or quality you can dredge up must be used. If you are strong physically, you use your strength, if you have charisma and inner dignity, you use them, if you have charm, you use charm. The smallest sign of servility, subservience, flattery, sycophancy or sneakiness is loathed by screws and cons alike. The screws will act on 'information received' but they won't thank the grass or protect him when he is duly punished by his victim.

The only unpleasant moment within my eye- or earshot came when a sixteen-year-old who was ungovernable in his stupidity, insubordination and insolence (I thought he was suffering from some sort of mental illness, for he would giggle and became so manic that it sent shivers down my spine) was, after pushing things too far, taken into the bathroom along from my cell by three of the screws. There was the sound of much pummelling and exceptionally dull thumping and I realised, with a shock, that he was being expertly beaten up. He came out alternately giggling and weeping. As he was led down the corridor, in great physical pain as he was, he tried to kick one of the screws. This was not a Jimmy Boyle refusal to be broken, this was not Shawshank resilience, this was illness.

I wanted immediately to write to the Home Secretary and talked to Barry, a witty Welshman whose cell was opposite to me, about doing so.

'They reads your letters, see. Won't do no good. And when you're out of yurr you'll forget all about it.'

He was right of course. When I left, I made no representation to anyone.

Barry, as it happens, couldn't read at all, so I set about teaching him. He it was who dubbed me 'The Professor', which was to become my prison nickname. Most people are 'that cunt' but the possession of a nickname puts you a little higher up the ladder than the others. I was lucky enough to have a whole cell to myself, back in those days of disgraceful prison undercrowding, and would alternately sleep on the top and the bottom bunk to help demarcate the days.

We had the treat to look forward to every Sunday of a visit from the prison chaplain, who, bizarrely, went by the name of the Reverend Chaplin and, more bizzarrely still, looked exactly like Charlie Chaplin: exceptionally thin, with tight black hair and a toothbrush moustache. With the usual inmate irony he was referred to as Ollie, as in Hardy. He let me play the piano for the Sunday service, attendance at which was optional, but which became, on account of the eccentricity of my playing, the hottest event of the prison week. I was allowed six hours off work a week without loss of pay so that I could practise the hymns. I entertained hugely by performing, not accurately ('Anyone can play accurately, but I play with wonderful expression. As far as the piano is concerned, sentiment is my forte') but with massively self-important arpeggios and symphonic style endings.

Thus, after 'The church's one foundation' for example I would end with a *Daaaaaah-dum! Da-dum-da-dum-da-um-da-dum-daaaaa-aaaaah DUUU-MMMMM!* And just as everyone was sitting down, I would add a high *Dum-di-dum-di-dum. Dum DUM! Dum.* (Pause) *Dum* (Pause) *Dum* (bigger pause, followed by a tiny) *Dim* . . . That surely must be the end, but no . . . a sudden quick bass *Tara-tara-DOM.* And finally it was over.

The Bishop of Malmesbury came to visit one Wednesday. A group of us was selected to sit round him in a circle while he asked us to speak frankly about prison conditions and how we were being treated and what we thought of ourselves. There were screws standing against the walls, eyeing the ceiling and we all knew better than to complain. All except Fry, of course.

'I would like to draw your lordship's attention to one thing that has been bothering me,' I said. 'It is, I fear, a very grave matter and the source of aggravation and discomfort to many of us here.'

There was a hissing in of breath from the others and a meaningful clearing of the throat from one of the senior screws.

'Please,' said the Bishop, 'please feel free.'

'I am sure,' I said, 'that Her Majesty has many calls on her time and cannot be expected to know everything that goes on in her name within the walls of institutions such as this.'

'No indeed,' agreed the Bishop, blinking slightly.

'However, I must urge you to draw her attention to the quality of the soap available in our bathrooms.'

'The soap?'

'The soap, my lord Bishop. It lathers not, neither does it float; it doesn't smell nice, it doesn't even clean you. The best that can be can said for it, I am afraid, is that it keeps you company in the bath.'

This was from an old Morecambe and Wise book I had bought years ago at Uppingham.

The Bishop burst out laughing and the screws dutifully joined in with smiles, shaking their heads at the jollity of it all.

'If your lordship will undertake to make urgent representation in the right quarters?'

'Certainly, certainly! Um, may I ask you, young man, I know this not good prison form and you really don't have to answer, but may I ask you none the less, . . . what, ah, are you *in* for?'

'Oh the usual,' I said carelessly. 'Churchmen.'

'I beg your pardon?'

'The senseless slaughter of clerics. I murdered four minor canons, two archdeacons, a curate and a suffragan bishop in a trail of bloody carnage that raged from Norwich to Hexham last year. Surely you read about it in the *Church Times*, my lord? I think it made the third page of the late racing extra.'

'All right, now. That's enough of that, Fry.'

'Yes, sir. I'm sorry, Bishop, you must forgive my freakish humours. In here we laugh that we may not weep. It was theft I'm afraid, my lord. Plain old credit-card fraud.'

'Oh. Oh, I see.'

I continued to teach Barry to read, while I practised the piano, zoomed along the corridors with my silver electric polisher and wrote letters to Jo Wood and other friends.

Barry had, when I had collected my wage packet at the end of my first week as a con, told me that the best way to make your burn go further is to pre-roll the cigarettes and lay them out to dry on the radiator pipe of your cell. I had dutifully done this and returned from Association to find every single one of my beautifully rolled cigarettes gone.

'Lesson number one, matey,' he said. 'You can't trust no one on the inside.'

What an *arse*. The cell door is left open during Association, it is only closed when the occupant is 'banged up' inside. The idea that in a building full of thieves I could cheerfully have left tobacco lying around and expected it to be there on my return

was absurd. Barry enjoyed my cigarettes and every now and
then would let me have half of one as that first pitiful burnless
week dragged by.

We were walking towards Association one evening the
following week when Barry and I thought it would be amusing
to drag our heels on the floor, which always left a black rubber
mark. I stopped doing it as I heard approaching footsteps and
Barry was caught mid-streak.

'Hughes! Off Association two days.'

'But, sir!' said Barry.

'Don't whine, you miserable *cunt*. Three days.'

'Sir, I feel I should confess that I am just as guilty,' I said. 'I
was doing exactly the same thing before you came round the
corner. In fact I made the worst marks.'

'Is that right, lad? I didn't see you, though did I? I didn't see
it, you didn't do it. Extra hour's Association for honesty.'

'Lesson One, matey,' I said to Barry as the screw passed by.
'Baffle them.'

Every two or three days or so I would receive a visit from my
court appointed probation officer. The great question facing
me was the nature of the sentence likely to be passed down
from the bench. Most of the experienced cons told me to expect
DC, Detention Centre – the 'short sharp shock' that Home
Secretary Roy Jenkins had proudly added to the judiciary's
roster of available sentences. DC came in three-month
packages, from a three months' minimum to a maximum, I
think, of nine months or possibly a year. It sounded foul. Up
at five, run everywhere, gym and physical jerks at all times,
running to dining halls, ten minutes to eat while standing up,
more physical jerks and weight training, and what would now
be called zero tolerance of all offences. The DC inmate
emerged physically powerful, immensely fit and utterly
zomboid in manner. An ideal candidate in fact for a job on the
outside such as the bouncer at a seedy night-club, which would
usually get him back on the inside for aggravated assault within
a matter of weeks. This time he would be in Big Nick and a full-
blown member of the criminal classes.

Borstal was the other option, an indeterminate sentence,

which was completed by the inmate rising up the ranks, winning a series of different coloured ties, until such time as the governor thought him fit to be freed. That sounded ghastly too.

'Or of course, there's just good old Nick. Six months, prolly,' some of them reckoned.

Mr White the court-appointed probation officer, who generously left me a pack of B&H at the end of every visit, was less pessimistic. He believed that it was essentially down to his report and he saw no reason so far not to recommend two years' probation. These were first offences, I had solid upright parents, I had learned my lesson.

I had learned my lesson, hadn't I?

I nodded seriously. I had learned my lesson, all right.

I cannot claim that prison politicised me in any way. It was not until years later, starting with those inevitable late-night student conversations at university, that I began to look seriously at the world through political eyes, but I do remember shivering with embarrassment at something that was said to me. Embarrassment is not a political emotion, it may be the British national emotion, but it is not political: rage is political, hatred can be political and so too can love, but not, I think, embarrassment.

What was said to me and I can't remember who said it (one of the Londoners I think, for Pucklechurch, in spite of that preponderance of West Country and Welsh inmates was also used as an overspill prison for Wormwood Scrubs, taking moderate and non-dangerous offenders, usually those who were serving sentences for the non-payment of fines) but it was said none the less, just as it had been said to Oscar Wilde.

'Person like you shouldn't be in a place like this,' the con said to me.

'What do you mean?'

'Well, you've got an education.'

'Not really. I've got some O levels, but that's it.'

'You know what I mean. These places aren't for the likes of you.'

I wish I could pretend he hadn't used that phrase 'for the

likes of you', but he really did. This is how Oscar Wilde relates a similar experience in *De Profundis*.

> – the poor thief who, recognising me as we tramped round the yard at Wandsworth, whispered to me in the hoarse prison-voice men get from long and compulsory silence: "*I feel sorry for you: it is harder for the likes of you than it is for the likes of us.*"

A hundred years on and still Britain is Britain. I tried to reply with the obvious, but none the less deeply felt by me, reply that I thought I deserved prison if anything *more* than he did. I had had every opportunity, every love, every care lavished on me. He heard me out in that non-listening way that convicts have and said:

'Yeah, but still, eh? I mean, it's not right, is it? Not really.'

The day for my court appearance drew near. I had received advance notice by letter from my mother that their old friend Oliver Popplewell, at that time not yet a judge, but a Queen's Counsel none the less, would be speaking for me in court.

It was immensely kind of him to do so, but how I wished he would not: the idea made me writhe with embarrassment. A West Country magistrate's court was not his milieu. He was not even a criminal barrister, he specialised in commercial and insurance law. It must have embarrassing for him too, knowing (for he was no fool) that the Swindon bench would go out of their way *not* to be impressed by this smart London silk, brought in by middle-class parents to keep their son out of the hands of the penal system. Maybe they might think that they had *paid* for him, paid the staggering sums that QCs cost. How alienating and infuriating *that* would be . . .

I arrived feeling very nervous and deeply pessimistic. Popplewell did a magnificent job however, no forensic rhetoric, no Latin, no appeals to law or precedent, merely straight, slightly nervous (real or cunningly assumed I cannot tell) representation. He had done this out of friendship for my parents and he performed the task with great humility: whether they asked him or he offered, to this day I do not know. He spoke to the bench as one who had known me from my birth and one who knew my parents as friends. He was aware that their worships would take the probation officer's report into consideration and hoped that they would take into consideration too the remorse and foolishness felt by an intelligent child who had gone off the rails, more as an act of teenage rebellion than as a threat to society. That the stability and unreserved love of his parents would also be taken into account, he was sure, as would be the very real promise that a young man of such intelligence showed the very real good he might do, at this turning point in his life, to the society he had scorned in this temporary fit of adolescent mutiny.

Oliver sat down in a swirl of black gown. The three members of the bench nodded to each other and asked for the probation officer, Mr White, whose report they had now read, to ask what sentence he thought proper.

White came through like a good 'un and said that he saw no reason, especially in view of the long custodial remand period I had served, for any sentence to be handed down other than an order for two years' probation.

'He has somewhere to live?'

Popplewell rose. 'With his parents, your worships, who will undertake to see that he obeys any order the court sees fit to make.'

More head-knocking and babbling before the beak in the middle cleared his throat and glared at me.

'Stand up, please. You have led a very privileged life, young man. You have been expensively educated and you have repaid the patience and devotion of all those around you with dishonesty and deceit. Let us be clear, the crimes you have committed have not been schoolboy japes. They have been very serious offences indeed. In the light of the probation officer's report, however, and various other representations it is the sentence of this court that you be placed on probation for a period of two years, during which time you are to reside . . .'

I don't remember the rest. It wasn't Big Nick, Detention Centre or Borstal, that was all that mattered to me, I was to all intents and purposes, a free man.

I turned slightly in the dock and caught my mother's eyes

which were bright with tears. What was I going to do now, I wondered?

And for how long was I going to ask myself what I was going to do, as if I were someone else, a stranger observing myself with curiosity and puzzlement.

The long drive back to Norfolk was friendly and unstrained. I don't know what either of my parents thought would happen next. I think they only knew for certain that there was nothing that they could make happen. My mother, always more optimistic, believed, I am certain, that things could only get better.

I fell into my sister's arms. She had been furious with me, furious for the grief I had caused Mother and furious for the atmosphere that had dwelt at Booton while I was away, but she hugged me and forgave me and wept. Roger, crisply short-back-and-sided shook his head with a smile and said that I was a clot.

The first thing I had to do was await the visit of the local probation officer appointed to take over my case. His name was Boyce and he had a snowy white beard. I had to visit him initially once a week, I think, and chat. He encouraged me to write while I was thinking what to do, so I wrote a strange updating of the old Greek myth of Theseus and Procrustes. I will not even begin to lower my hands into the steaming pile of psychological implications lying there, but just leave it at that. I gave it to Boyce to read and he passed it back professing himself completely unable to make head or tail of it. Reading it now, nor can I.

More urgently, I had discovered that Norwich City College was having its final enrolment day. They offered a one year course of A levels in most of the major subjects. I rushed to join the queue and found myself in the office of a twinkly little man who was head of arts admissions.

'I would like to apply to do English, French and History of Art A levels,' I said.

He shook his head sorrowfully as he read my application form. Next to the question, Attainments? I had written 'Prep-school sub-prefect and 3rd XI scorer'.

'I'm afraid,' he said, 'that English and History of Art are both full up. If you had come on the first day of enrolment . . .'

The first day of enrolment had been the day of my sentencing.

'I must tell you this,' I said, more urgency and concentration and power in my voice than had ever been there before. 'If you admit me on to those courses I will get A grades in each subject. I will take S levels in all subjects and get Grade Ones. I will take Cambridge Entrance . . .'

'We don't do Cambridge Entrance here . . .'

'Nevertheless,' I said. 'I will go to the library, take out past papers and, if I have to, take a job in the evening to be able to pay one of your staff to invigilate while I sit the Cambridge Entrance. I will be given a place to read English at Queens' College. If you take me on, this is what will happen.'

He looked at me with his blue twinkly eyes.

I looked back. My entire destiny was in the hands of this man. What had he had for breakfast? What were his views on failed public school boys screaming for the assistance of state-funded City Colleges? Did he have children? Were they difficult or good? Had he been to Cambridge or did he loathe Oxbridge and everything it stood for?

His blue unreadable eyes just twinkled back, as inscrutable and potent as a Siamese cat's.

'I must be mad,' he said, scribbling his signature on my form with a sigh. 'Take that to the office next door. Term starts on Monday. I'll be taking you for Chaucer.'

Catching Up

I WAS DOWN IN THE basement rooms of Norwich's Bohemian hang-out, Just John's Delicatique. On what dark night of the soul the word Delicatique was born no one knew and John refused to say, but his coffee shop was *the* place in Norwich to talk art, music and politics.

I had not been able that morning to bear the suspense any more of waiting for the postman and news from Cambridge. The promised A levels and S levels had been achieved in the summer, that glorious summer of '76, and the following November, alone but for a single invigilator in a huge hall at City College, I had sat the Cambridge Entrance exam. After two weeks of scaring the postman off his bike, I told my mother that I had had enough.

'I can't take this any more. I'm going into Norwich. If there's anything in the post, feel free to open it. I'll be at Just John's at lunchtime.'

The post in Booton didn't arrive until at least ten in the morning and the only bus into Norwich left the corner of the lane at seven-forty on the dot, so the choice was Postman or Norwich.

It was good to be back in Just John's. The usual crowd were there: Jem, impossibly, Byronically handsome worshipper of Blake and Jim Morrison; Nicky, Rugby School expulsee and amiable conversationalist; Greg and Jonathan, two twinkly and amusing brothers and the small gang of other café society regulars. We sat, drank coffee, nibbled carrot-cake and sipped at communally paid for shared glasses of frighteningly expensive

Urquell Pilsner, talking of this, that and everything in between.

'You look nervous,' said Greg.

He pointed out that every twenty seconds I had been looking at my watch and that my right leg had been bouncing up and on down on the ball of its foot – a mannerism Hugh Laurie to this day constantly upbraids me for. He used to believe that I did it to put him off when we played chess together at Cambridge (see photograph): in fact I am never aware that I do it. Hugh's way of putting me off was to checkmate me, which is great deal less sporting.

'It's nothing,' I said. 'Just that . . . no, there can't be anything. It's ten past one. If there *was* a letter my mother would have called straight away.'

Just then Just John himself appeared halfway down the stairs: 'Stephen!' he yelled across the buzz of frothy talk and frothing cappuccino. 'Telephone for you!'

I jumped to my feet and streaked towards him, sending my chair backwards on to the floor.

Somehow I managed to overtake John on the narrow stairway and I leaped for the dangling receiver.

'Mother! Did a letter come?'

'No, darling. No letter.'

'Oh . . .'

Bless her, but damn her too, *why* did she have to call if there was no letter? She must have known my heart had been in my throat all morning. She wants me to buy some bloody salami or something . . .

'No letter at all, I'm afraid,' she said again. 'Just a telegram.'

'A *what*?'

'A telegram.'

Who on *earth* could be sending me *telegrams*? Christ, maybe it had something to do with the court case. A new charge? A discrepancy in my statement. It was a whole year ago now, but these things could happen.

'I'll read it to you,' said my mother, and then in her best and clearest for-foreigners-and-the-deaf voice, she enunciated: 'Congratulations stop Awarded Scholarship Queens' College stop Senior Tutor.'

'Read that again! Read that again!'

'Oh darling . . .' she said with a sniff. 'I'm so proud. I'm *so* proud!'

What did Paul Pennyfeather do? What did W. H. Auden do? It was the only thing *to* do.

I emerged from London's Green Park tube station two days later and strolled past the Ritz Hotel. Perhaps I should go in and say hello to Ron, tell him how useful his beloved Reitlinger had been in preparing me for the History of Art paper. Maybe later. My appointment was for eleven o'clock and it would not do to be even a second late. I passed Albany Court and peeped up, thinking of Jack and Ernest, Raffles and Bunny.

Turning left into Sackville Street I searched the doorways until I saw the brass plaque I had been looking for:

GABBITAS & THRING
SCHOLASTIC AGENCY

They wouldn't spurn a good public school fellow, a Cambridge Scholar Elect. There must be a prep school out there somewhere in need of extra staff. In need of someone who knew the system and was prepared to step in at a moment's notice to teach a little Latin, a little Greek, a little French, English and History. Someone who would muck in, referee a rugby match, help mount a play. A typical Uppingham product: a good, solid, all-round chap.

I rang the bell.

'*Thrrrrring!*'

I thought of the great whiskers and the Chapel. I thought of hurrying past those great whiskers to see where *he* might leave his briefcase in the colonnade. Had I really been caught in such a net of madness for so long? And was that stab I felt inside still a stab of longing? No, no. Surely not.

My whole life spread out gloriously behind me.

I knew how to work now. Preparing for the Cambridge Entrance exam I had read every Shakespeare play and written pages and pages of notes on each: scene breakdowns, character lists, cross references, everything. I knew how to concentrate. No need for Lentizol and constipation to keep me attentive.

Was I exuberant? Was the spring back in the step? When I arrived at Cambridge I would be older than the others in my year. I would be twenty and they would be eighteen. Jo Wood, Matthew, all of those Uppingham friends, they had already left. I would be out of place amongst a milling crowd of youths who, *pace* Churchill, wanted to sow wild oats while all I wanted to do was grow sage.

'*Thrrrrring! Thrrrrring!*'

'Wizzit?'

'Um, I have an appointment for eleven o'clock. To see a Mr Howard?'

'*Gabbitas!*' The electric door latch snapped open with a triple clunk and I bounded up the stairs.

No. I was *Stephen*. I was always going to be Stephen. I would always be that same maddening, monstrous mixture of pedantry, egoism, politeness, selfishness, kindliness, sneakiness, larkiness, sociability, loneliness, ambition, ordered calm and hidden intensity. I would cover my life with words. I would spray the whole bloody world with words. They were still all that I had but at last they were getting me places.

Go and sin no more? I'm sorry, Mr Cromie, but there are sins out there I haven't even *heard* of yet – not even me: cleverclogs, smart-arse, read-it-all, know-it-all, done-it-all, seen-it-all me.

You bet I was fucking exuberant.

Afterword

MOST HUMANS manage their path from cradle to crematorium without seeping their lives and the lives of their families all over perfect strangers. I suspect that everybody who ever does come to write an autobiography wants to borrow David Copperfield's opening words.

> Whether I shall turn out to be the hero of my own life, or whether that situation will be held by anybody else, these pages must show.

I suppose I am, according to Ihab Hassan's definition, the anti-hero of my own life, with those 'problems of estrangement and communion, sincerity and simulation, ambition and acquiescence . . . clowning his sentimental way . . .'

If I am lucky I may be yet just halfway through the passage of my time on this earth. I shall be forty years old this very next weekend. Perhaps I shall be ready one day to write down some memories of the twenty years that have passed since I stood outside the offices of Gabbitas and Thring and asked for employment as a prep-school master.

I know that my early life was at one and the same time so common as to be unremarkable, and so strange as to be the stuff of fiction. I know of course that this is how *all* human lives are, but that it is only given to a few of us to luxuriate in the bath of self-revelation, self-curiosity, apology, revenge, bafflement, vanity and egoism that goes under the name Autobiography. You have seen me at my washpot scrubbing at the grime of years: to wallow in a washpot may not be the same thing as to be purified and cleansed, but I have come away from this very draining, highly bewildering and passionately intense few months feeling slightly less dirty. Less dirty about the first twenty years of my life, at least. The second twenty, now *that* is another story . . .

Stephen Fry – Norfolk, August 1997

Acknowledgements

APROBLEM THAT bedevils the autobiographer is that he cannot guess with any confidence whom he will offend by inclusion in his book and whom by exclusion. Some who have figured and continue to figure in my life may have felt greatly put out to see their names written down here, others will have been affronted by my negligence, ingratitude and forgetfulness in leaving them out. I must beg all who know me, or have known me, to believe that the foregoing unravelling of reminiscence is bound to contain inaccuracies, omissions and conflations: memory is a most inaccurate and unstable entity, and autobiography can never be the same thing as history. My own memory, often praised, is good for trivia games and for learning dramatic roles quickly, hopelessly unreliable with the dates and facts of my own life but, I think, dependable and honest when it comes to the recall of emotional states and atmospheres.

I owe a great debt to Anthony Cromie, who was kind enough to write a letter that answered many of my questions about the lives and proper names of some of the Stouts Hill staff, any errors in those passages in the book are my own. That one piece of assistance and days of endless rummaging through my old scrapbooks and letters aside, I have allowed my memory and my memory alone to dictate every scene and situation. I have explained already within the book that some names have been changed: sometimes to protect the guilty and sometimes to protect the innocent.

As always, Sue Freestone at Hutchinson's was angelically

patient as she awaited the final, overdue outchug from my printer; Lisa Osborne (no relation . . .) and her calm, cheerful, brilliant, literate and knowledgeable copy-editing under the highest pressure were of indispensable assistance; Anthony Goff my literary agent remained a model of calm, kindly understanding and my sister Jo, who runs my life more efficiently and more sweetly than is credible, knows that were she not there I would be as a balsa twig in a tornado. She was no older than eleven at the time of my return from Pucklechurch so she does not feature here in much detail. In fact, my life could neither have been led nor written without her.

My parents and my brother Roger may flinch at this book, this further example of the Stephenesque, as it used to be called within the family. They always taught me to be polite so, exhausted of further words, I can only say.

Sorry

and

Thank you.